Demonizing a President

Demonizing a President

THE "FOREIGNIZATION"
OF BARACK OBAMA

Martin A. Parlett

BLOOMSBURY ACADEMIC
NEW YORK • LONDON • OXFORD • NEW DELHI • SYDNEY

BLOOMSBURY ACADEMIC
Bloomsbury Publishing Inc
1385 Broadway, New York, NY 10018, USA
50 Bedford Square, London, WC1B 3DP, UK
29 Earlsfort Terrace, Dublin 2, Ireland

BLOOMSBURY, BLOOMSBURY ACADEMIC and the Diana logo
are trademarks of Bloomsbury Publishing Plc

First published in the United States of America by ABC-CLIO 2014
Paperback edition published by Bloomsbury Academic 2024

Jacket design by Silverander Communications
Cover photos: Seal of the United States. (Ben & Kristen Bryant/Thinkstock);
Concrete wall. (matsilvan/Thinkstock); President Obama. (Brooks Draft/Corbis)

Library of Congress Cataloging-in-Publication Data
Parlett, Martin A.
Demonizing a president : the "foreignization" of Barack Obama / Martin A. Parlett.
pages cm
Includes bibliographical references and index.
ISBN 978–1–4408–3055–6 (hard copy) — ISBN 978–1–4408–3056–3
(EISBN) 1. Obama, Barack—Public opinion. 2. United States—Politics and government—
2009—Psychological aspects. 3. United States—Race relations—Political aspects.
4. Political psychology—United States. 5. Public opinion—United States. I. Title.
E907.P37 2014
973.932092—dc23 2014021696

ISBN: HB: 978-1-4408-3055-6
PB: 979-8-7651-2847-3
ePDF: 978-1-4408-3056-3
eBook: 979-8-2160-7310-9

To find out more about our authors and books visit www.bloomsbury.com
and sign up for our newsletters.

To Lydia
By my side, chasing rainbows

Contents

Preface

> I have obviously failed to galvanize and prod, if not shame, enough Americans to be ever vigilant not to let a Chicago communist . . . subhuman mongrel like the ACORN community organizer, gangster Barack Hussein Obama, to weasel his way into the top office of authority in the United States of America.
>
> —*Ted Nugent, January 17, 2014*

If each book has a discrete point of conception—a moment of cartoonesque light bulb inspiration—then *Demonizing a President* might be traced, with some accuracy, to an unexpectedly memorable doorstep in northern Virginia.

To provide some context, it was my first time in the United States, and the consummation of a long-distance love affair between a British student and America's democratic promise. Whether it was the shared history of our two countries, our common tongue, or some genetic overlay from a since-forgotten Georgian ancestor, I had always in some small part considered myself a pretended American. And so, in the summer of 2008, as I heard Barack Obama's call for a realignment of international politics, for the enactment of a more perfect union, and for *ordinary people to achieve extraordinary things,* that sound mingled with the latent whispers of an America I had heard about for all of my life. Mixed with some youthful naiveté and a palpable Millennial zeitgeist, my clothes and hopes were packed into a nearby suitcase with a wanderlust of severe rapidity. Less than 24 hours later I was touching down at Washington's Dulles airport, as a foreign and voluntary foot soldier for a man whom I had never met, and for an election in which I could not vote.

And so there I stood, under the August sun, upon the threshold of an unassuming suburban family home complete with an obligatory white picket fence. Glancing down at my clipboard, I could see from previous contact with the campaign that the household was inhabited by "undecided" voters, presenting the opportunity for a meaningful and potentially persuasive conversation. I rang the bell and waited, adjusting my identification badge, which had become a sort of nervous tic during these (admittedly breviloquent) doorstep dialogues. The silhouette of a well-built man appeared behind the frosted glass and, after a short but pregnant moment, the door was unlocked and opened.

Soon after embarking upon some preliminary introductions and polite doorstep preamble, I turned the discussion to key issues in the upcoming election. The man scanned my Obama pin and literature, and then met my eyes in a gaze that signaled a brewing interior rage. As I continued to speak about the Illinois senator's platform—on the economy, healthcare, veteran affairs—he broke his purposeful silence.

"Do you want to speak to my gun?" he asked, glowering now without even the suggestion of horseplay.

I'd surely misheard. *Did I want to meet to his son? Partake in a stick of gum? Or consult a local nun?* I offered a tentative smile, which was—in hindsight—no doubt infuriating for my opposite.

"Would I like to speak with whom, sir?" I asked.

He repeated. "I said: would you like to speak to my gun."

I must confess, the words seemed crystalline upon their second utterance. As I turned to look around for my out-of-sight walking partner, I clocked a collection of previously overlooked Confederate soldier models on the lawn, beneath the right hand window. For a moment, my body was stupefied while adrenalin bombarded my synapses to formulate the right response. And then, with complete retrospective foolishness, I said it.

"Only if your gun can vote, sir." The retort was a rapid effort to harness the tension-melting power of a well-timed witticism. But this drew no laughter. As he moved to reach for something behind the door, I hastily retreated, apologized for the disturbance, and informed him with all deference that he would be taken off our contact database to avoid future calls or mailings. He yelled for me to get off his private property, convincingly informing me that he would "*never* vote for a black man."

As I made it to the corner, *sans* physical altercation or gunshot, I realized that I had stumbled into a phenomenon of acute and personalized political hatred. It was a crystallizing lapse of ordinary decorum, and a lasting motif of the way in which Obama's mere being inspires a suspension of rational political debate. While this was a very real and powerful introduction to the negative identity politics leveled at Barack Obama during this campaign—and indeed throughout his presidency—it was not, alas, an event of rare occurrence.

Over the next weeks, I was surprised at the regularity of these underground experiences of intense prejudice and negative identity politics. Volunteers were distressed when respondents dismissed Obama as a worthless "nigger" before hanging up the phone or slamming the door. Locally, a roadside banner was defaced with "KKK" in black-painted lettering before being burned down the following night. A large inflatable campaign sign was slashed on countless occasions before being permanently removed due to safety concerns. We heard informal reports from nearby counties and states about lacerated car tires, blades being thrown at vehicles, and campaign office vandalism. During the organization of an upcoming campaign rally featuring Barack Obama and Joe Biden in Fredericksburg, the local T-shirt printing shop refused to fulfill my order for our volunteer staff because, in her own words, Virginia didn't "want anything to do with Obama" and she would not memorialize him in a cotton and polyester blend. I recall one elderly resident, who brought me a recent mailing that had landed on her door mat, who was concerned about the ongoing pattern of demonization. The campaign leaflet—paid for by the Republican Party of Virginia—was a glossy indictment of Obama on the basis of his relationship with William Ayers: "TERRORIST. RADICAL. FRIEND OF OBAMA." Photographs of the Democratic candidate were placed alongside Ayers's police mug shot, and black-and-white pictures of protests and burning buildings. Bold text announced, "Obama has close ties to domestic terrorist," and warned, "Barack Obama: Not Who You Think He Is."

Where I had been concerned about the effect of my British accent on the doorstep, the real battle for the campaign worker was the resistance to the very idea of a *black* man in the *White* House. Countless moments of demonization and foreignization were quotidian experiences for those on the ground, but—as a conscious strategy—such encounters were invariably silenced from the realms of local and national media. In one sense, this book aims to importantly break through that strategic but damaging quietude of persistent and knowing prejudice.

Following my return to England soon after the election, I continued to observe how these rejections of Obama on the basis of his race and identity became more manifest, pernicious, and mainstream. The Tea Party; virulent Birtherism; calls for Obama's college records; suggestions of alternative paternities; Obama's depiction as Stalin and Hitler; calls for the president to return to his "native" Kenya; accusations of Islamic extremism, domestic terrorism, communism, fascism, anti-colonialism, and European socialism; and talk of death panels and re-education camps became the touchstones of a right-wing conspiracy theory of Obama's non-belonging that pushed him beyond the limits of American normalcy.

To be clear, these pages are not intended as hagiography. They are not meant to sanctify the 44th President of the United States, to beatify his policies, or to canonize his legacy. Nor is it my intention to shroud Obama in a veil of victimhood, although personal victimization there has surely been. Rather, this volume aims to provide a comprehensive examination of the various frames of Obama's extreme demonization as deployed by his political enemies. Beyond cataloguing these central strategies of Obama's "othering"—through the denigration of his birth, race, religion and politics—I hope to contextualize this modern political demonization through examination of presidential history and antique American prejudices that come to be subtly and overtly resurrected in the Obama era.

In that sense, the forthcoming pages are an attempt to unravel the current psychology of the political divide between Obama and his detractors, particularly where this diametrical relationship is energized by attacks on the president's personal identity in place of, or as a vehicle for, partisan disputation. Using the philosophical lens of the concept of "the Other" and the historical American experiences of societal fracture, this volume is driven by a personal (but shared) concern and fascination with the extent to which seemingly ordinary Americans are willing to engage in the extraordinary and racially implicated demonization of the first African American president; a man who seems to simultaneously encapsulate our collective progress and underline our continuing historical entrapment in the politics of identity.

Chapter 1

The "Other" in American Politics

Without alienation, there can be no politics.
—*Arthur Miller, January 1988*

INTRODUCTION

The blue-black evening sky framed Chicago's Grant Park dais, and was broken only by the flash of mobile devices and the repetitive luster of press photography. The panoramic stage—classical in its simplicity—hosted a multitude of star-spangled banners, which bowed and lifted nervously in the night breeze, behind the vacant lectern. As news organizations blanketed television screens across the globe with this suspenseful image, alongside the reflective chatter of election-night analysts, an anonymous broadcasting voice reverberated from Illinois to London, from New Delhi to Nairobi: "*Ladies and gentlemen, the next First Family of the United States of America.*"

It was November 4, 2008, and the melting-pot crowd erupted into wild gesticulations, raising hands, banners, flags, and screams as Barack, Michelle, Sasha, and Malia Obama emerged onto the international stage. "Yes We Can" rippled and roared throughout the throng, finding its rhythmic peaks and troughs like a Pacific Ocean wave. The moment was pregnant with celebration and historical quietude. For there they stood, like a human quartet of progress. Four black faces, haloed by joy, expectation, and difference, flashed upon the retinas of millions, as the visual proclamation of change. For many, this stunning tableau represented a restorative panacea in the uneven history of American racial justice. From slave to president, the black outsider—if viewed through this ephemeral lens—had made a significant degree of progress.

Indeed, in that moment, it was difficult not to be drawn into the narrative of large-scale racial transformation. One and a half centuries after the Emancipation Proclamation and the foreclosure of Reconstruction-era freedoms, 40 years after Martin Luther King, Jr., spoke of the mountaintop and the Promised Land, and 100 years after the founding of the National Association for the Advancement of Colored People, Barack Obama assumed the mantle of the executive office, which for so long had been the bastion of racial oppression and inequalities. As he spoke, it was difficult not to imagine the visage of the young Illinois senator in history books and on classroom walls, providing a stark and demarcating point of contrast in the long line of his 43 white forebears. It was difficult not to smile or weep at the irony of an African American president taking residence in a building constructed, in part, by the industry of slaves, the least powerful stratum of American historical life. It was equally difficult to fathom the visual rhetoric of Obama's inauguration taking place at the site where a tent city once stood for the slaves and workers who built the U.S. Capitol. The journey of emancipation, miscegenation, enfranchisement, desegregation, and civil liberties appeared to be sustained and even completed by the popular election of the first black president. The ballot box was no more the site of racial exclusion, but rather the very means of African American progress. Before he took the oath of office, and before the last vote was counted, Obama—as an heir to Lincoln, King, and the civil rights movement—suggested, by his mere existence, the creation of a post-racial America.

Barack Obama had understood, and cradled, his candidacy as having the capacity to engender a politic of post-racial transcendence. In the wake of the national and international divisions rendered by the George W. Bush era, and calling upon the history of social and racial separatism, Obama framed his campaign as the enablement of a seismic "change we can believe in" toward a "more perfect union" that moved beyond tribal red and blue Americas, and indeed all divisive dichotomies. Obama extended his own iconicity—as a mixed-race symbol for multivariate change and racial, social, and geographical hybridity—through, for example, the deployment of his central slogan "Yes We Can," which signified a positive response to the status quo, negative frames of institutional discrimination.

As Obama stood in Grant Park, the speech he delivered that night was meticulously orchestrated to provide a post-racial gravitas to his—and the crowd's—moment in history. "If there is anyone out there who still doubts that America is a place where all things are possible," he began, "who still wonders if the dream of our founders is alive in our time, who still questions the power of our democracy, tonight is your answer" (Obama 2008). Defining the crowd as a symbolic coalition of difference—"young and old, rich and poor, Democrat and Republican, black, white, Hispanic, Asian, Native American, gay, straight, disabled and not disabled"—he placed his audience at the front row of history: "Tonight, because of what we did on this date in this election at this defining moment, change has come to America." The resonance with the civil rights rhetoric of the mid-20th century was unmistakable. Revivifying King's March on Selma speeches, Obama spoke of the "arc of history" and the oasis-laden journey of racial justice: "The road ahead will be long. Our climb will be steep. We may not get there in one year or even in one term. But, America, I have never been more hopeful than I am tonight that we will get there." Drawing heavily from the presidential rhetoric of John F. Kennedy and Abraham Lincoln ("As Lincoln said to a nation far more divided than ours, we are not enemies but friends. Though passion may have strained, it must not break our bonds of affection"), Obama spoke as if he embodied the cosmic inheritor and cure for the entire timeline of racial inequality. As tears fell upon the cheeks of Jesse Jackson, Oprah Winfrey, and countless anonymous faces across the globe that night, America and its meritocratic promise seemed born anew.

And yet the world could not have been more mistaken.

The frenetic moments of Obama's election and inauguration—halcyon, bipartisan, harmonious, cinematic even—betrayed a recent past that had laid bare one of the most fractious and disturbing electoral campaigns in living memory. They provided no premonition of the profoundly polarized citizenry and Congress that Obama would inherit, nor did they give any indication of the wild conspiracies, campaigns, and fissures in sanity and logic that would give rise to the foreignization and alienation *ad absurdum* of an incumbent commander in chief. If Obama had given the impression of now being on the "inside" of national acceptance, that impression was naïve and transitory. For what millions of people did not see on the night of the Grant Park victory speech was that Barack Obama, the first African American president of the United States, spoke from an invisible cage of bulletproof glass. It was a 2-inch-thick, 15-foot-high physical representation of the inside-outside boundary that had defined Obama's entire political career, and that would come to represent the (often imperceptible) "us" and "other" mentality of a 21st-century America that struggled to adapt to the very symbol of progress it had created.

Obama had recognized from a young age that a kid with big ears and a funny-sounding name would be the fodder for some measure of identity politics. But little could he have imagined the patterns of his own foreign-ization from the 2008 candidacy to the current day, and the varied and complex lenses of alienation and "othering" utilized by his political opponents to reject and delegitimize the aspiring public servant—sometimes crude, sometimes subtle or pernicious. Obama is caught in a binary world of post-racial, yet racial-centric thinking, where for some the event of his election is the end of racial injustice and for others *the source* of its modern manifestation. The frames applied to Obama as a radical Muslim, socialist, European, terrorist, fascist, closet homosexual, angry and lazy, academic fake, Arab, Bill Ayers zealot, food-stamp president, Kenyan spearchucker, Indonesian citizen, shucker and jiver, satanic, son of Frank Marshall Davis, chairman of death panels, and clandestine Republican—to name but a few—were applied, despite the internal inconsistency of these labels' collective philosophies and implications, to dehumanize and scourge the first African American president. These disgraceful *ad hominem* attacks were (and are) structured to cast Barack Obama—and by extension his family—as outside of the comfortable and accepted normalcy of the upright, patriotic, democratic, heterosexual, and Judeo-Christian American paragon. To paraphrase the voluminous vitriol: He may be a president, but he is not My President. He is Other.

These were not the whispers of conspiracy junkies or the unread "contributions" on obscurist forums, though there certainly abound a great number of these. Rather, they were the key messages of campaign organizations, media personalities, and party activists who approached and permeated the mainstream with the message of the "Other."

As far back as 2004—and only two weeks after Obama's formative Democratic convention speech catapulted him into a position of national prominence—a relatively unknown Illinois political candidate, Andy Martin, released a statement calling on the media to attend a press conference that provided a false fact-check upon Obama's family history. "I feel sad having to expose Barack Obama," Martin wrote, "but the man is a complete fraud." Selectively drawing upon elements of Obama's genealogy, Martin concluded that Obama "is a Muslim who has concealed his religion" with a name that is both "Arabic and Koranic" in association—pushing him beyond the border limits of the "Land of Lincoln" (Martin 2004). The overall implication was that the Illinois senator posed a significant threat to American values and the Jewish state, as an unknown entity surrounded by (manufactured) whispered associations. Reassuringly, Martin (a serial litigator) abandoned this assertion late in

2008, only to depressingly spearhead a new incompatible theory: that Obama's true father was not the supposedly hardline Muslim Barack Obama, Sr., but rather the American political activist Frank Marshall Davis.

Despite the originator's U-turn, almost all Obama-as-Other narratives found their genesis in Martin's cyberspace campaign of suspicion and alienation. In 2006, Martin's original slander was re-energized by Ted Sampley's *U.S. Veteran Dispatch* article, "Barack Hussein Obama: Who Is He?" which returned to the unsubstantiated claims, accompanied by a cartoon image of Obama wearing a blue fez featuring the Christian cross and the Islamic star and crescent with the caption, "Christian/ Muslim" (Sampley 2006). In that punctuation, that forward slash between two potential religions, is revealed the double-speaking agenda of the Right's insinuation of Obama's oscillating, hidden or Janus-faced identity. Anonymous political chain emails began to incestuously quote Martin and Sampley, embellishing the tenuous claims for Obama's religious status with new demonizing details. One claimed that "Obama was enrolled in a Wahabi school in Jakarta," where he was indoctrinated in "the RADICAL teaching that is followed by the Muslim terrorists who are now waging war against the Western world" (PolitiFact.com 2007). In 2008, Jerome Corsi, one of the pacesetters for Obama conspiracy theories, quoted Martin's original claims in his *New York Times* bestseller, *The Obama Nation,* which postulated that "Obama's extensive connections with Islam and radical politics" precluded him from assuming citizenship, let alone representative political office (Corsi 2008, xv).

The growing trend of Obama's foreignization as a dubious outsider reached a fever pitch during the 2008 general election cycle, though it was initially the supporters of an increasingly desperate Hillary Clinton campaign, rather than the McCain political machine, that grasped the Willie Horton-esque stratagem as a "Hail Mary" political maneuver. Though the controversy surrounding Obama's long-time pastor, Jeremiah Wright, was ultimately damaging to the Obama campaign, it had at least reaffirmed the Christian credentials that the candidate had professed in response to the lingering crypto-Muslim slurs. Yet an anonymous Clinton supporters' email began to make the rounds, with the modus operandi being to position Obama as constitutionally ineligible for the presidential office, erasing his American status and rights on a fictitious technical point. Resurrecting the centuries-old trope of African slave diaspora and the inequalities of black and white Americans, the email cast Obama as the child of a sophisticated identity cover-up: "Barack Obama's mother was living in Kenya with his Arab-African father late in her pregnancy," the email read. "She was not allowed to travel by plane then, so Barack Obama was born there and his mother then took him to Hawaii to register his birth" (Swaine 2011). It was this unsourced, unsubstantiated, and anonymous claim that arguably fired the starting pistol and launched Birtherism, a movement that, thanks to Orly Taitz, Donald Trump, and members of the American Right, remains alive, well and disproportionately influential in Obama's second presidential term.

Claims of Obama's non-American citizenship raced and clashed in the Hadron Collider of the 2008 election cycle: that Obama's middle name was secretly "Mohammed," that he maintained multiple and therefore disqualifying citizenships, that his family had orchestrated misleading newspaper announcements in the Hawaiian press, that he was adopted from abroad, that his time in Indonesia voided his American citizenship, that no birth certificate existed, or that a birth certificate had existed but was now amended or destroyed. Prompted by such aspersions and by calls from both Democrats and Republicans to put the birth issue behind him, the Obama campaign released a digitally scanned image of the senator's short-form birth certificate on June 12, 2008, via the *Fight the Smears* website. Birtherism evidently had electoral clout. Partisan opponents denounced the certificate as a fake almost immediately, an elaborate continuation of the grandiose conspiracy, while FactCheck.org and the state of Hawaii handled the original document and confirmed its authenticity. Despite Obama's confirmation as president-elect on January 8, 2009, and his subsequent inauguration that same month, Obama's citizenship status continued to be litigated across the country, with almost 20 lawsuits contesting the president's entitlement to his assumed constitutional office filed before the end of 2008 alone. Orly Taitz, who came to be known as the Birther Queen in recognition of her misguided diadem of tenacity, released a rudimentary counterfeit Kenyan birth certificate bearing Obama's name, enacting the very same forgery of which Obama was accused without even the grace of acknowledged irony. Throughout 2009 and 2010, the issue spluttered on, with *World Net Daily* continuing to distribute billboards, bumper stickers, and other merchandise branded with Birther slogans and themes. Sarah Palin declared that she thought the ongoing doubts were "fair game" and legitimate for political candidates to raise as "the public rightfully is still making it an issue" (Smith 2009). In March 2011, Donald Trump, teasing the (im)possibility of his own candidacy, stated that he still had personal doubts about the verisimilitude of the short-form birth certificate in the public domain. Michele Bachmann, floating her own presidential run, proclaimed that the very "first thing" she would do following her formal announcement would be to release her full *American* birth certificate (Pareene 2011). A poll of

GOP voters indicated that 45 percent believed that President Obama was not born in the United States, with a further 22 percent of respondents expressing uncertainty about Obama's origins (Condon 2011). The memory of Obama's infancy—the core of his essential innocence and identity—was poisoned, wrapped in the swaddling blankets of sore losing, institutional whiteness and racial attacks cloaked as patriotic concern.

Demonstrating the potential damage posed by this collective dismantling of his legitimacy, Obama made an official request of Loretta Fuddy, Director of Hawaii's Department of Health, for certified copies of his original long-form certificate, known as the Certificate of Live Birth, in 2011. Obama's personal counsel, Judith Corley, had the peculiar honor of visiting the department in Honolulu to pay the processing fee on behalf of the sitting president and to collect the two requested copies of the certified long-form version. A PDF image copy of the certificate was posted on the official WhiteHouse.gov website, and paper copies were provided to journalists. Despite its endorsed legitimacy and its corroboration of the previously released short-form version, the long-form birth certificate was rejected by the Birthers as an *a priori* electronic fake, retrospectively made with image editing software at Obama's request. The *Drudge Report* was rapid in putting forth the argument that strange layer components were proof of Adobe manipulation, as others called upon image software specialists to undermine the credibility of the document. Donald Trump, who took full credit for forcing the White House to succumb to the certificate's release, was "proud" of the achievement. When in October 2012 he offered Obama $5 million to a charity of his choice in return for the publication of his college and passport applications, Trump revealed that the birth certificate pursuit was merely an optioneered vehicle for a movement that at its heart desired only to demonize and alienate the first black president by pulling away the president's supports of legitimacy and belonging from kindergarten through to the U.S. Senate.

If suggesting that the president of the United States belonged in Kenya resurrected the historical associations of the powerlessness of the transportation of sub-citizen African slaves in centuries past, then the sensational act of a sitting president, twice affirmed by the American people, forced to stop in the course of ordinary business to produce his own birth certificate (relentlessly attacked as a subversive forgery) was to revivify the "show me your papers" mentality of a Jim Crow-era America. In the pathos-laden words of Obama himself, "We've posted the certification that is given by the state of Hawaii … People have provided affidavits … and yet this thing just keeps on going" (Obama 2011).

This systematic foreignization of the president as a primitive but powerful form of partisan argumentation is sustained not only by the determination of right-wing activism, but also by the willingness for senior media and political forces to do nothing in the midst of such rumor. In 2008, for example, Sarah Palin stoked the fires by highlighting Obama's supposedly anti-American ethos, by pointing to his unproven association with the Weather Underground leader, William Ayers. In Colorado, Palin told devotees, "This is not a man who sees America like you and I see America"; rather, she claimed, Obama was "palling around with terrorists who would target their own country." Town hall and rally audiences became wrapped up in the fervor of the rhetoric, shouting "liar," "socialist," "terrorist," and "Kill him" (investigated by Secret Services) as confirmation that the message of rejectionism had penetrated the conservative base. Such occurrences, in the words of Myra Mendible (2012), "turned the race for the presidency into the mythic battle between 'real' Americans and socialists and terrorists"—and, it made great television.

One moment stands out—and it is surely tragic that there is only one—where the mythic alienation of Barack Obama was nationally challenged by a leading member of the conservative movement. John McCain, as the Republican nominee for the U.S. presidency, hosted a town hall rally on October 10, 2008, in which audience members parroted the increasingly offensive narratives of Obama's alienation, manufactured from the far Right. First a man took the microphone: "We're scared of an Obama presidency," he began, fashioning the fear engendered by an identity politics based upon demonization. "I'm concerned about someone that cohorts with domestic terrorists such as Ayers" (Spiegel 2008). Face to face with the questioner, McCain had little room to pretend that he did not hear the hyperbolic accusation and instead moved to rehumanize his opponent; "First of all ... he is a decent person and a person that you do not have to be scared [of] as president of the United States." Boos erupted from the audience as McCain's message did not comport with the established narrative of Obama-as-Other. "Come on John!" an anonymous voice erupted with incredulity. Others retreated to the easy refrains of alienation—"terrorist!" "liar!" McCain moved on, placing his hope in a middle-aged woman at the other side of the room, but was little rewarded. "I can't trust Obama," she started, "I have read about him, and ... er ... he's an Arab." Her voice was shaky and her delivery a little unsure, but the sentiment was loud and clear. It was the pinnacle statement of a crowd mentality that was entrenched in the conspiracy of Obama's "otherness." For even the casual observer, it was a breakthrough moment where the dog whistle rhetoric reached the volume of a trumpet call on the national stage. McCain, clearly disturbed, grabbed the microphone and cut the questioner off before she could continue: "No, ma'am; no, ma'am. He is a decent family man—citizen—that I just happen to have disagreements with on fundamental issues, and that is what this campaign is all about." McCain's resistance to the explicit sentiment of alienation was, by now, so extraordinary that it gained national attention as a threshold moral stand. Wary of the electoral impact of defending his opponent, McCain clarified, "I don't mean that has to reduce your ferocity; I just mean to say you have to be respectful" (Speigel 2008). Hopes from the Left, the moderate Right, and racial activists that McCain's rejection of the trope of alienation signaled a move away from negative identity politics were, however, short-lived. In subsequent days, McCain and Palin continued to hit Obama for palling around with "unrepentant terrorists," running ads that proliferated the old refrain that "Senator Obama's political career was launched in Mr. Ayers's living room."

It is a tactic that could be evidenced in these pages *ad finitum*. Throughout the healthcare legislation battle, Obama was rendered as the reincarnation of both Lenin (via Jim DeMint, Michele Bachmann, Mike Huckabee, and others) and fascist leaders including Hitler (see Hank Williams, Jr., on Fox News comparing Obama and John Boehner playing golf to Israeli Prime Minister Netanyahu fraternizing with Adolf Hitler). These fusions of identity continue to be levied despite their philosophical incompatibility, and the prima facie absurdity, for example, of casting a black president as the reincarnation of Arian eugenics. This was Godwin's Law, going *off piste*.

If not Hitler, then why not Satan himself? Taking Obama's demonization to the nth degree, watchers of The History Channel's hit miniseries *The Bible* noticed a bizarrely uncanny resemblance between President Obama and the representation of the devil. In 2013, the Egyptian newspaper *Al Wafd,* opposing the United States' planned response to the Syrian use of chemical weapons, produced an image of a be-horned Obama against a backdrop of burning skies emblazoned with the fiery imprint of "6 6 6." In a Public Policy Polling survey conducted earlier that year, an astonishing 13 percent of Americans believed that Obama was undoubtedly the Antichrist, with a further 13 percent remaining on the fence as to whether the president was the prince of Christ's enemies. A Mitt Romney robocall had defined Obama as "a threat to our religious freedom" in 2012, and YouTube user "ppsimmons" posted a video of Obama's 2008 nomination acceptance speech claiming that when played backward, it implored the listener to "Serve Satan." This video, which has racked up more than 3 million individual hits, is one of countless online that claim Obama engages in subliminal satanic back-masking—a technique popularized in the more psychotropic corners of the music recording industry, as well as in the 1973 film *The Exorcist,* in which the vocalizations of the possessed reveal messages from the Antichrist when played in reverse. In a perverse metaphorical extrapolation of the body politic, the depiction of Obama as a malevolent, possessive political force is to suggest that America's essential identity locus, or soul, has been infiltrated and overtaken by a foreign and unwelcome "Other."

Back in 2007, when America was still grappling with the unlikely notion of an African American nominee, George Stephanopoulos sat down with Obama on ABC's *This Week* for a wide-ranging interview in which Stephanopoulos (who had been Clinton's first-term communications director) seemed intrigued by Obama's noticeably "very cool style when you're doing those town meetings" and asked if such a temperament was "tied to your race." Stephanopoulos's question introduced the notion that Obama's style—if not also his policies—was informed by a racially determined difference. This impulse, when internalized by the machines of hyperpartisanship, has resulted in the seemingly limitless rejection of Obama through insinuation, slurs, denigration, and explicit bigotry, based on the overt and implicit racial stereotypes exhibited in America's past (and present).

Recall, in late 2008, the Chaffey Community Republican Women Federated Group distributed a newsletter brandishing the image of fake currency, known as "Obama Bucks," featuring the head of Obama on the body of a donkey, surrounded by the supposed paraphernalia of the black community—fried chicken, ribs, Kool Aid, and a watermelon wedge. These new bank notes were no longer American dollars bearing the proud portraits of American leaders, but rather "United States Food Stamps," the supposed currency of the black underclass and a symbol of Obama's animalistic influence on (socioeconomic) American decline.

Remember the "parody" song *Barack the Magic Negro* released six weeks before the 2008 election; it was written by Paul Shanklin and aired for public broadcast (on numerous occasions) by radio host Rush Limbaugh. This rewriting of *Puff, the Magic Dragon* involved racist lyrics masquerading as comical satire. It was sung from the perspective of the former presidential candidate, the Reverend Al Sharpton, who lamented the power of a magical Negro such as Obama in being acceptable to whites " 'Cause he's not from the hood." This controversy was reinvigorated in December 2008, when Chip Saltsman, while campaigning for the chairmanship of the Republican National Committee (RNC), mailed recordings of the song on a Christmas CD, called *We Hate the USA*, to 168 RNC members while canvassing for their support. In an ironic conclusion, Michael Steele, the first African American to chair the RNC, won the election after Saltsman dropped out of the race.

Bring to mind the words of Jason Thompson, the son of the former Wisconsin governor, who said, at a brunch attended by the subsequent RNC Chairman, Reince Priebus, in 2012: "We have the opportunity to send President Obama back to Chicago—or Kenya!" Thompson's deportation jibe was greeted with applause and laughter from the Republican audience, a member of which glibly interjected, "We're taking donations for that Kenya trip."

Remember similarly, in the summer of 2013, when Obama visited both Arizona and Florida, how the president's foreignization was evident as a form of popular political engagement. While he was in Phoenix to talk through his blueprint for a new mortgage financing system, hundreds of protesters gathered outside of Desert Vista High School. According to the *Arizona Republic*, those gathered chanted, "Bye, bye, black sheep," as the president of the United States spoke, bringing a note of simplistic schoolyard ostracism to the level of political racism. Deanne Bartram, a 17-year-old protester, held a unambiguous banner, brandished with the words "Impeach the Half White Muslim." She explained, "Obama is ruining American values. He is ruining the Constitution. He needs to go back to where he came from because obviously, he is a liar" (Pierce 2013). Later that week, as Barack and Michelle Obama arrived in Orlando to speak at the convention of Disabled American Veterans, a string of banners (held in the majority by middle-aged white people), welcomed the president with messages including "Kenyan Go Home," "Obama Lies," and "Honk to Impeach Obama." It is as though the title cards from D. W. Griffith's *Birth of a Nation*—insensitive manifestations of an epic racial drama—are transplanted onto an American era struggling, to some extent, with the juxtaposition of Obama's presidency and ever-present racial complexes.

Remember how the fractious debate on the Affordable Healthcare Act, despite the legislation being passed as law and upheld by the U.S. Supreme Court, was also tied to Obama's identity in the powerful portmanteau *Obamacare*—worn as a badge of honor by Democrats and leveled as a political slur from the GOP. Members of the far Right called the new healthcare program by that sobriquet so as to align it with the very identity they perceived as illegitimate and to transfer the poison of Obama's personal invalidity to the law itself. Extremists on the Right shut down the federal government in 2013 in a futile battle against the law's implementation precisely to avoid the dual legitimization of both president and law tied together in a forced rhetorical marriage. No government at all was the preferred choice over a government that held values foreign to a narrow perception of the modern republic.

Recall the words of the Senate minority leader, Mitch McConnell, in 2010 on the eve of the midterm elections: "The single most important thing we want to achieve is for President Obama to be a one-term president." Obama's annihilation became the essential policy platform of the Grand Old Party, which sought to eradicate his tenure by proclaiming it to be an aberration of history, a momentary lapse of *real* American representation. In 2011, McConnell, the highest-ranking Senate Republican, maintained that his major objective remained steadfast: "That's my single most important political goal, along with every active Republican in the country." The words repeated the calls in 2009 from Rush Limbaugh on his own radio show, and Fred Thompson on CNN for Obama, and his policies, to comprehensively fail. It was a curious strategic construction, stressing less the importance of right wing victory, but allowing the wish of Obama's personal failure to become the father of Republican thought. The personal sabotage of Obama, still manifest at the brink of America's default, economic, and job crises, reveals an ethic of identity politics at the very heart of the Right's strategy, even to the deficit of national progress.

One notable trend has been for right-wing political and media personalities to elicit racial prejudice without explicit reference. Whether it is John Sununu in July 2012 wishing that "this president would learn to be an American"; Mitt Romney in 2011 stating, "Sometimes, I just don't think that President Obama understands America"; or Sarah Palin's Facebook post claiming, "Obama's Shuck and Jive Ends with Benghazi Lies" (calling upon the parlance of slave field workers and their supposedly evasive behavior toward the ruling whites), many have insinuated that Obama's racial status precludes him from appreciating the core of (white) American values, placing him at the un-American fringe instead. It is clear that these are not simply fundamental disagreements based on the color-blind assessment of Obama's policies, but rather rejectionist, racially informed vocalizations striking at the heart of Obama's identity as *the* disqualifying factor.

In the ultimate extension of this strategy of personal and political alienation, calls for impeachment continue to emanate from the Tea Party and mainstream opposition leaders as a legitimate opportunity for Obama's defeat, though consistently lacking the foundation of the "high crimes and misdemeanors" defined in Article II of the U.S. Constitution. Though patently unsuccessful in their ends, such efforts sustain an air of vague illegitimacy surrounding Obama's right to govern. Where some attempted to remove Obama from the United States, others have sought to remove the United States from Obama. Only three weeks after his re-election in 2012, with the reality of Obama's legitimization made more real, almost 1 million people representing all 50 states had signed petitions calling for state secession. Residents of states including Alabama, Florida, Georgia, Louisiana, North Carolina, South Carolina, Tennessee, and Texas all (in an ironic twist) used the White House's own website petition feature ("We the People") to rack up more than the 25,000 signatures required each for a formal administration response. The Texan petition, which garnered over 125,000 signatories, claimed, "It is practically feasible for Texas to withdraw from the union, and to do so would protect its citizens' standard of living and re-secure their rights and liberties in accordance with the original ideas and beliefs of our founding fathers which are no longer being reflected by the federal government" (Holpuch 2012). Institutional whiteness was facing catastrophe, and many were unhappy with the portended doom of a racial paradigm shift. The Tea Party website petition to "Impeach President Obama & Remove Him from Office," in its first five months after being launched in May 2013, resulted in over 300,000 letters to Congress. These letters stated, "[Obama] has divided the country like in no time in history since the Civil War. He has pitted men against women, gay people against straight people, and used un-American, Marxist class warfare that has no place in a free America. He has caused racial strife by unjustifiably labeling anyone who disagrees with his USSR-style governance as a 'racist.' "

From the xenophobic, racist, misjudged, and deliberately foreignizing, we move to the quite frankly bizarre realm of Obama's "othering." Could Obama be a reptilian alien who has taken the reins of government on behalf of an otherworldly secret animalistic species? Might he be working with the Federal Emergency Management Agency (FEMA) to use refugee sites as proxies for communist "re-education camps" aimed at the nation's children? Has he actually spirited Osama Bin Laden out of Pakistan so as to keep him alive in a government-sponsored safe house? Is Obama's immigration policy the enabling factor to create a Muslim America replete with Sharia law? Was Obama's 2008 campaign bankrolled by socialist heavyweights, such as the now-deceased Venezuelan president, Hugo Chavez?

A slightly newer conspiracy of alienation from the Judeo-Christian American ideal, sustained by Jerome Corsi at *World Net Daily* (WND), focuses on Obama's "hidden" homosexual orientation. The "evidence" for this claim involves a ring Obama wore in college, and his appointment of gay and lesbian public servants within the administration. Incontrovertible, surely? "Was he married before he was married?" Corsi asks. "Was he married to a guy? What's the deal? I think these are legitimate questions" (Wong 2012). In 2012, Corsi stated, "[O]ver the past several months, WND investigators have interviewed a number of members of the church who claim the President benefited from [the Reverend Jeremiah] Wright's efforts to help black men who engage in homosexual activity appear respectable in black society by finding them a wife." Linked to this theory is the accusation that Obama attended gay bath-houses in Chicago with his first chief of staff, Rahm Emanuel, and that he had a love affair with his Pakistani Occidental roommate as well as his former personal assistant, Reggie Love. According to some propo-nents of this theory, Obama has ordered the murder of numerous prob-lematic witnesses to his gay past, including the killing of the openly gay choir director at Wright's Trinity Church, Donald Young; the execution-style elimination of Larry Bland, a black gay Trinity congre-gate; and the slaying of Nate Spencer, another member of Trinity Church. Erik Rush, also of *World Net Daily*, has attempted to implicate the sitting president in the murder of a hustler, a nurse, and journalist Michael Hastings, demonstrating that "the 'Chicago Way,' Marxist ruthlessness and autocracy rule the day." Obama is not just an immoral homosexual president in this Tea Party alternative-identity universe; he is a secret murderous one at that.

It is not only the Internet, blogosphere, right-wing press, and Tea Party representatives who proliferate damaging and poorly evidenced mistruths in an attempt to "other" the president, in lieu of genuine political argu-mentation. Walk into any bookshop or search for Obama-themed titles on Amazon, and you will find volumes such as *Where's the Birth Certifi-cate?*, *The Amateur*, *Gangster Government*, *The Roots of Obama's Rage*, *Conduct Unbecoming*, *Fool Me Twice*, *The Manchurian President*, *Divider in Chief*, *The Secret Life of Barack Hussein Obama*, *The Great Destroyer*, *Democracy Denied*, *The Communist*, *Dreams from My Real Father*, and *Radical in Chief*. The list is admittedly sophomoric, yet this book, in some small part, is intended as a retort to the content of such pages that masquerade as the stuff of nonfiction. The impact of such writings on the American psyche and its orientation toward the first African American president should not be underestimated or written off as the little-regarded fringe of political argumentation. Indeed, Joel Gilbert's DVD *Dreams from My Real Father: A Story of Reds and Deception*—which argues that Obama's real father was a Communist Party activist—was distributed to more than 1 million targeted voters in Ohio and Florida during the 2012 election. Books such as Corsi's *The Obama Nation* (2008), D'Souza's *Obama's America*, and Aaron Klein's *Fool Me Twice* continue to rise to the echelons of the *New York Times* bestseller list.

It seems a long way from that November 2008 night in Grant Park.

At the center of this foreignization, alienation, and racism-in-lieu-of-genuine-political-argument are, of course, Obama's mixed-race status and the unavoidable reality of an African American citizen becoming the U.S. head of state. Obama's ascension as an individual to the dizzy heights of political power was also a symbolic marker of general societal progress from the bounds of white American hegemony. His election signified an event of racial significance in the redefinition of the historical-societal dynamic of the black population. Whereas the national touchstones of slavery, the Civil War, Jim Crow, the civil rights movement, riots, assassinations, and lynchings had positioned the black individual over centuries as "less than" or barely equal to the value of whiteness, Obama's position of American and international preeminence dramatically shifted the paradigm of traditional racial signification; it wrapped the American Dream in the skin of a black man, forcing the reality of black representation upon some who would happily return to the Liberian deportation arguments of the late 19th century. Where right-wing opposition to Democratic policy intersects with remnant racist tendencies and the retreat to the long-established meaning of whiteness, the framing of Obama's foreignization as some racial "Other" is born and nourished. Almost all attacks on Obama based on race revert to the tropes, images, and code words of minority subjugation and alienation inherited from those historical fault lines of American racial oppression.

THE "OTHER" AND AMERICAN (UN)BELONGING

The foreignization of the first black U.S. president—and importantly the first *non-white* president in American history—is a manifestation of a philosophical concept known as the "Other," a concept strengthened and maintained by an historic American cultural equation of whiteness with belonging. Through its damaging manipulation, Obama has been written by the far Right (the "Tea Party anarchists") as the antithesis of America's promise, the undoing of the American Dream, and a dramatic reversal of the immigration mythology of America's founding.

Othering is a concept of 20th-century continental philosophy, though its existence undoubtedly runs in parallel to the very evolution of human identity. Othering is a central means of constituting one's identity in relation to another—the definition of the self in subjective contradistinction to an external locus of identity. To "other" as a form of societal or personal action is to bind self-identification within a transactional context of differentiation—between the known and the unknown, the near and the far, the home and away, the black and the white, the me and "not me." There is nothing structurally malignant in the process of othering; rather, it is the method by which we are able to constitute our own selves through the knowing of difference. It is how we form national identification in an international identity space, and how we affiliate with certain sports teams and engage in playful rivalries with others in the league. However, in practice, and in its association with a Eurocentric imperialist philosophy, to "other" is to positively position the self in distinction to a negative or unequal Other, whereby segregation, negative stereotyping, and actions of non-admittance strengthen the identity of the person, group, or society in question to the detriment of another. Othering stands in sharp opposition to the cooperative ethos of globalism and international interdependency; it is phenomenon that has contributed to the scarring landmarks of the Crusades, colonization, the transatlantic slave trade, the Gulags, the Holocaust, the Cold War, and the War on Terrorism. To other is to increasingly deny the ownership of characteristics and qualities that constitute the 'same'.

According to Myra Mendible, in her own study of race and class in the Age of Obama, the criticism surrounding the current president

often involves this amorphous "Othering" process: references to Obama's "questionable" birth certificate raise doubts about whether he was "really" born in America; allusions to his "Kenyon father" the "Luo tribesman" arouse suspicions about Obama's "Africanness"; use of the word "socialist" in conjunction with any policy Obama proposes, regardless of how centrist or moderate or capitalist, spooks middle-class Americans into opposing what might benefit them economically; and opportune uttering of his middle name, Hussein, works to denote Muslim or Middle Eastern affiliations with all that entails in post-9/11 America. Thus distortion and misinformation persist, circulated via popular conservative media outlets, talk radio, internet blogs, and even prominent political leaders. Not surprisingly, a Harris poll conducted in March of 2010 shows that 67% of Republicans believe Obama is a socialist, another 57% that he is a Muslim, and 45% that he was not born in the United States and is therefore ineligible for the presidency. (Mendible 2012)

While Obama has been cast by the Right as a demonized outsider, perversely disconnected from American and political normalcy, his opponents, especially in 2008 and 2012, have framed their own candidacies as bearing the hallmarks of righteous otherness, positive disconnectedness from the core of national power. John McCain, Sarah Palin, and Mitt Romney, for example, rode upon steeds of Washington-outsiderness, of straight-talking, non-elite, maverick hockey moms and ordinary businessmen, presenting themselves as positive alien forces, while negating Obama on the same grounds. The outsider trope seems both semantically fluid and racially inclined.

The origins of the Other as an intellectual concept are found within foundational continental philosophy. In Hegel's *Phenomenology of Spirit*

(1807), the "Other" is a feature of the philosopher's well-known parable of the master and slave dialectic, denoting a mode of recognition within the self-consciousness, rather than the harsh constitution of identity barriers that we find in modern-day usage. Jean-Paul Sartre also used the "Other" as a basis for his theories of human intersubjectivity—that is, the conceptualization of the psychological interaction among people(s)—in his work *Being and Nothingness* (1993). Here, the potential manifestation of another causes the self to interpret itself as an object within the view of that "Other." Sartre would later infamously state that "Hell is other people"— an appropriate slogan, perhaps, for the members of the far Right who continue to perceive President Obama as a devilish manifestation of incompatible, un-American difference.

Emmanuel Levinas, the French philosopher and ethicist, neologized the term "Other" in its modern usage, using it in his philosophical thought to describe the intersubjective relationship of humanity established through the face-to-face encounter. This encounter is the essential means of firmly establishing one's subjective relationship with the Other, which impacts "unlike any worldly object or force" (Bergo 2013). Psychoanalyst Jacques Lacan promulgated the concept of the "mirror stage" of childhood psychological development, in which the ego is formed as the infant meditates upon his or her own reflection in a mirror. The infant consequently misrecognizes the self as an "Other," which "marks a decisive turning-point in the mental development of the child ... it typifies an essential libidinal relationship to the body-image" (Lacan 2003 [1953], 300). In his seminal philosophical travelogue *Tristes Tropiques*, anthropologist Claude Levi-Strauss contemplates the relationship between man and an observer-Other arguing, from his anthropological perspective, that there are two distinct reactions to encountering difference:

If we were to look at them from outside it would be tempting to distinguish two opposing types of society: those which practice cannibalism who believe, that is to say, that the only way to neutralize people who are the repositories of certain redoubtable powers, and even to turn them to one's own advantage, is to absorb them into one's own body. Second would come those which, like our own, adopt what might be called anthropoemia (from the Greek *emein*, to vomit). Faced with the same problem, they have chosen the opposite solution. They expel these formidable beings from the body public by isolating them for a time, or forever, denying them all contact with humanity, in establishments devised for that express purpose. In most of the societies which we would call primitive this custom would inspire the profoundest horror: we should seem to them barbarian in the same degree as we impute to them on the ground of their no-more-than-symmetrical customs. (Levi-Strauss 1961, 386)

Levi-Strauss underscores his recognition of a Western "comfort" with the
expulsion and denigration of fellow human beings (metaphorical interpersonal vomiting), as opposed to their social (re)integration and total
assimilation (metaphorical interpersonal digestion).

   In recent decades, the phenomenon of othering has been understood in
the context of imperialism, as a result of the historical "unequal human
and territorial relationship" informed by Eurocentric "ideas of superiority and practices of dominance" (Gregory, Johnston, Pratt, Watts, and
Whatmore 2009). The colonializing impulse of those early international
empires—the Portuguese, Spanish, Dutch, French, Russian, and Italian
territories—was energized by the explorative promise of Renaissance
Europe and formed through the dominion of the aggressor and the subor-
dination of the conquered. The act of othering is a fundamentally binary
praxis of power dynamics, whereby a superior "we" is formed against a
conceptually inferior "they." This conceptual polarization was formed
in the rapid cut and thrust of landing, defeating, and controlling new-
found lands and associated resources in a process that permitted only
the narrowest glimpse into the native identity, denying all complexity
and shared humanity. Like the Lacan-esque child peering into the mirror
for the first time, those early explorers similarly contemplated a fellow
human community as a distant Other, an object that we interpret as distinct to our own identity and as somehow alien or foreign. This misrecog-
nition of the native object was tied to the essential motivation of those
early explorers, including Drake, Raleigh, Columbus, Pizarro, Vespucci,
Cortes, Marquette, and Hudson: to secure the totalizing ownership of
the exotic and wealth-making resources of "virgin" lands, and to justify
their treacherous crossings with the international enhancement of their
power, prestige, trading routes, and religious congregation. The identity
and dominance of invading forces were established physically through
enslavement, torture, murder, pillage, and colonization; forced linguisti-
cally through the introduction of English and Latin languages as the *lingua franca* of defeat; and visually compounded by a cartographic
psychological obsession with enlarging and centering Europe as the
"source" of civilization itself and asserting the preeminence of the
Northern Hemisphere.

   Imperialism is a historical event that demonstrates the impulse of othering to strengthen the homeland identity at the initial point of interaction
with an alternative human society. The very act of colonization displayed
the *prima facie* might and transportational skill of the respective
European power, providing a formative contradistinction to the passive,
supposedly non-explorative inhabitants of the colonized region. Othering
has been understood as an act of emphasizing the alleged weaknesses of

minority and marginalized groups as a means to enhance the perceived strength of those in positions of majority and power. These sociopolitical polarizations are extended to affirm the hierarchy of (generally white) groups of privilege, when such groups are faced with the crisis realization of alternative cultures: familiar versus strange, rich versus poor, weak versus strong, civilized versus savage, and human versus animal. Such exaggerated opposites were informed less by significant alterity than by what Freud termed the "narcissism of minor differences." These unequal binaries bolstered the invaders' colonial identity and justified their continuing dominion over the Other. Empire building was sustained only by the oxygen of these opposing paradigms, the trenchant prejudice and active discrimination that created a legacy of cultural elimination, segregation, resource poverty, ghettoization, and under-education. It is a story written throughout the pages of early anthropology, whereby the European author's gaze determined the hierarchical dynamic of the subject-object relationship between the observer and the observed. Colonial powers denied the international communities which they came into contact with of voice, respect, and knowledge. It is the utter manifestation of the clichéd Foucauldian institute of power—the regime of so-called truth, which continues to rig our discourse, including that of American racial politics—to this day.

Whereas colonial powers had imposed the "us versus them" dialectic upon the Americas and Africa to rationalize native subjugation, the 18th- and 19th-century movement known as Orientalism exercised a similar paradigm in the Middle East and Asia. Orientalism, as defined by Edward Said's seminal 1978 publication, is a means of "coming to terms with the Orient that is based on the Orient's special place in European Western experience" (Said 1978, 1). In simple terms, Orientalism is the artistic and literary imagining and representation of Arabic and Asian peoples that emphasizes the East as exotic, erotic, uncivilized, and corrupting. From Beckford's *Vathek,* Byron's *Turkish Tales,* Coleridge's *Kubla Khan,* and Johnson's *Rasselas,* to Verdi's *Aida* and Gilbert and Sullivan's *Mikado,* to the paintings of Jean-Auguste-Dominique Ingres and John Frederick Lewis, to the flying carpets of Aladdin, we find the formulaic justification of the West's fear, superiority, intervention, and proselytizing. The oriental Other is composed of sandscapes, harems, laden camels, hedonism, pyramids, and sheikhs that serve as metonyms for Eastern inferiority. Such characterizations retrofitted the Oriental Other to suit the historical incidence of European colonization of the Arabic and Asian regions of the world. As Bernasconi has written, "To characterize the other as primitive or exotic is in a sense to silence the other; it is to enclose the other in a cocoon from which he or she does not and cannot speak to me as an equal" (Bernasconi, 2012, 153–54). The Othering of non-European societies involved the silencing of the subjective perspectives of those at the receiving end of such prejudice.

The America of Obama's political inheritance is one that bears witness to a legacy of many instances of large-scale foreignization and alienation, as these concepts have been used to constitute the true American identity versus some "Other." American belonging has been, and continues to be, structured within institutions of whiteness, the hereditary consequence of a nation formed and sustained through colonization, conflict with Native American tribes, the importation and enslavement of Africans, and an economy based upon the physical and cultural domination of white hegemony. The early British colonization of the Eastern seaboard established a predominantly white European culture as supposedly moral, civil, superior, and, more often than not, spiritually chosen. Native American and West African cultures were defined in directly converse terms, often in want of white repair or redemption. That said, those early justifications for subjugation—that African forced labor was a necessary evil for a competitive colonial economy, that black skin and other physical differences denoted mental and moral inferiority, that God had created the African race for the explicit purpose to serve the white master, and that as non-Christians such persons (if they were indeed lucky enough to be considered as such) were desirous of spiritual reformation—were not always as clear cut, or as permanent, as they would come to be.

Though certainly never viewed as equal to the "high civilization" of white Europeans, Native Americans and imported black populations were not always immediately subjugated or enslaved during their initial interactions with the British settlers of the New World. In 1607 and during the establishment of Jamestown, Virginia, as the first permanent English colony of the Americas, for example, the subjects of James I were not initially motivated by an othering logic or a well-conceived notion of whiteness. They were dispatched in part to resist the Spanish domination of North America, and to seek profit and resources for British utilization. The diary of George Percy, who was among the inaugural 104 men and boys who settled Jamestown, reveals how the Powhatan tribe welcomed the travelers with dance, tobacco, grain, bread, and orations. The settlers were not well placed for agricultural success; indeed, they relied for many winter months upon the generosity of the native tribe for essential corn (Southern 2004). The marshy environs of Jamestown combined with the settlers' lamentable farming expertise resulted in high disease and mortality rates. Soon, relationships between the settlers and the Powhatan tribe deteriorated, resulting in on-and-off skirmishes and the genesis of the

Native-as-savage narrative. Under Percy's own leadership, the population dropped to 60, and the settlement was on the verge of being abandoned. John Rolfe (of Pocahontas fame) introduced successful tobacco crop plantations in 1612, which eventually required greater labor forces than could be provided by England alone. In 1619, Dutch traders brought the first African slaves to Jamestown, though many men were treated as indentured servants, able to win some measure of freedom through the fulfillment of duty or dutiful conversion. Anthony Johnson was one such African servant to be freed; he, in turn, became a highly successful and slave-owning tobacco farmer in Virginia. Initial colonial relationships with African and American natives were far more dynamic and fluid in this primordial colonial soup than often depicted in some sources.

However, as settlements expanded with the capture and destruction of Native peoples, and as the importation of enslaved Africans increased, demarcations between colonial and "Other" parties became more polarized. The previously nonexistent legal construct governing slavery practice became formalized over the late 17th and early 18th centuries, resulting in the development of slave codes. Virginia was at the forefront of introducing the standards and expectations for slave statuses and behaviors. In 1659, slaves were denied arms; in 1662, the bondage or freedom of children born in Virginia was determined "only according to the condition of the mother"; in 1691, emancipation was prohibited unless the master was willing to cover the cost of onward transport; in the same year, miscegenation was criminalized; subsequently rights to vote and hold office were eliminated; Christianity became a determinant for liberty; and by 1705, Virginia's House of Burgesses had established the unforgiving framework regulating slavery where "All Negro, mulatto and Indian slaves within this dominion . . . shall be held to be real estate." Not only was an African diaspora created by the colonization of the New World, but newcomers to Spanish Florida, the Carolinas, New England, and Virginia enslaved many Native Americans or exported them to Caribbean plantations.

The binary polarizations of the colonial era became entrenched in law, economy, politics, and tradition. Almost no resistance to the institution of slavery by white colonists was recorded until the Revolutionary War era. Even the Quakers' official resistance to slavery was shelved for well over a century until the ignition of the abolition movement. As a consequence of generational dominance, the European American, though formed through immigration, was established as the paragon of citizenship, privileged through the infrastructure of education, land rights, franchise, immigration policy, and legal definition. Prejudice through racial othering was legitimated throughout slavery, Native American reservations and internment camps, segregation, Liberian deportation efforts, the collapse of Reconstruction, the strictures of the Jim Crow era, white supremacist movements, lynchings, and race riots. Progress made in the 20th century toward curing the racist othering that Einstein classed as America's "worst disease" was significant but no panacea. Inequalities of wealth, educational attainment, home ownership, unemployment, prison population, agricultural access, and political representation persist in the 21st century, with some inequalities continuing to widen in the wake of the economic collapse and credit crunch of 2007.

Against the backdrop of America's racial history, President Barack Obama's election held significance in terms of both the country's progress and its shortcomings. First, the ascension of a black man to the nation's supreme political office, elected by a greater percentage of white voters than voted for John Kerry in 2004, signaled a social and political degree of national restoration. Obama's rhetoric of transformation, change, and purposeful integration took the baton from the civil rights language of the 1960s, and built and sustained a diverse coalition of grassroots and electoral support to achieve unexpected victory. Obama's triumph was, symbolically at least, a partial cure for the illness of institutional racism. Yet the repercussions of Obama's meteoric rise were to make the symptoms of America's hereditary disease of othering more pronounced. As a man born of an African father, on the American outskirts, schooled for some time in Indonesia, with an Arabic-rooted middle name, the reality of Obama's preeminence raised the ghosts and anxieties of the rhythmic prejudices that had emerged throughout America's history. His very existence and national elevation represented a catastrophe for institutional whiteness, the legacy of the master-slave, black-white segregationist dialectic that persists at the explicit and implicit level in many areas of American life and psychology.

To understand how whiteness functions is to understand the historical and modern black experience as it is relevant to the sometimes racialized rejection of Obama's presidency. Whiteness studies, initiated by the work of W. E. B. Du Bois, take as their central tenet that whiteness is a historically informed social construction that governs the continuing structural discrimination of non-white peoples. "The white problem," Bruce Baum maintains, "remains a central and disabling feature of, and barrier to, struggles for social justice" (Baum 2011, 2). The white problem, as it has come to be described, is a product of America's colonial inheritance whereby non-whites "were framed as divinely, biologically, or culturally in need of either annihilation or subjugation" (Hughey 2012, 165). According to James Baldwin, author of the 1964 publication *The White Problem*, white Americans misremember that "[i]n this extraordinary endeavor to create the country called America, a great many crimes were committed" (Baldwin 1964a, 83). As Baum extrapolates, "American mythology enables white Americans to deny or minimize these crimes, which included the decimation of Native Americans and the enslavement of Africans" (Baum 2011, 9). There is, in other terms, a tendency to view the entire stretch of history, and the present, through white-tinted lenses.

Baldwin, echoing the remnant divisions of the colonial immigration experience, describes his own introduction to Great Depression era America as a black man as still structurally dichotomous. "I was brought here," he writes,

And when I got here, I did not, like the Irish and the Jews and the Russians and the Poles and the Czechs and the Italians immediately find myself in a slum and then by hard work and saving my pennies rise out of the slum into a position of relative economic security so that my idea of reality changed. The black experience is entirely different. You find yourself in a slum and you realize at a certain point that no amount of labor, no amount of hard work, no amount of soap is going to get you out of that slum. (Baldwin 1964b, 32)

The slum, of course, is as much metaphorical as it is physical when speaking to ongoing racial prejudice. Progress over the decades has undoubtedly been made, though true equality remains painfully elusive. Since the race riots of the 1960s and the murders of Martin Luther King, Jr., and Robert F. Kennedy, explicit racism has, in the main, been sent underground, receding somewhat from public acceptability, while becoming coded, subtle, and malevolent—often invisible to entire swathes of Americans. As Christopher Hitchens maintains, out-and-out racism after the civil rights movement era "became less respectable and, with the defection of white Southerners to the Republican party, more a matter of codes and signals" (Hitchens 2010a). As de jure segregation came to an end, so did the momentum of the national engagement with the black movement. The now-infamously racialized Willie Horton ad ushered in a period of pernicious coding, whereby "words achieve their intended effect by arousing the same kinds of anxieties that 'blackness' does in a racist, but without implicating the speaker in racism" (Mendible 2012). The Trayvon Martin case and its aftermath reverberated because it signaled an entire nation's racial blindness to the genuine quotidian experience of young black men, walking home in a neighborhood of unspoken, but sometimes deadly, prejudice. It is unmistakably clear that the rejection of Barack Obama comprises extreme demonization informed by, if not based upon, race differentiation and its attendant stereotypical associations. And while this frequently occurs in broad political daylight, it also often remains quiet and subtle, functioning below the radar of widespread recognition.

Whiteness, as the go-to structure of American identity, is the default setting of U.S. belonging. Despite the great diversification of the country's racial make-up, the advantage and historical power of whiteness flow through the very veins of America's normativity. The boisterous and loud prejudice of old is alive and well (and perhaps increasing in the age of Obama), but the post-civil rights era is also marked by the largely unreferenced discrimination against non-whites through the continuing elevation of whiteness—in law, education, institutional rules, and behavioral and political expectations. Because of the privilege that whiteness affords to whites, it is regularly activated without their perception. As David Owen explains, whiteness "systematically shapes all aspects of the social world, providing whites with unrecognized (to them) advantages and benefits, and persons of color with recognized (to them) disadvantages and burdens" (Owen 2010, 116). The George Zimmerman trial and the circumstances of Trayvon Martin's death crystallized, for a moment, the gulf of racial experience and the privilege of *thinking whitely* in modern America. The outcome of that case, despite the intricacies of Florida law, demonstrated, for some, the institutional racist bias that continues to be maintained 400 years after colonization of the New World began. Eugene Robinson, writing for *The Washington Post*, translated the inequalities with eloquence:

The assumption ... was that Zimmerman had the right to self-defense but Martin—young, male, black—did not. The assumption was that Zimmerman would fear for his life in a hand-to-hand struggle but Martin—young, male, black—would not. ... I call this racism. What do you call it? Trayvon Martin was fighting more than George Zimmerman that night. He was up against prejudices as old as American history, and he never had a chance. (Robinson 2013)

To extend this idea further, Obama—an African American in the company of 43 white presidents—stood little chance against the ingrained prejudices of some members of the far Right who buy into (or who can easily be persuaded to buy into) a mode of racial thinking. When a white man shouts, "You lie!" during a formal presidential address to Congress; when white men and women demand the submission of Obama's birth certificate; when Hillary Clinton's chief strategist describes Obama as "not at his center fundamentally American in his thinking"; and when Christians stress his middle name and overseas influence, Obama's opponents are encouraging their listeners to perpetuate a lens of whiteness, which holds that Obama is deserving of neither respect nor the office which he holds. This is an "Other" president, and the same rules do not apply. As the early civil rights activist and author James Weldon Johnson has said, "The main difficulty of the race question does not lie so much in the actual condition of the blacks as it does in the mental attitude of the whites" (Johnson 1912).

Obama himself, of course, has contributed to the phenomenon of his own demonization on the basis of race. Framing his candidacy as the stepping stone to a place of racial harmonization, and lauded as the representative of post-racialism, Obama's success prematurely foreclosed discussions of ongoing inequality and the dominance of whiteness and systematic othering. The symbolic position of Obama as a black paragon denied the everyday experience of non-presidential minorities. He rarely spoke, or speaks, about race, having provided only one (albeit powerful) deliberative oration on race in his 2007 "More Perfect Union" speech, which was forced by his need to limit the political damage from the Jeremiah Wright firestorm. Obama has refrained from pursuing any explicit agenda of racial equality, and he has deliberately framed himself as a "cool" and "calm" guy, resisting the associations of the militant or "Angry Black Man." Yet, because Americans largely "regard the gap in black-white socio-economic status in strictly individualistic rather than structural terms," Obama's election by national majority suggested that a collective failing had been overcome (Baum 2011, 16). In the wake of Obama's election, almost two-thirds of Americans surveyed believed that blacks had achieved racial equality and more than four-fifths believed that the post-racial moment had arrived. Dangerously, in reaction to Obama's success, whiteness was cast by some as a political handicap: "Obama is only in this position because he is black," said Geraldine Ferraro; "I'm only a white male," said a plaintive John Edwards in reference to the new "privilege" of Obama's blackness and Hillary's womanhood. Evidently, for some, Obama's election not only facilitated and expressed equality, but actually tipped the balance the other way. Christopher Hitchens put it best: "[N]obody with any feeling for the Zeitgeist can avoid any feeling for the symptoms of white unease and the additionally uneasy forms that its expression is beginning to take" (Hitchens 2010b).

Secession, impeachment, and assassination plots have been hatched as whiteness comes under attack from this "Other" president. Membership in paramilitary organizations, militias, and hate groups has multiplied in direct correspondence to Obama's election. Astonishingly, according to the Southern Poverty Law Center, the number of conspiracy-rich patriot organizations, including armed militias, has risen by 813 percent since Obama's election: from 149 in 2008 to 1,360 in 2012. "Patriotism" has become a byword for pre-2008 American values of whiteness and racially based opposition to the leadership of the mixed-race Obama. In 2010, the Southern Poverty Law Center reported alarm at the surge of identity-based violence:

Since the installation of Barack Obama, it reported, "right wing extremists have murdered six law enforcement officers. Racist skinheads and others have been arrested in alleged plots to assassinate the nation's first black president. . . . Most recently, a rash of individuals with anti-government survivalist or racist views have been arrested in a series of bomb cases." (Potok 2010)

The rejection of Obama has led to the wholesale rejection of government or federal power, because of the supposedly un-American status of its temporary representative—a fact that can only be dangerous to the institutional future of American democracy itself. In this new political universe, to identify as patriotic is to reject Washington, D.C., all government process and intervention, and Obama himself, all of which the right wing perceives as having collectively moved America away from the pure roots of its founding. Anti-Obama patriotism became a shibboleth for Republican membership and credibility. This perspective is why the Affordable Healthcare Act is tied to Obama's identity as "Obamacare": for the extremists, it is not a real law, but rather an antipatriotic law outside of the normative values of real Americanness. It is stamped with the name of the Other president. It is why Obama is robbed of his childhood, of an American story, of an ordinary Christian heritage, of presidential respect. A new patriotism has arisen, whose initiation ceremony is to metaphorically burn the effigy of the 44th president. Mendible puts it well:

Americanness in the age of Obama invokes "patriotic" themes associated with historically Anglo-American myths of cultural belonging. . . . It invokes an imagined community united by religious (Judeo Christian) and economic (capitalist/ free market) kinship. Differentiating Obama depends on excluding him from these foundational narratives—portraying him as an outsider who holds no authentic ties to "American" history or values. (Mendible 2012)

The Tea Party—a moniker for a broad range of conservative views, but now increasingly extreme—was established as the vanguard of supposedly real American values, in direct response to the election of Barack Obama and the perceived growth of federal power. Anti-government, anti-taxation, and overwhelmingly white, the Tea Party poses as the defender of an ever fragile Americanness against tides of demographic change, progressive societal values, and the relative secularization of society. With a laser focus on delegitimizing President Obama, the Tea Party has amassed significant electoral support (in the 2010 midterm elections), sparked mass protests, incited violence and hatred, shut down the U.S. federal government, threatened the debt ceiling, and embarrassed presidential authority in the name of patriotic value.

The Tea Party movement, draped with flags and antique American imagery, purposefully conjures up the lexicon and values of the colonial age. It is a form of mass psycho-political reversion therapy that seeks to return to a time in which Obama's presidency was a legal and social impossibility. It attempts to reclaim a period of history famous for its antiestablishment revolt, for its casting off of the shackles of conventional authority, and for iconic, destructive protest. The recoding of the Boston Tea Party protest, which was a precursor to the American Revolution, reminds the nation of an era of unwelcome, and soon rejected, un-American rule. In this new parlance of far Right rhetoric, Obama is cast as the distant, foreignized autocrat, to be overthrown by sustained revolution. Similarly, the Tea Party brings to the fore images from an age of mass African American enslavement—indeed, the complete subjugation and devaluation of non-white peoples—in juxtaposition to a century of relative racial progress. The original rejection of the British Tea Act of 1773 pivoted upon the "No taxation without representation" slogan expressing 18th-century colonial grievances. This ethic of noncompliance with a political leader to which the group does not feel fiduciary allegiance is no doubt a purposeful echo to the modern age in which the 21st-century Tea Party rejects Obama's policy as misrepresentative of American value. As the logic goes, if the Massachusetts Sons of Liberty could tip British tea into the harbor waters (a grave insult to monarchical power), then their modern counterparts could systematically jettison policy, spending, implementation, negotiation, compromise, gun reform, and logic as if still navigating revolutionary, pre-bipartisan times. In October 2013, for example, as the federal government shutdown and its associated gridlock persisted, some in the GOP refused to negotiate without the repeal of the Affordable Healthcare Act and (hiding behind claims of patriotism) seemed to accept the associated damage to the nation. Virginia Congressman Morgan Griffith compared the evidently reckless political stratagem of the far Right with the violence of the Revolutionary ethos:

what may be distasteful, unpleasant and not appropriate in the short run may be something that has to be done. . . . I will remind you that this group of renegades that decided that they wanted to break from the crown in 1776 did great damage to the economy of the colonies. They created the greatest nation and the best form of government, but they did damage to the economy in the short run. (Lavender, 2013)

Tea Party members rhetorically anchor themselves to this era, with their opposition to Obama—often on relatively minor issues—extrapolated to suggest the weight of an epic historical battle in some pre-modern time zone where a black progressive presidency cannot, or should not, exist.

As Christopher Parker found during his research for *Change They Can't Believe In: The Tea Party and Reactionary Politics in America,* "people who supported the Tea Party tended to be more racist, sexist, homophobic, xenophobic, and anti-Obama" (Klein, 2013). Roll these impulses into one, and you have the basic motivations behind the multi-variate idea of Obama's foreignization. The Tea Party is not simply a useful borrowed name, claimed by serious, small-government, low-tax conservatives; rather, it is increasingly synonymous with craziness, immovability, and irresponsibility, fueled by the politically, racially, and xenophobically motivated nonacceptance of Obama's reality. The Tea Party others the president as a means to retain the sense of historical American (white) dominance in an oft-perverted, medieval sense of patriotism, wreaking the colonial trauma upon the modern political landscape in the name of the republic's values. The Tea Party proliferates, and is sustained by, the fear of Obama as an alien, un-American political antihero, resurrecting a history of national turmoil and revolution to incite and legitimize Tea Party members' extremist language and opposition. Such national demonization builds upon the American perception of modern international pandemonium—a world in which Obama's presidency bears witness to a global landscape peopled with murderous dictatorships, anonymous terrorists, and imperceptible enemies.

THE AXIS OF OTHER: FOREIGN(IZED) ENEMIES IN THE WAKE OF 9/11

The fear of the Other is a stable and recurring vignette in America's internal narrative, an arguably unavoidable mechanism within a national symbolic construct. Its prominence has ebbed and flowed throughout the history of the republic—forged in settlement and colonization, formalized in a two-party political system, revived in the Civil War, piqued in the McCarthy hearings, roused in civil rights clashes, and torturously made manifest in the falling towers of 9/11. Obama's presidency and the rise of political extremism via the Tea Party and other right-wing groups have arrived in the context of one of America's greatest periods of anxiety, in which cognitive binaries between good and evil, us and them, form much of the political framework deployed and internalized to comprehend the country's situation and vulnerability in the *international* landscape.

No words can translate the flame, malevolence, dust, screaming, hero-ism, collapse, perplexity, and loss experienced on September 11, 2001. News organizations had little information to provide to their publics, as initial assumptions that "This must be some horrific accident" gave way to "We are under attack." Varying reports about more planes haunting that piercing blue sky, breaking news of an explosive crash at the Penta-gon (the center of U.S. defense), a (false) report of a car bomb at the U.S. Capitol, and the thunderous crash of United Airlines Flight 93, com-bined to create a sense of complete global chaos. As Sue Veres Royal, co-director of the U.S. in the World Initiative, has written, "The events of September 11, 2001 struck an unexpecting, yet already weary American public whose view of the rest of the world was that of a world filled with problems, disorder and dangerous people" (Veres Royal 2011, 405). This was not an attack on soldiers stationed overseas or a U.S. embassy; it was the encroachment of that danger into the heart and soul of America itself. The sheer unlikelihood and unpredictability of the terrorists' scope, organization, and lethal accuracy prompted the resurrection of "a dis-torted narrative ... that fell in line with precarious stereotypes—dehumanizing entire populations" (Veres Royal 2011, 405).

With the dearth of any standard enemy locus—no state, no dictator, no defined territory—the George W. Bush administration moved to endow terrorism with a certain corporeality to establish the abstract "War on Terror" as a legitimate binary opposition for American comprehension and reaction. The worldview paradigm of complexity, danger, and may-hem was cascaded into a simple ordered duplex of friend and enemy, same and other, American and un-American. This linguistic strategy rec-onciled the public's interpretation of international chaos in the wake of that attack into a fundamentally crude fairy-tale narrative, supporting the tenet of cognitive science that human beings are innate story-tellers and story-receivers, navigating narratives as modes of comprehension. This narrative was so easily established as an organizational structure because it reverted to latent stereotypes of foreign, Arab, and Muslim worlds and reaffirmed America as the home of liberty and virtue, opposed directly by the dark forces of what President Bush would term an "axis of evil."

Orientalist narratives that had sustained the mythic figure of an anti-thetical Arabic figure were essential for the adhesion of this organizing principle. Bush's depiction of the 12 terrorist actors extended the cookie-cutter narrative of Arabic peoples as hateful, suspicious, and reli-giously alien that was perpetuated in literature, television, and film. In the political resurrection of this stereotype, "Actions, policy, and politi-cal debate now found a replacement for evil or the enemy, whose place on the field had been left open (or at least had been a constantly revolving door) for a decade after the collapse of the USSR. The new opponent/ enemy now had a face—that of a twenty-to-thirty-five-year-old Arab man" (Veres Royal 2011, 407).

Arguably the impact of the 9/11 terrorist attacks and their ramifications for the public interpretation of danger are at the core of Obama's presidency and set the tone for the opposition that has come to define it. Whereas Bush's position in this dichotomy of good and evil was secured and protected by the othering impulse at 9/11's epicenter, Obama—as a mixed-race, young man with a Kenyan father and an Arabic middle name, with a conciliatory approach toward the resolution of Middle Eastern disputes—perversely revived the primordial fears of an America under threat. The hyper-personalization and racialization of America's newest international enemy encouraged the everyman's interpretation of national security in very individual terms. The ensuing level of terror-personification created the space for the identity politics that formed the basis of the hard Right's anti-Obama attacks. As Veres Royal (2011, 408) maintains, "in times of heightened fear and anxiety, stereotypes are exacerbated, identity with one's own group increases, suspicion of other groups is heightened, and we hold tightly to familiar/default scenarios." In the days following 9/11, the corporealization of terror in the aftermath's rhetoric meant that terrorism could now technically inhabit any potential host body, like some anti-American epidemic ready to destroy the *body politic*. To conclude that this impulse is both real and culturally manifest, one need not only look to Obama's demonization by Tea Party extremists, but also to its fictional reflection in the hit television drama *Homeland*. In this cable series, a young U.S. Congressman and war hero, Nicholas Brody, emerges as a clandestine and murderous jihadi, simultaneously an attractive and dangerous ascendant political personality who rapidly approaches (vice)-presidential office. The series, as with Obama's opposition, turns upon the relative uncertainty of the politician's true identity, perpetuated by scant evidence, latent fears, and the problematic binary formation of an America's post-9/11 psyche.

The state of emergency into which America lurched resulted in the (temporary) abandonment of ordinary process, protocol, and etiquette; it changed the landscape of appropriate interpersonal relationships. Greater airport security, locked cockpits, racial profiling, the Patriot Act, and the Guantanamo Bay prison were introduced with sometimes surprising ease, despite their essential contrariness to pre-9/11 libertarian philosophy. There was a necessary suspension of traditional national logic, whereby discrimination became an entrenched facet of effective national security. World Initiative focus group research conducted in

2009 in conjunction with the Topos Partnership revealed that respondents were generally content with a level of racialized annoyance for the benefit of national security: "If Muslim and Arab Americans are patriotic Americans," they pondered, "they won't mind the extra inconvenience" (Veres Royal 2011, 413).

Such a reality begs the question as to whether such a suspension of rationality has been extended into the realm of presidential critique, whereby to hamper the executive office with requests for birth certificates, college transcripts, secession, and impeachment are legitimate "inconveniences" in a landscape of familiar demonization and emergency. Participants' somewhat nonchalant recognition but acceptance of discriminatory practice perhaps provides some insight into the seeming under-the-radar status of Obama's alienation. We have been prone to let it slide, perhaps, because a man with certain qualities is barred from respect and equal treatment, even if he is elected as head of state. Many in America are trapped to a larger extent than others in the post-9/11 cognitive framework of patriotic mistrust of characters associated with a place of global chaos.

Certain neuroscientific research would support that such a construct and its robustness are products of how the physical brain itself is wired to cope with perceived danger or fear. The seat of our rational consciousness and empathy can be momentarily overtaken by a stimulus of imminent danger or legitimate trepidation. The fight-or-flight mechanism supersedes nonessential thought processes, stripping away the "soft" brain functions that define our humanity and justifying action on the basis of survival alone. "When hyperaroused, the brain's fear system literally commandeers consciousness," Veres Royal summarizes, "it guides and influences our thinking and in some instances determines … 'whether we are able to "think" at all' " (Veres Royal 2011, 411). If an emergency atmosphere is sustained by the ill-defined and amorphous continuation of a War on Terror, we might extrapolate these neuroscientific principles to the political world, whereby Obama's threat to the hard Right's political survival has manifested a collective suspension of ordinary or rational conduct.

In 2010, for example, Terry Jones, a pastor of the ironically named Dove World Outreach Center in Florida, gained international attention when he claimed that he and some compatriots planned to burn 200 copies of the Quran on the anniversary of the 9/11 attacks. Jones was arrested in 2013 with thousands of kerosene-soaked copies of the Holy Book in his possession. Michele Bachmann demanded an investigation in 2012 into the influence of the Muslim Brotherhood within Obama's Departments of Justice and Homeland Security, as well as into Obama's plans to impose Sharia law onto the American people. The country grappled with the prospect that a mosque might be constructed near the Ground Zero site, raising the ghost of that 9/11 panic and bringing un-American xenophobic arguments to the fore. Our collective prefrontal cortex may remain hampered by the never-ending perception of a fearful Other, based on instinctive judgment to the detriment of careful consideration of the evidence.

CONCLUSION

We have established that President Barack Obama has been subjected to extraordinary methods of rejection, alienation, and demonization; that such impulses are informed by a human desire to define the "Other" as part of the formation of group identification; that Obama's othering is informed by America's specific racial and divisive histories; that whiteness (and its associations) remains the dominant structural and political lens for the interpretation of events in the United States; and that the perception of international chaos has reoriented the American psyche to fear forms of foreignness and to suspend pre-2001 behavioral normativity. The attacks upon Obama as a Kenyan, terrorist, socialist, Muslim, lying foreigner, for example, find their motivation in some, or all, of these dynamic sociopolitical forces at play during the 21st-century presidency.

Never before has a single candidate or president been so outrageously and systematically maligned by so many, in such sundry ways—and yet won. This volume, in some small part, aims to understand this Obama-as-Other paradox. That is, it seeks to decipher how Obama's candidacy and elections, as unparalleled modes of national legitimization, inspired a converse cult of delegitimizing *ad hominem* rhetoric, at the center of which was an unprecedented level of discourse anchored in the rejection of political identity, based on antique modes of American belonging.

This book is arranged to assess the central methods and motivations behind Obama's unparalleled demonization as a political leader and to elucidate his continuing success in reorienting such attacks to his own electoral and popular advantage.

Chapter 2 examines the genesis myth of Obama's alienation—that he is a president from foreign soil. It assesses Obama's biography against the multitude of narratives that have been created to perpetuate the racially inclined rejection of Obama as a legitimate American citizen and representative. It traces the emergence of Birtherism and the diverse array of conspiracy theories surrounding the location of Obama's infancy, including the forced submission of a presidential birth certificate as a landmark event of elite racism. This chapter also examines the extent to which the birth certificate trope aims to rekindle ancient associations of black origin, vivifying the ghosts of extreme racial subjugation (such as slavery), and reintroduces a "show your papers" standard as established during the Jim Crow era. In delegitimizing Barack Obama by virtue of birth, a predominantly WASP political constituency is wielding an unprecedented racial yardstick.

Chapter 3 examines the role that Obama's mixed-race status has played in his biography, elections, presidency, and modes of foreignization, providing assessment of the utter contradistinction of Obama's promise of a post-racial America with one of the most racially fractious political dynamics in modern times. The chapter examines the role that whiteness continues to play in reconciling the first non-white president in American history, and the assertions from Gingrich, Sununu, Romney, and others that Obama is too black, too stupid, too Kenyan, too lazy, or too angry to legitimately represent America and its citizenry.

The demonization of Obama as a covertly Islamic president is examined in Chapter 4. Owing to his unusual middle name, Kenyan father, and sometimes overseas education, opponents have—in a perverse application of 9/11 fear—depicted the president as Muslim, as an Islamic fundamentalist, and even as a jihadist. This chapter addresses the dehumanization of Obama within the age of terror-anxiety as well as the extent to which Obama's pursuit of sustained military operations in the Middle East—and his ordained killing of Osama bin Laden—have altered the Obama-as-Muslim dynamic.

Chapter 5 reveals the tactics of the Right in transmogrifying Obama's Democratic political identification into a form of maligned (European) communism. Examples are drawn primarily from the fervent partisanship surrounding Obama's healthcare legislation, through which Obama was painted as a militant Marxist, under European influence, destroying America from within. This chapter examines the framing of health legislation as Obamacare as a method of tying the fate of medical progress to Obama's own problematic legacy, as well as the exaggerative demonic tropes that emerged, such as death panels. The notion of the communist enemy within is, once again, a reinvigoration of historical American othering. This chapter explores how it has been given new life by attaching Obama to leading communist influences, such as his "true" secret father (Frank Marshall Davis) and a redistributive philosophy.

The final chapter examines the paradox upon which this entire volume turns—that is, how President Obama has been able to, from his youth, recognize the problematic markers of his potential marginalization and transform them, through rhetorical manipulation, strategic intent, and social media, into positive electoral attributes. Obama's success is to be understood as a result of anti-foreignization survival instincts, tuned to overcome the nascent barriers of American institutions and culture. More specifically, this chapter underlines how Obama uses elements of his own "otherness" to appeal to different, and often alienated, constituents in building one of the most formidable coalitions of support in the last century.

REFERENCES

Baldwin, James. "The White Problem." In *100 Years of Emancipation*, edited by Robert A. Goldwin, 80. Chicago: Rand McNally, 1964a.

Baldwin, James. In James Baldwin, Nathan Glazer, Sidney Hook, and Gunnar Myrdal. "Liberalism and the Negro: A Round-Table Discussion." *Commentary* 37 (1964b): 25–42

Baum, Bruce. "Barack Obama and the White Problem." Paper presented at the Annual Meeting of the Western Political Science Association, San Antonio, TX, April 21–23, 2011.

Bergo, Bettina. "Emmanuel Levinas." In *The Stanford Encyclopedia of Philosophy*, edited by Edward N. Zalta. Summer 2013. http://plato.stanford.edu/archives/sum2013/entries/levinas.

Bernasconi, Robert. "Othering." In *Critical Communities and Aesthetic Practices: Contributions to Phenomenology,* Vol. 64, edited by Francis Halsall, Julia Jansen, & Sinead Murphy, 151–157. New York: Springer, 2012.

Condon, Stephanie. "Poll: One in Four Americans Think Obama Was Not Born in U.S." *CBS News* (April 21, 2011). http://www.cbsnews.com/news/poll-one-in-four-americans-think-obama-was-not-born-in-us/.

Corsi, Jerome. *The Obama Nation.* New York: Simon and Schuster, 2008.

Gregory, Derek, Ron Johnston, Geraldine Pratt, Michael Watts, and Sarah Whatmore, eds. *The Dictionary of Human Geography,* 5th ed. Oxford, UK: Wiley-Blackwell, 2009.

Hegel, Georg W. F. *Phenomenology of Spirit.* Digireads.com Publishing: 2009.

Hitchens, Christopher. "From the N-Word to Code Words." *Slate* (September 20, 2010a). http://www.slate.com/articles/news_and_politics/fighting_words/2010/09/from_the_nword_to_code_words.html.

Hitchens, Christopher. "White Fright." *Slate* (August 30, 2010b). http://www.slate.com/articles/news_and_politics/fighting_words/2010/08/white_fright.html.

Holpuch, Amanda. "White House Petition for Texas Independence Qualifies for Response." *The Guardian* (November 13, 2012). http://www.theguardian.com/world/2012/nov/13/white-house-petition-texas-independence.

Hughey, Matthew W. " 'Show Me Your Papers': Obama's Birth and the Whiteness of Belonging." *Qualitative Sociology* 35, no. 2 (2012): 163–181.

Johnson, James W. *The Autobiography of an Ex-Colored Man.* Boston: Sherman, French & Company, 1912. http://www.ibiblio.org/eldritch/jwj/auto.htm.

Klein, Ezra. "People Don't Fully Appreciate How Committed the Tea Party Is to Not Compromising." *Washington Post* (October 4, 2013). http://www .washingtonpost.com/blogs/wonkblog/wp/2013/10/04/people-dont-fully -appreciate-how-committed-the-tea-party-is-to-not-compromising/.

Lacan, Jacques. "Some Reflections on the Ego." In *Influential Papers from the 1950s,* edited by Andrew C. Furman and Steven T. Levy, 293–306. London: Karnac, 2003 [1953].

Lavender, Paige. "Morgan Griffith, GOP Rep, Compares Default to American Revolution." *Huffington Post* (October 12, 2013). http://www.huffingtonpost .com/2013/10/12/default-american-revolution-morgan-griffith_n_4089911 .html.

Levi-Strauss, Claude. *Triste Tropiques,* translated by John Russell. London: Criterion, 1961.

Martin, Andy. "Columnist Says Barack Obama 'Lied to the American People'; Asks Publisher to Withdraw Obama's Book." *Free Library* (August 11, 2004). http://www.thefreelibrary.com/Columnist Says Barack Obama 'Lied To The American People;' Asks. . .-a0120417594.

Mendible, Myra. "The Politics of Race and Class in the Age of Obama." *Revue de recherche en civilisation américaine* 3 (March 2012). http://rrca.revues. org/489.

Obama, Barack H. "Victory Speech." Speech given in Chicago, IL, November 4, 2008. *BBC News.* http://news.bbc.co.uk/1/hi/world/americas/us_elections _2008/7710038.stm.

Obama, Barack H. "Remarks by the President." Speech given in Washington, DC, April 27, 2011. The White House. http://www.whitehouse.gov/the -press-office/2011/04/27/remarks-president.

Owen, David. "Othering Obama: How Whiteness Is Used to Undermine Authority." *Altre Modernità* 3 (March 2010): 112–119. doi: 10.13130/2035-7680/517.

Pareene, Alex. "How Can Michele Bachmann Be President If She Won't Release Her Birth Certificate?" *Salon* (March 17, 2011). http://www.salon.com/ 2011/03/17/bachmann_birth_certificate/.

Pierce, Charles P. "What Is Not about Race." *Esquire* (August 8, 2013). http:// www.esquire.com/blogs/politics/The_President_In_Arizona.

Politifact.com. 2007. "Obama Attended an Indonesian Public School." December 20, 2007. http://www.politifact.com/truth-o-meter/statements/2007/dec/ 20/chain-email/obama-attended-an-indonesian-public-school/.

Potok, Mark. "Rage on the Right: This Year in Hate and Extremism." *Southern Poverty Law Centre Intelligence Report* 137 (Spring 2010). http://www .splcenter.org/get-informed/intelligence-report/browse-all-issues/2010/ spring/rage-on-the-right.

Robinson, Eugene. "Black Boys Denied the Right to Be Young." *Washington Post* (July 15, 2013). http://www.washingtonpost.com/opinions/eugene -robinson-black-boys-denied-the-right-to-be-young/2013/07/15/d3f603d8 -ed69-11e2-9008-61e94a7ea20d_story.html

Said, Edward W. *Orientalism.* London: Routledge & Kegan Paul, 1978.

Sampley, Ted. "Barack Obama: Who Is He?" *U.S. Veteran Dispatch* (December 29, 2006). http://www.usvetdsp.com/dec06/obama_muslim.htm.

Sartre, Jean-Paul. *Being and Nothingness,* translated by Hazel E. Barnes. New York: Washington Square Press, 1993.

Smith, Ben. "Palin: Obama Birth Certificate 'a Fair Question.' " *Politico* (December 3, 2009). http://www.politico.com/blogs/bensmith/1209/Palin_Obama _birth_certificate_a_fair_question.html.

Southern, Ed. "Observations Gathered out of a Discourse of the Plantation of the Southern Colony in Virginia by the English, 1608. Written by That Honorable Gentleman, Master George Percy." In *The Jamestown Adventure: Accounts of the Virginia Colony, 1605–1614*, 20–36. Winston-Salem, NC: John F. Blair, 2004.

Speigel, Lee. "McCain Confronts the Anger." *ABC News* (October 10, 2008). http://abcnews.go.com/blogs/politics/2008/10/mccain-confront/.

Swaine, Jon. "Birther Row Began with Hillary Clinton." *The Telegraph* (April 27, 2011). http://www.telegraph.co.uk/news/worldnews/barackobama/ 8478044/Birther-row-began-with-Hillary-Clinton.html.

Veres Royal, Sue. "Fear, Rhetoric, and the 'Other.' " *Race/Ethnicity: Multidisciplinary Global Contexts* 4, no. 3 (2011): 405–418.

Wong, Curtis M. "Jerome Corsi, Tea Party Activist, Reports Obama Is Gay and Familiar with Chicago Bathhouse Scene." *Huffington Post* (September 12, 2012). http://www.huffingtonpost.com/2012/09/12/obama-gay-rumors -chicago-jerome-corsi-_n_1877990.html.

Chapter 2

The Origin Myth: The President from Foreign Soil

The *ad hominem* delegitimization of President Obama has centered itself—more often than not—on the ideology of the nursery, rather than the Oval Office. In the existential panic of the right wing's predicted and actual electoral defeats in 2008 and 2012, many conservatives (some extreme, some less so) have questioned the status, location, date, legitimacy, and parentage of the president's birth as a means of racializing and revoking his American identity and citizenship as a sport of opposition. Although Obama was 47 years old when he assumed presidential office, with a credible biography and accomplished résumé, the extreme rejection of the Democratic politician was facilitated by a form of othering at the retrospective site of his conception and birth. Strategically and rhetorically, to push Obama's nativity to a fore-history of intrigue and deception was to transmogrify his origins into a series of varietal mythologies, which in turn became open to widespread and universally negative exegesis. Such work of the Birther movement, and others within the Tea Party and the conspiratorial far Right, was to "poison the well" of Obama's political and personal existence, *in statu nascendi*.[1] To contaminate the reality of Obama's birth (the source of his existence) is the first step in the ongoing and pervasive project of Obama's biographical demonization as a naked partisan tactic. The Birther movement—a sociopolitical phenomenon motivated entirely by negative identity politics—has used the accusation of foreign birth, forged citizenship,

---

[1]Translation: "From the point of birth."

and disqualifying parentage, to name but a few angles, to shift the critique of Obama to a place without political agency; in other words, it seeks to delegitimize the president on the basis of passive nativity, rather than active policy. To disqualify the very genesis of Obama's coming into American being is to reduce him to an annulled state of natal, foreign silence and to pull the carpet from under the feet of representative government on the basis of a technical disavowal of birth right citizenship, devoid of logic.

Speaking of illogicality, the entire Birther construct hinges upon an extraordinary suspension of judicious thought; it defies the smallest modicum of common sense and betrays the identity-politics-at-any-cost ethic in the age of Obama's ascent and presidency. For whether it is the assertion that Obama was born in Kenya; or that his father is Malcom X, Frank Marshall Davis, the devil himself, or some other dangerous foreigner; or that his birth certification (short and long forms) has been doctored; or that the Hawaiian newspaper birth announcements were somehow staged, the Birthers make an outrageous foundational assumption: that Obama was destined, from his conception, to become the president of the United States almost 50 years later, as a result of cabalistic New World Order providence. A mixed-race child, with the name Barack Hussein Obama, born to an 18-year-old unconventional mother and (mostly absent) African father, schooled for a time in Indonesia, and born in an age where the notion of a black president was unimaginable to the political majority, Obama does not seem like the natural choice for a grand-scale Jason Bourne style political manipulation. One might ask, was there not a more conventional political wunderkind candidate waiting in the wings in middle America for this rarefied presidential grooming? The Birther narrative relies on a form of political clairvoyance of such epic proportions that a moment's thought would dispel it from the impartial mind. Its remaining prevalence in the parlance of the Right's opposition demonstrates the fixedness of identity-based conspiracies in an age of hyperpartisanship and remnant racial attitudes geared to reject Barack Obama at any cost, or to use the strategy as a proxy for questioning his trustworthiness and American core.

Soon after the director of Hawaii's State Department of Health provided an affidavit (yet again) as to the veracity of Obama's birth certificate in 2009, Robert Gibbs, then White House press secretary, addressed the insanity of the Birther story head on:

A pregnant woman leaves her home to go overseas to have a child—who there's not a passport for—so is in cahoots with someone . . . to smuggle that child, that previously doesn't exist on a government roll, somewhere back into the country and has the amazing foresight to place birth announcements in the Hawaii newspapers? All while this is transpiring in cahoots with those in the border, all so some kid named Barack Obama could run for president 46 and a half years later.

Gibbs was astonished. "You couldn't sell this script in Hollywood," he exclaimed.

The addiction to a symbolic construct of Obama-as-Other as proliferated by the Birther movement is borne out by the statistics. One month after Obama's 2008 election, an AOL poll found that 52 percent of some 90,000 national respondents stated that they thought there was merit in the controversy surrounding the basis of Obama's citizenship. In the same month, *World Net Daily* (the Web epicenter of Birtherism) asked its readers: "Are you satisfied Obama is constitutionally eligible to assume the presidency?" In response, 97 percent answered "no." A year later, 58 percent of the Republican Party said they doubted that Obama was born in the United States (DailyKos.com 2009). In April 2011, shortly before Obama released his long-form birth certificate, a poll found that only 38 percent were definitely sure that the president was born in America (USAToday.com 2011). One year into Obama's second term in 2013, almost two-thirds of polled Republicans stated that it was "probably true" that Obama was hiding information about his origins (PublicMind.fdu.edu 2013). This same poll—incidentally—found that the Birther myth is the most popular and stable conspiratorial framework in the American psyche—beyond Roswell, JFK, and the moon landing. It is a form of fantasy sustained through its relationship to historical modes of African American treatment, because of the continuous stoking of the fires by those politicians wooing the Tea Party wing, and by the legitimization of the claim in mainstream media discussion, perpetual legal cases and the pejorative anti-Obama literature, which collectively send out smoke where there is no fire.

The smoke was initially brought to the presidential arena not by McCain, Palin, Trump, Taitz, or Gingrich, but rather by Obama's Democratic Primary opponent, Hillary Clinton. A weekly strategic review memo written by Clinton's campaign manager, Mark Penn, on March 19, 2008, advised the campaign to portray Obama as essentially alien. Specifically, Penn advised Clinton to stress Obama's "lack of American roots" while foregrounding her own American essence:

All of these articles about his boyhood in Indonesia and his life in Hawaii are geared towards showing his background is diverse, multicultural and putting that in a new light.

Save it for 2050.

It also exposes a very strong weakness for him—his roots to basic American values and culture are at best limited. I cannot imagine America electing a president during a time of war who is not at his center fundamentally American in his thinking and his values. He told the people of New Hampshire yesterday he has a Kansas accent because his mother was from there. His mother lived in many states as far as we can tell—but this is an example of the nonsense he uses to cover this up.

How we could give some life to this contrast without turning negative:

Every speech should contain the line you were born in the middle of America to the middle class in the middle of the last century. And talk about the basic bargain as about the deeply American values you grew up with, learned as a child and that drive you today. Values of fairness, compassion, responsibility, giving back.

Let's explicitly own "American" in our programs, the speeches and the values. He doesn't. Make this a new American Century, the American Strategic Energy Fund. Let's use our logo to make some flags we can give out. Let's add flag symbols to the backgrounds. (Green 2008)

Penn's memo suggests that the time for American acceptance of Obama's multicultural, diverse identity is not now and that 2008 is a year ripe for its prejudicial manipulation. Penn's urging for a rhetoric and symbolism of over-the-top Americana for Clinton would create an implicit binary of home and away, familiar and foreign, to contrast the Democratic candidates. Penn never advised the deployment of explicit Birther narratives, but the motivation and objective of the Clinton campaign and the subsequent Birther movement were identical. Penn had tapped into a sociopolitical phenomenon: the notion that American voters are more ready to associate patriotic identity with whites over ethnic minorities (Devos and Banaji, 2005; Devos, Ma, and Gaffud 2008).[2] Clinton disregarded Penn's guidance, but in outlining such a strategy as a legitimate anti-Obama campaign, Penn dragged Birther gutter talk into the strata of serious electioneering. Although Clinton sensibly did not pursue it, Penn fired the starting pistol for legitimate Republican utilization of the de-Americanizing strategy he outlined.

Naturally, such laser-like focus upon the matter of Obama's birth has infantilized the very scope of political discourse, hijacked the early biography of America's first African American leader, and rekindled the complicated relationship America has with the very definitions of national

---

[2]Participants polled in a study titled "Enough to Be the Next President? The Role of Ethnicity and National Identity in American Politics" (Devos, Ma, and Gaffud 2008) were found to more firmly associate American values with Hillary Clinton over Barack Obama when provided with visual stimuli.

belonging. Each of the frames of Obama's othering (political, racial, religious) taps into latent historical instances of prejudice and easily revived patterns of (un)belonging. In this case, the Birther movement's proliferation of anxieties surrounding Obama's Hawaiian birth and family history corresponds with a centuries-old angst regarding American genealogy, the definitions of citizenship, electoral eligibility and the plight of racial acceptance.

This chapter reviews the history and claims of the Birther movement alongside the facts of President Obama's biography. Although the conspiracies associated with Obama's childhood are numerous, they can be divided into two main streams of "thought." The first claims that Obama was born in Hawaii, but to a foreign father, of African roots and British citizenship. To support this assumption, the movement claims to follow a *jus sanguinis* code (birth right through blood) in defining the eligibility of presidential candidates who must be natural-born citizens, as per the Constitutional dictate. Simply put, according to these conspiracy advocates, if Obama Senior is foreign, then Obama Junior inherits his disqualifying otherness. The second line of thought goes further to postulate that Obama was not born in Hawaii, or indeed in any American state, but rather upon foreign (and usually African) soil. As a result, these Birthers claim that Obama's eligibility is invalidated from a *jus soli* (birth right through soil) perspective. This theory has resulted in relentless accusations of a network of counterfeit documentation and a multilayered conspiracy of government infiltration by an alien interloper.

These contrasting (yet often parallel) strategies will be assessed here by tracing the motivations, historical impulses, and legal perspective of such claims. Furthermore, this chapter is concerned particularly with the rhetorical implication of the demand (and release) of Obama's birth certification, as a reminder of the ever-present racialization of American citizenship, a trope that is revived from slave law, the black codes, and Jim Crow laws, with concerning effortlessness to demonize the 44th President.

BIRTHERISM: OBAMA'S BIOGRAPHY MALIGNED

Obama was born as the result of an unlikely and progressive whirlwind romance.

His *father* was an African, the son of a Kenyan mission cook *cum* tribal herbal doctor, born upon the shores of Lake Victoria and a member of the Luo ethnic tribe. He herded goats in his father's fields and demonstrated academic prowess in the classroom. At the age of 23, having developed a characteristic British accent and a signature charm, the man won a prestigious scholarship—later supported by John F. Kennedy, among others—intended to fund Kenyan students' transformative advancement at Western institutions. Representing a post-independence wave of young Africans, he set his sights on Honolulu to study economics, traveling to the island in 1959 to become the first African student admitted to the University of Hawaii.

His *mother*, meanwhile, was still at high school in Seattle and would arrive in Hawaii one year later. Born in Wichita, Kansas, in the epitome of small-town, mid-Western America, she was an only child (and distant cousin of Wild Bill Hickok). Soon after the attack on Pearl Harbor, her father signed up to the war effort while her mother assisted on the Boeing assembly line in California. With World War II ended, she moved with her parents to the state of Washington, where they established a successful family-run furniture business. When Hawaii became the 50th state to be admitted to the Union in August 1959, the family—intrigued by new shores, new experiences, and new markets— set sail.

The lives of (Stanley) Ann Dunham and Barack Obama, Sr., collided, unpredictably, when both stepped into the same Russian language class at the University of Hawaii (cue Soviet conspiracy here). In the intense fixing of their eyes upon each other, an American presidency and era were unconventionally born. In an age when miscegenation was still outlawed in numerous states, the Trans-Atlantic pair became romantically involved, fell pregnant, and, on February 2, 1961, married. Barack Obama, Jr., was born on August 4, when his mother was only 18 years old. The birth was announced in Honolulu's main newspapers (*The Sunday Advertiser* and *The Honolulu Star Bulletin*), but while Hawaii was "as successful as any place in accommodating a multicultural environment" (Barack Obama 1995 interview), the union was neither expected nor widely supported. The marriage did not last the ages, with Obama's mother spending time with friends in Seattle and his father moving to Massachusetts and eventually back to Kenya, when the future president was only 2 years old. From this point on, Obama's father became a mythic figure for the young boy, a paternal collage of passed-down stories, second-hand memories, and dog-eared photographs. Obama's only personal memories of his father were formed during his brief visit to Hawaii when the president was 10 years old. At that point, Obama Senior had been virtually blacklisted in his native Kenya, subject to a personal and political vilification that, unbeknownst to him, his son would inherit during his ascent to prominence.

Soon after the Obamas divorced, Ann married a Javanese geographer, Lolo Soetoro, in 1965. Consequently, Obama was moved to Indonesia with his mother for a period of four years, where he was educated at a Catholic and Indonesian public school. He was then sent back to the United States to live with his grandparents and attend the Punahon School in Hawaii. His mother and new stepsister, Maya, rejoined Obama a year later in 1972, allowing Ann to continue with her studies and her children to enjoy some hitherto rare measure of continuity. Obama's early nomadism has been the source of many modern controversies.

So formative was Obama's childhood experience that he wrote an entire memoir devoted to its unraveling—a curious experiment for the supposed Manchurian Candidate. A third of *Dreams from My Father* (1995) is devoted to the exploration of Obama's roots and childhood, traced with pathos and honesty, facing the reality of being composed from a father "black as pitch" and a mother "white as milk" (10).

In a Birther's world of confirmation bias, however, the reality of Obama's coming into being has been widely and wildly disparaged from his candidacy to his second presidential term, in a process of unparalleled personal harassment. Obama's birth certification has been demanded, received, pasted over the entire globe, and rejected as fake. His citizenship has been "assessed" as ineligible on the basis of misapplied constitutional and legal interpretation. His "real" father has been theorized to be Frank Marshall Davis, Malcom X, or some undetermined foreigner. His autobiography has been trashed as an elaborate if well-written hoax, supposedly authored by the radical campaigner, Bill Ayers. A counter-documentary, *Dreams from My Real Father*, has been screened across the nation as a Tea Party campaigning tool, comparing the nose and lips of Obama with those of his revealed communist father as conspiratorial "evidence." Jerome Corsi's fact-light book *Where's the Birth Certificate?* (2011), published by *World Net Daily*, reached number six on the *New York Times* bestsellers list; it demanded all manner of identity documentation to support the overall conspiracy of Obama's foreign, "Other" status, his radical politics, and his Muslim religion.[3] Bumper stickers,[4] political mailings, yard signs, television adverts, T-shirts—a whole host of communication paraphernalia—insinuate or scream that Obama is not American born. Dinesh D'Souza, Mike Huckabee, and Newt Gingrich, for example, have suggested that Obama's foreign origins result in the first truly non-American president, governing as a foreigner. Former House Speaker Gingrich pondered, "What

---

[3]In fact, Obama released his birth certificate one week prior to the book's publication.
[4]Thrifty Bumper stickers, Buffalo, New York.

if Obama is so outside our comprehension, that only if you understand Kenyan, anti-colonial behavior, can you begin to piece together [his actions]?" (Costa 2010). If that were not enough, the conservative group Fellowship of the Mind has recently demanded the birth papers for Obama's own children to prove their claim that both girls were actually fathered by Obama's Chicago pastor, Dr. Jeremiah Wright. A democratized media landscape, a mainstream hyper-aestheticization of partisan conflict, a political trend of polarization, a culture of all-access, rumor-plagued, tabloid-driven celebrity, the influx of dollars from right-wing SuperPACs, a history of racial documentary control, and an established ethic of holding presidents to public account have all contributed to the proliferation of one of the most extraordinary and sustaining extremist strategies of the far Right, built upon biographical fiction and proliferated as axiomatic truth.

A NATION OF BIRTHERS: PRESIDENTIAL ELIGIBILITY CHALLENGES THROUGH TIME

The Birther impulse has been manifest throughout American presidential history, utilized by political opponents as a by-word for treachery, non-allegiance, and foreign, un-American values. While Obama's birth eligibility challenges are unique in their application to racialized citizenship and civil rights, he is not the first president or candidate to have his origins questioned as a method of disqualifying, partisan attack.

The only other president not to have two U.S.-citizen parents was Chester A. Arthur, a somewhat forgotten leader who succeeded President James Garfield after the latter's assassination in 1881. During Arthur's vice presidential campaign in 1880, a New York attorney named Arthur Hinman (an early incarnation of Orly Taitz, perhaps) began to investigate the candidate's background as a means of opposing his eligibility. Initially, Hinman suggested that Arthur had been born and raised in Aberdeen or Belfast, and not Vermont, though such nonsensical rumor was not supported by the facts of his parent's emigration to the United States in the early 1820s. Like the Birthers today, demonstrating ingrained confirmation bias, Hinman simply changed the premise to arrive at the same conclusion: perhaps he was Canadian instead. *The New York Times* was sufficiently intrigued to report the actions of Hinman:

A stranger arrived here a few days ago, and registered at the American House as A. P. Hinman, of New-York. Since then he has been very busy in the adjoining town of Fairfield, ostensibly collecting materials for a biography of Vice-President-elect Arthur. He has privately stated to leading Democratic citizens, however, that he is employed by the Democratic National Committee to obtain evidence to show that Gen. Arthur is an unnaturalized foreigner. He claims to have discovered that Gen. Arthur was born in Canada, instead of Fairfield; that his name is Chester Allen ... that he was 50 years old in July instead of October, as has been stated, and generally that he is an alien and ineligible to the office of Vice-President. (*New York Times* Archive 1880)

Hinman ultimately published a polemic biography entitled *How a British Subject Became President of the United States* (1884), which was essentially a rambling series of unfounded biographical claims. Hinman included uncertified correspondence, affidavits, testimony from Arthur's aunt, and reported conversations as evidentiary proof of Arthur's Canadian status; he excluded all opposing arguments and relied heavily upon rumor and selectivity for his application of Article II of the Constitutional eligibility requirements. Beginning his pamphlet, Hinman wrote, "It will be still more interesting and entertaining to trace the genealogy of the man who did not want to recall it for himself" (Hinman 1884, 4). President Arthur refused to engage with Hinman's vitriol.

The parallel between the relentless opprobrium of Hinman and the modern Birther strategy is unavoidable. The tone of Hinman's work is entirely personal, yet veiled as patriotic concern. It surveys not only the president's birth and parentage, but also the validity of his education, having sought written confirmation of his standing at various scholarly institutions. Likewise, where today's members of the Right pose as victims of a grand conspiracy and cast Obama as the villain infiltrator, Hinman closed *his* work with a remarkably solipsistic three-stanza poem, "The Death Struggle" (copied from *Harper's Weekly*, August 12, 1872, and undersigned A. P. Hinman). In this poem, the fight against Chester Arthur is cast as a cosmically heroic feat, just as Birthers today pursue Obama's disqualification as an intrepid American duty:

> My back is to the wall,
> And my face is to my foes;
> I've lived a life of combat,
> And borne what no one knows.
> But in this mortal struggle
> I stand, poor speck of dust,
> Defiant self-reliant,
> To die—if die I must. (Hinman 1884, 90)

Self-effacement, it seems, is not the defining symptom of the Birther malaise.

President Martin Van Buren, though American born, spoke Dutch as his first language, leading some to believe that he was born in Holland.

During the 1916 presidential election, which was won narrowly by
Woodrow Wilson, the eligibility of his Republican opponent, Charles
Evans Hughes, was questioned because his father remained a British subject. Breckenridge Long, one of Wilson's campaign activists, published an
article titled "Is Mr. Charles Evans Hughes a 'Natural Born Citizen' within
the Meaning of the Constitution" (Long 1916) in the *Chicago Legal News*;
in this article, he concluded that Hughes held a split allegiance and could
not be considered "natural born." The controversy did not catch the public's imagination, however; Hughes had served as a U.S. Supreme Court
Justice before accepting the Republican nomination, bolstering his status
as a legitimate candidate. He was also nominated to serve as Secretary of
State in 1921 and as Chief Justice of the Supreme Court from 1930.

Barry Goldwater's 1964 presidential campaign saw his 1909 birth in
the Arizona Territory (before it became a state) examined for consistency
with the Constitution.

George Romney—who was the GOP nominee in the 1968 election—
had been born in a Mormon colony in Mexico, where his polygamous
grandfather had emigrated in 1886. As Romney's parents had maintained
their U.S. citizenship and returned to America in 1912 during the Mexi-
can Revolution, George Romney's eligibility credentials were largely
accepted throughout his time in the public sphere.

Lowell Weicker departed from the Republican primary campaign in
1980 before the issue of his foreign birth (in Paris) and his British mother
(born in India) became significant eligibility concerns.

John McCain—the lead participant in a 2008 campaign that pursued
the tactics of foreignization of Barack Obama—had his own eligibility
questioned in 2000 and 2008 in light of his birth in the Panama Canal
Zone in 1936, on Coco Solo Naval Air Station. Potentially because of
the real possibility of a McCain presidency, the long-term senator's eligibility garnered greater legal and political attention than Goldwater's
or Romney's origins, for example. Although McCain was born to two
U.S.-citizen parents, during a U.S.-directed military posting, the military
facilities located in the unincorporated territory of the Panama Canal
Zone were not classified as American soil at the time of his birth. In February 2008, *The New York Times* floated the possibility of McCain's
ineligibility, in an article claiming that "the issue is becoming more than
a matter of parental daydreaming" (Husle 2008). However, as many
pointed out, if there was ambiguity, it was seemingly clarified by the
retroactive definition of American citizenship within the Panama Canal

Zone by the passage of 8 U.S.C. § 1403 in 1937. Section A of that law states:

Any person born in the Canal Zone on or after February 26, 1904, and whether before or after the effective date of this chapter, whose father or mother or both at the time of the birth of such person was or is a citizen of the United States, is declared to be a citizen of the United States.

In April 2008—two months before Obama was compelled to release his own birth certification—the Senate passed a simple Resolution 511, "recognizing that John Sidney McCain III, is a natural born citizen" under the definitions of the Constitution. As part of the Resolution, Senator Patrick Leahy (Democrat-Vermont) appended a summary statement on McCain's natural-born citizenship qualification:

John Sidney McCain, III, was born to American citizens on an American Naval base in the Panama Canal Zone in 1936. Numerous legal scholars have looked into the purpose and intent of the "natural born Citizen" requirement. As far as I am aware, no one has unearthed any reason to think that the Framers would have wanted to limit the rights of children born to military families stationed abroad or that such a limited view would serve any noble purpose enshrined in our founding document. Based on the understanding of the pertinent sources of constitutional meaning, it is widely believed that if someone is born to American citizens anywhere in the world they are natural born citizens. [...]
    I recently asked Secretary of Homeland Security Michael Chertoff, a former Federal judge, if he had any doubts in his mind. He did not.

The Resolution was introduced by Senator Claire McCaskill (Democrat-Missouri) and co-sponsored by one Republican and four Democrats, including Hillary Clinton and, somewhat ironically in retrospect, Illinois Senator Barack Obama.
    Despite Obama co-sponsoring this resolution, which provided unambiguous collegiate support for McCain's presidential eligibility and nullified the Birther-ist' whispers against his future Republican opponent, McCain would come to systematically foreignize Obama on the basis of his origins. In October 2008, for example, McCain roused an angry crowd in Albuquerque, New Mexico, by asking "Who is the real Barack Obama?" in a speech that was overt and euphemistic in describing Obama's perceived duplicitousness. "I didn't just show up out of nowhere," McCain said, teasing the contrast between his own biography and Obama's. "At this late hour in the campaign, there are essential things we don't know about Senator Obama or the record he brings to this campaign." Throwing grenades of character aspersion into the

throng, McCain joked, "For a guy who's already authored two memoirs, he's not exactly an open book." As Cindy McCain laughed and applauded behind her husband, the crowds booed every mention of Obama, some shouting "liar" and another crying "send him home."

Where Obama had aided McCain in providing an iron-clad, government-sealed confirmation of the Arizona senator's legitimacy, McCain propagated a directly contrary fog of uncertainty surrounding the validity of his adversary. It was a form of political betrayal, for sure, but also emblematic of the latent inequalities in the treatment of established WASP politicians and African American candidates when it came to the matter of acceptable "real" American identities. By contrast, Barack Obama's eligibility was never corroborated by Senate Resolution, and Obama never used McCain's birthplace as the foundation for his own negative campaigning.

CASE CLOSED? THE LEGAL HISTORY AND FAILURE OF BIRTHERISM

The Birther movement, since its formal inception by Obama's Illinois opponent, Andy Martin in 2004 (and its resurrection by a Hillary Clinton campaign group email in 2008), has conducted itself with great litigiousness, logging countless lawsuits and election ballot challenges against Obama's eligibility in a pretense of legitimacy. No such lawsuit has ever been successful in moving dominant opinion in the case of Obama's birth status, yet the Birthers continue to appeal and resubmit their cases, accusing uncooperative legal officials as complicit in the Obama conspiracy. Back in the heat of the 2008 election campaign, and in an attempt by the Obama organization to clear the field of disparaging birth-conspiracy talk, the campaign released a copy of Obama's Certificate of Life Birth from Hawaii, posting it online for the doubters to download. The document details the birth of Barack Hussein Obama II to Stanley Ann Dunham (identified as Caucasian) and Barack Hussein Obama (identified as African) on August 4, 1961, at 7:24 p.m. Although this certificate is the standard and accepted documentation for official birth in Hawaii, and "State law prohibits the release of a certified birth certificate to persons who do not have a tangible interest in the vital record," its release only sparked even greater conspiratorial debate and litigation (Health.Hawaii.gov 2011).

The first major legal contestation arrived in the form of federal case *Berg v. Obama et al.,* which ran for more than a year beginning in August 2008. Philip J. Berg, a Democratic former deputy state attorney general in Pennsylvania, filed a suit seeking a declaratory judgment that Obama was ineligible for the office of president, an injunction to ban

Obama from running from presidential office, and an injunction to keep the Democratic National Committee from nominating him. The "grab bag of claims"—as the Appeal Court ultimately described it—named the presidential candidate in the case as follows: "Barack Hussein Obama, a/k/a Barry Soetoro, a/k/a Barry Obama, a/k/a Barack Dunham, a/k/a Barry Dunham." The list was intended to suggest that Obama's identity was not fully known, splintered into "others," and that the "real" Obama could be lurking under any of these foreign-sounding and evasive pseudonyms. The complaint alleged that Obama was born in Kenya and, therefore, was unable to claim the status of a natural-born citizen, and that Obama's newly released birth certificate was a counterfeit. In the initial case heard by U.S. District Judge R. Barclay Surrick, the complaint was dismissed because of Berg's lack of standing and his lack of persuasive arguments to the contrary. Attempts to elevate the case to the U.S. Supreme Court followed and failed. In November 2009, the Third Circuit Court of Appeals reaffirmed the district court's dismissal on the basis of standing. "A prerequisite of standing," the court defined, "is that the litigant has suffered or will suffer an injury in fact that is caused by the complained-of conduct by a defendant that can be redressed by court." The court's impatience with Berg was evident:

The electoral votes have since been cast, without objection to Obama's qualifications by any members of Congress, and Obama was inaugurated. Berg nonetheless persists in this litigation ... Berg's worry that Obama, if elected, might someday be removed from office was not an injury cognizable in a federal court because it was based on speculation ... Berg's wish that the Democratic primary voters had chosen a different presidential candidate, and his dissatisfaction that they apparently did not credit the evidence he tendered, do not state legal harm. Because there is no case or controversy, we will affirm the District Court's order dismissing Berg's action.

Most federal cases ended the same way, concluding that political disagreement or individual voter grievance did not constitute legal harm or standing. Federal-level claims brought by Daniel John Essek (2008), Mario Apuzzo (2008), Alan Keyes and Captain Pamela Barnett (2009),[5]

---

[5]Filed on the day Obama was sworn into office, demonstrating the often reactiveness of litigation against the reality of Obama's political legitimization. The plaintiffs were active, inactive, or retired military personnel; private individuals; state representatives; and one person claiming to be Obama's relative. The defendants included President Obama, First Lady Michelle Obama, Vice President Joe Biden, Secretary of State Hillary Clinton, and former Secretary of Defense Robert Gates.

Gregory Hollister with Berg (2009),[6] and Taitz (various),[7] for example,
failed the basic litmus test of legal credibility. State-level efforts during
Obama's first and second terms, also failed to find their own legitimacy.
Andy Martin (resurrecting his old claims) requested sight of the long-
form certificate for his own research into the matter, but was denied in
October 2008. Leo Donofrio's triple suit against the eligibility of Obama,
McCain, and Roger Colero was denied a hearing at the U.S. Supreme
Court. Cort Wrotonowski complained that Obama's birth certification
was forged and that the citizenship status of Barack Obama, Sr., rendered
Obama ineligible for the presidency; the Supreme Court appeal was
denied. Alan Keyes's attempt to use the reported words of Obama's
step-grandmother as witness to Obama's ineligibility was dismissed and
refused further hearing.

The fact that Obama had been elected by the popular vote, served his
first term, released his long-form birth certificate, and received the
Democratic Party's reelection nomination in April 2012 might have presented the ultimate case for the president's now-well established legitimacy, particularly when viewed alongside the consistently failed legal
attempts of the Birther movement. However, the litigious spirit of the
conspiracy-hunting activists was roused to an even greater extent to challenge Obama's very placement on the ballot in the 2012 election cycle.
Betraying desperation and signaling the identity politics at play, these
legal challenges were laced with an othering ethic of significant volume
and hyperbole. In Alaska, Obama's appearance on the ballot was rejected
by Gordon Epperly on the basis of an explicit race-based argument,
which sounded as though it belonged to the lexicon of pre-
Emancipation America:

As Barack Hussein Obama is of the "*Mulatto*" race, his status of citizenship is
founded upon the Fourteenth Amendment to the United States Constitution.
Before the [purported] ratification of the Fourteenth Amendment, the race of
"*Negro*" or "*Mulatto*" had no standing to be citizens of the United States under
the United States Constitution. As the Fourteenth Amendment is only a grant of
"*Civil Rights*" and not a grant of "*Political Rights*," Barack Hussein Obama II

---

[6] Judge James Robertson: "The issue of the President's citizenship was raised, vet-
ted, blogged, texted, twittered, and otherwise massaged by America's vigilant citizenry during Mr. Obama's two-year-campaign for the presidency, but this
plaintiff wants it resolved by a court." Robertson described Berg and his fellow
attorney as "agents provocateurs." The judge viewed the case as demonstrating
a purpose to harass.
[7] "Tilting at windmills," "toying with the Court or displaying her own stupidity,"
"Sisyphean quest."

does not have any "Political Rights" under any provision of the United States Constitution to hold any Public Office of the United States government. (*Epperly v. Obama* 2012)

This antiquated claim is nothing short of outrageous. Epperly, who has also written of his rejection of female political office holders, contends that Obama's ineligibility is writ large in his skin color as well as his birth.

Similarly, in Alabama, Albert Hendershot and Harold Sorenson regurgitated old statements about fake birth certificates and ballot ineligibility in front of Jefferson County Circuit Judge Helen Shores Lee. Sorenson submitted a request for Judge Lee to recuse herself "due to racial bias, lack of judicial discretion as well as lack of knowledge of the U.S. Constitution, Article II, Section 1, Clause 5" (Velasco 2012). The suggestion was that Lee could not—or would not—by virtue of being black, comprehend the "true" intent of the Constitutional Article. In the eyes of the Alabama Birthers, neither black presidents nor judges could be deemed valid for fear of an anti-white cabal.

The tenor of Birther efforts was no better in Indiana, where the ubiquitous Orly Taitz challenged Obama's 2012 ballot appearance because of his "false" surname, stolen Social Security number, and constitutional status. She accused the Indiana Election Commission of complicity in a pro-Obama cover-up, at one point interjecting, "You're all out of order," during proceedings. It was a strategy that Taitz would continue on her whistle-stop tour of state election commissions. In Mississippi and New Hampshire, election bodies that dismissed Taitz's various litigations were inculpated for involvement in the conspiracy. Taitz wrote to the speaker of the New Hampshire House of Representatives, urging the immediate removal and indictment of Secretary of State Bill Gardner for fraud, forgery, aiding and abetting, and treason:

Gardner committed fraud and treason, by placing on the ballot in the state of New Hampshire a foreign citizen with citizenship of three other foreign nations and no verification of US citizenship, no valid US identification papers, no valid US birth certificate, no valid US Social Security number. Elections fraud and possibly treason is clear based on application. (Taitz 2011)

In September 2012, betraying the growing animus and racialization of this issue, Taitz assisted Joe Montgomery in his efforts to remove Obama from the Kansas ballot. Upon Montgomery's withdrawal of the complaint, Taitz was denied the opportunity to formally address the state board; after the session, she became embroiled in an argument with Obama supporter T. J. Vaughan in Memorial Hall. Taitz claimed that she had been encircled by approximately 20 black men who "acted like wild animals." The statements were refuted by witnesses and described as "racist." This is not the first or only case of civil disobedience that has been perpetrated or incited by Birther representatives (some of whom have been subjected to criminal prosecutions). Subsequent Birther suits were also lodged by the Liberty Legal Foundation, Todd House, Charles Tisdale, H. Brooke Paige, Gordon Epperly, and Susan Daniels, for example. In September 2012, Arnold Begay, an incarcerated sex offender, filed a lawsuit in the U.S. District Court in Phoenix, Arizona, demanding the release of Obama's DNA for analysis and comparison against Saddam Hussein and Osama bin Laden. If anything speaks to the dubious irrationality of the Birther movement's blind pursuit of Obama's foreignization into powerlessness, this might be it.

The accusations pertaining to Obama's birth legitimacy have not only been employed as a mode of raw political opposition, but elaborated to question his patriotic and military credentials as the incumbent commander in chief. Three notable cases of "conscientious objection" have been lodged against Obama on the basis of his perceived illegitimacy and foreignness (*Cook v. Good*, *Rhodes v. MacDonald*, and the court-martial of Terrence Lakin). Stefan F. Cook, a major in the U.S. Army Reserve, was a willing supporter of the Birther movement when in February 2009 he offered his support to Orly Taitz's lawsuit. Three months later, Cook voluntarily requested deployment in Afghanistan and was ordered to report for service on July 15, 2009. Yet, one week before his deployment, Cook (via his attorney, Taitz) brought a transparent lawsuit against Colonel Wanda L. Good of the Army Human Resources Command, citing Obama's disqualifying birth status and ineligibility to serve as the military's commander in chief, to gain his status as a conscientious objector. Proceeding to deploy, he argued, "would be acting in violation of international law by engaging in military actions outside the United States under this President's command." Cook's orders were subsequently revoked—a fact twisted by Birtherism and Fox News into an admission of Obama's ineligibility.

Later that year, in September 2009, Orly Taitz returned to the same judge who heard Major Cook's complaint to request a restraining order on Captain Connie Rhodes's upcoming deployment in Iraq as a physician, as (she argued) any such order stemming from Obama's authority was voided by his own illegality. Taitz reacted negatively to the dismissal of the case by Judge Clay Land as a waste of military time and a speculative witch hunt, accusing the court of treason and submission to the "dictatorship" of President Obama. Subsequently, Captain Rhodes claimed that Taitz had pursued the case without her approval or knowledge.

Judge Land denounced Taitz, describing her approach as "breathtaking in its arrogance and borders on the delusional" and levying a fine of $20,000 for attorney misconduct.

Most recently, in April 2010, Terrence Lakin, a surgeon in the Army Medical Corps, refused to deploy for his second tour of duty in Afghanistan on the grounds of Obama's unproven status as a natural-born citizen and legal commander in chief. His intention had been recorded in a YouTube monologue, uploaded by the American Patriot Foundation, in which he claimed that in light of "troubling but compelling information," America deserved "the truth about President Obama's constitutional eligibility." In the same video, Lakin declared that until such proof was made available, he would place his 18-year service history at peril, rather than submit to illegal orders. Lakin was initially supported by the former U.S. senator from New Hampshire, Robert Smith, who stated, "I don't have a problem with that [constitutionality question] being answered." Astonishingly, three retired military generals (two of whom were Fox News analysts) also provided positive backing for Lakin's pursuit of the Birther conspiracy. Lakin's refusal to deploy ultimately led to a criminal prosecution under the Uniform Code of Military Justice, where Judge Colonel Denise Lind ruled that Lakin's presidential concerns were not relevant to the objection to his orders or to the remit of the military court. Lakin pleaded guilty to the charge of disobeying orders and was convicted on a count of missing movement by design. After he was sentenced to six months in a Kansas Correctional Facility, the Kansas State Board of Healing Arts revoked Lakin's license to privately practice medicine as a result of his non-deployment, which was interpreted as an event of placing fellow soldiers at risk. Questions were also raised concerning Lakin's future alignment with healthcare legislation associated with President Obama, when he had already evidenced perilous medical behavior.

This quasi-military subset of the Birther movement has served as a proxy for the more general foreignization of Obama, intent on casting this presidency in the hue of the enemy, an unreliable locus for the leadership of America's military interests. Persistent in prosecutorial attack, defamation, and personal demonization, the Birther movement has also attempted to veil itself in a garb of all-encompassing victimhood—both as a public relations stratagem and as a tactic to suggest legal "standing." The rhetorical contortion is nowhere more evident than on the homepage of the Birthers.org website, the closest one might get to an official hub for the movement. The mission statement is worth quoting in some detail:

We are the Birthers, we are those who are under attack by the Mainstream Media ... They want to mock us by giving us a label to discredit and marginalize us. This is nothing new, when people have no direction they attack those who do. Labelling and ridiculing the opposition is a tactic of the communist union organizer Saul Alinsky ... Obama is the grandmaster of Alinsky smear tactics and ridicule ... A community organizer is simply a euphemism for a leader and trainer of radical agitators and street type demonstrations.

[...]

Lenin and Stalin had the "Bourgeois," Hitler had the 'Untermenschen," Pol Pot had the "Intelligentsia," and now Obama has the "Birthers." People like this have always needed someone to blame for their own inadequacies, a scapegoat for their failures.

[...]

We accept their name, the Birthers for wanting to give rebirth to that which we as Americans hold dear. To return the favor of giving us a name in which we can find a common identity, we in turn give them a name that must be our polarizing opposites, "the O-Borters." For they are seeking to abort the fabric that has held America together, the Constitution of the United States of America. (Birthers.org)

The statement, read by any reasonable person on the Left or the Right, is both politically and intellectually illegible. Aligning Obama with Lenin, Stalin, Hitler and Pol Pot stretches the Birthers' concern with Obama's natural-born citizenship status to the level of foreign dictatorship at the center of the American complex. Without any self-awareness or reflection, the Birther movement, in this statement and in its actions, is guilty of the very crime of demonization and vilification that the Birthers allege to be perpetrated against them. To claim to be "under attack," marginalized, subjected to "smear tactics and ridicule," and scapegoated by "radical agitators" and "purveyors of cheap words" is to look into the very mirror of the Birther soul.

BIRTHERISM REBORN: THE HISTORICAL FEAR OF FOREIGN PRESIDENTIAL BLOOD

The Right's relentless demonization of Obama's birth narrative as a means of besmirching his adult presidential eligibility is a modern manifestation of a very historical American paranoia of identity politics. For while today the conspiratorial and racially imbued scrawlings of the Birther movement are conveyed through a hyper-transactional social media landscape, they have been in many ways written into the fabric of the U.S. Constitution. Whereas the framers aimed to create a governmental framework protected from the monarchical grab of foreign powers, reflecting the acute sensitivities of an Independent America, the Birther movement pretends to represent its 21st-century perpetuation by regurgitating centuries-old quotations, seizing upon antique prejudices, and misinterpreting the Constitutional and legal position to historicize and legitimate the Birthers' factually incoherent and racially packaged rejection of Obama's birth status.

The Birther movement is able to facilitate its rhetorical and legal challenge to Obama's natal credentials primarily through its capitalization upon the lexical ambiguity in Article Two, Section One of the Constitution itself. For a group almost idolatrous in its fidelity to the literalism of the founding documents, it is a romantic notion that its modern political enemy might be undone by yellowed parchments of old. In this part of the Constitution, the 18th-century drafters defined certain identity requirements for all future presidential office holders:

No person except a natural born citizen, or a citizen of the United States, at the time of the adoption of this Constitution, shall be eligible to the office of President; neither shall any person be eligible to that office who shall not have attained to the age of thirty five years, and been fourteen Years a resident within the United States.

The final clauses, requiring a minimum age threshold and prescriptive residency duration, echo the constitutional eligibility requirements for representatives and senators as defined in Article One. As Obama clearly met both obligations at the time of his election, there has been little controversy on these points. The "natural born citizen" clause, however, which refers exclusively to the office of the president, has become the very lifeblood of the Birther conspiracy. For without contemporaneous definition, a constitutional glossary, or any minutes of the discussion conducted by the Committee of Eleven on the logic for the phrase's inclusion, Birtherism has been allowed to disproportionately transmogrify an 18th-century safeguard against a return to foreign or monarchical rule into a hyper-racialization and alienation of Obama's political identity. Birtherism in its various manifestations uses the "natural born citizen" clause, and monopolizes upon its ambiguity, to justify its *jus soli* (right of the soil) and *jus sanguinis* (right of blood) disqualification of Obama's birth right, by claiming (1) that the president was not born in Hawaii or (2) that through the inheritance of his father's DNA, he is not an American in his veins.

The impulse in this decade to foreignize Obama on the basis of his birth is given faux legitimacy by invoking the 18th-century animus toward despotic colonization. To understand why this process of othering has been able to anchor itself to nascent American concern and constitutional ambiguity, I will trace the broad history of the "natural born citizen" clause and its subsequent interpretations and application. In ascertaining the motivation of the framers of the Constitution in inserting this clause (which has become the Holy Grail of Birtherism), the *Federalist Papers* are illustrative.

Alexander Hamilton, the presumed author of *Federalist Paper 69*, "The Real Character of the Executive," and a Constitutional Convention delegate from New York, lobbied the Convention to ensure that the structuring of the presidential office and its limitations would contrast sharply with the excesses of foreign empires. Hamilton wrote:

The President of the United States would be an officer elected by the people for four years; the king of Great Britain is a perpetual and hereditary prince. The one would be amenable to personal punishment and disgrace; the person of the other is sacred and inviolable. (Hamilton #69)

Writing in comparative adjacency pairs, Hamilton sought limitations to strip the trappings of monarchical privilege from the office of the chief executive, countering the perspective of some "who would persuade us that things so unalike resemble each other." While recognizing the importance of the differentiation, Hamilton greatly opposed the exaggerated foreignization of the powers afforded the president in the Constitution and attempted to expose the hyperbole deployed by detractors of the Constitution:

Calculating upon the aversion of the people to monarchy, they have endeavoured to enlist all their jealousies and apprehensions in opposition to the intended President of the United States; not merely as the embryo, but as the full-grown progeny, of that detested parent ... He has been decorated with attributes superior in dignity and splendor to those of a king of Great Britain. He has been shown to us with the diadem sparkling on his brow and the imperial purple flowing in his train. He has been seated on a throne surrounded with minions and mistresses, giving audience to the envoys of foreign potentates, in all the supercilious pomp of majesty. The images of Asiatic despotism and voluptuousness have scarcely been wanting to crown the exaggerated scene. We have been taught to tremble at the terrific visages of murdering janizaries, and to blush at the unveiled mysteries of a future seraglio. (Hamilton #67)

Hamilton's assessment of the anticolonial and orientalist imagery deployed by opponents of the proposed presidential powers, might almost read as a description of a 21st-century anti-Obama mailing circular from the more extreme Tea Party presses. The explicit foreignization of the president—though theorized here and removed from personal identity—was evidently present at the moment of Constitutional incorporation. This Founding Father, who also authored *Federalist Paper 68*,

"The Mode of Electing the President," understood the intense concern surrounding international duplicity:

Nothing was more to be desired than that every practicable obstacle should be opposed to cabal, intrigue, and corruption. These most deadly adversaries of republican government might naturally have been expected to make their approaches from more than one quarter, but chiefly from the desire in foreign powers to gain an improper ascendant in our councils. How could they better gratify this, than by raising the creature of their own to the chief magistry of the Union. (Hamilton #68)

The development and inclusion of the "natural born citizen" clause must be interpreted in this context of understandable colonial paranoia, wherein priority number one was to protect the healing nation from further foreign and corruptive influence. The fear surrounding the infestation of government was, in the 18th century, quite real and informed by the experience of English secession law, which permitted the enthronement of foreign-born monarchs. In reinterpreting this intense Constitutional debate over the formation of powers for an imaginary future president, the Birther extremists have justified their own lexicon of enemization as applied to the very real human incumbent. In other terms, the Birther conspiracists have interpreted the abstracted emotion—the reactionary ethos of a country recently unfettered from the shackles of the British Empire—as the intent and meaning of the clause and subsequent legislation. There is no doubt, of course, that the citizenship clause was included to ensure American fidelity, but it is erroneous to suggest that such a clause might be harnessed to forbid Obama's access to executive office.

The clause's inclusion is generally understood as originating from a letter sent to George Washington from John Jay (of New York) in 1787, on the matter of ensuring national security through the identity of the chief executive. "Permit me to hint," he wrote:

whether it would not be wise and seasonable to provide a strong check to the admission of Foreigners into the administration of our national Government and to declare expressly that the Commander in Chief of the American army shall not be given to, nor devolve on, any but a natural born Citizen. (Jay 1787)

Following the receipt of this letter, the Committee of Eleven altered the original requirement for eligibility from merely "citizen" to "natural born citizen," without extant justification. It seems that Jay's decision to lobby Washington (the presiding member of the drafting Committee) led to its direct inclusion without significant debate. The phrase must have been established well enough so that its interpretation was shared, without the necessity for internal documentary definition. The Birther community, however, almost universally substantiates its rejection of Obama's citizenship eligibility by claiming that the Founders were influenced not by an American or English legal framework, but rather by the French words of the Swiss philosopher, Emer de Vattel, from his 1758 publication *Le Droit des Gens,* or *The Law of Nations.* This individual source of continental philosophy stands almost isolated among contemporaneous writings and *jus soli* legal definition.

Vattel argues that "naturels" or "indigenes" are defined as those born in a particular country to citizen parents, placing a *jus soli* and *jus sanguinis* stipulation on presidential officeholders. This definition raises many problems. While many of the framers were fluent in 18th-century French (and Benjamin Franklin purchased three copies of Vattel's text), and recognizing that Vattel's tome had some influence on America's founding philosophy, it remains true that neither Vattel's original nor his translation came close to using the phrase "natural born citizen" until a decade after the eligibility clause was enshrined in the U.S. Constitution. In the numerous translations that were produced between 1759 and 1797, none translated the phrase in a way consistent with the Birthers' interpretation. There is no attribution to Vattel's philosophy in the Constitution or surrounding documents, and no ink spent on flagging the use of a phrase that differed significantly from the more broadly understood terms of citizenship of English common law. Furthermore, Vattel himself conceded that on the matters of determining citizenship, "civil and political laws may, for particular reasons, ordain otherwise" (Vattel 1797, 102).

The Birthers' modern extraction of a chronologically inconsistent phrase seems, at best, politically motivated and shoddily researched. Indeed, one need look no further than to the wisdom of James Madison, the fourth president of the United States and, appropriately, recognized widely as the Father of the Constitution. Two months after the Constitution was ratified, Congress was due to consider the very first issue of a contested House election, whereby the question of representative eligibility was considered and unanimously defined on the basis of *jus soli.* Following William Loughton Smith's election in South Carolina to the 1st Congress (1789–1791), his opponent David Ramsay contested the result, arguing that Smith was not an eligible citizen of the United States for the requisite seven years established in the Constitution. The House referred the case to the Committee on Elections, which was established in April 1789, and in the process provided a very clear opportunity for the House to set a resounding and foundational precedent.

Smith had been born in Charleston, South Carolina, in 1758, but had spent a 13-year period abroad (1770–1783), creating sufficient ambiguity on which Ramsay's "team" (including an ardent rival of Smith, Thomas Tudor Tucker) sought to capitalize. Although he had been abroad at the time of the founding of the United States, the committee confirmed Smith's election, and the House rejected Ramsay's petition by a 36-1 majority. Madison, who played a decisive role in the ultimate judgment, reaffirmed the political construct's investment in birthplace over parentage in deciding matters of eligibility:

From an attention to the facts which have been adduced, and from a consideration of the principles established by the revolution, the conclusion I have drawn is, that Mr. Smith was, on the declaration of independence, a citizen of the United States; and unless it appears that he has forfeited his right, by some neglect or overt act, he had continued a citizen until the day of his election to a seat in this House ... It is an established maxim, that birth is a criterion of allegiance. Birth, however, derives its force sometimes from place, and sometimes from parentage; but, in general, place is the most certain criterion; it is what applies in the United States; it will, therefore, be unnecessary to investigate any other. Mr. Smith founds his claim upon his birth right; his ancestors were among the first settlers of that colony. (Madison 1789)

With the same verve as his 21st-century Birther colleagues, Ramsay did not easily accept the reality of his opponent's ruled eligibility. He published a further pamphlet entitled *Observations on the Decision of the House of Representatives* (1789) that served as an embittered critique of Smith and the validity of the judgment.

Despite the *Smith v. Ramsay* ruling, the Naturalization Act of 1790 cast momentary doubt on the dominance of *jus soli* and, as a result, is often called upon by Obama's citizenship deniers as further testimony in their favour. The relevant clause states:

the children of citizens of the United States, that may be born beyond sea, or out of the limits of the United States, shall be considered natural born citizens: Provided, That the right of citizenship shall not descend to persons whose fathers have never been resident in the United States.

While this act signaled that there remained some consideration of *jus sanguinis* shortly after the ratification of the Constitution, the Naturalization Act was subsequently revised to remove any reference to the "natural born citizen" and ultimately repealed in 1802. Consequently, the act has not been law in the United States for more than two centuries and is superseded by the 14th Amendment. Even if the act remained standing, the fact that Barack Obama, Sr., was resident in the United States prior to his son's birth would surely render the citation moot.

Early legal opinion surrounding the natural-born citizenship clause emphasized the prevalent investment in a *jus soli* interpretation of U.S. citizenship, recognizing birth location as the greatest testimony to national allegiance. Judge Zephaniah Swift, author of the first legal treatise in America (*A System of the Law of the State of Connecticut*) and U.S. Representative from Connecticut, wrote in "Of the People Considered as Foreigners and Natives":

It is an established maxim, received by all political writers, that every person owes a natural allegiance to the government of that country in which he is born ... The children of aliens, born in this state, are considered as natural born subjects, and have the same rights with the rest of the citizens. (Swift 1795, 163)

Fellow jurist St. George Tucker (from Virginia) corroborated Swift's opinion, describing the Constitution's presidential eligibility clause as "a happy means of security against foreign influence" (Blackstone, Tucker, and Christian 1803, 323). Tucker quoted "a very respectable political writer" in stating, "Prior to the adoption of the constitution, the people inhabiting the different states might be divided into two classes: natural born citizens, or those born within the state, and aliens, or such as were born out of it." James Kent, a prestigious legal scholar and author of *Commentaries on American Law* (1826–1830), defined "natives" as "all persons born with the jurisdiction and allegiance of the United States" (Lecture 25, Part 4), such that

As the President is required to be a native citizen of the United States, ambitious foreigners cannot intrigue for the office, and the qualification of birth cuts off all those inducements from abroad to corruption, negotiation, and war, which have frequently and fatally harassed the elective monarchies of Germany and Poland, as well as the pontificate of Rome. (Kent 1826, 255)

Kent's contemporary, William Rawle, U.S. District Attorney for Pennsylvania (as appointed for George Washington), provided even greater clarity on the established understanding of the natural born citizen clause in his 1829 work, *A View of the Constitution*:

[E]very person born within the United States, its territories or districts, whether the parents are citizens or aliens, is a natural born citizen in the sense of the Constitution, and entitled to all the rights and privileges appertaining to that capacity ... Under the Constitution ... the principle that the place of birth creates the relative quality is established to us. (Rawle 1829, 86)

One year later, Joseph Story, an associate justice on the U.S. Supreme Court, addressed the issue of citizenship and birth allegiance in his opinion in *Inglis v. Trustees of Sailor's Shrug Harbour.* "Nothing is better settled at the common law," he wrote, "than the doctrine that the children even of aliens born in a country while the parents are resident there under the protection of the government and owing a temporary allegiance thereto are subjects by birth."

As far as case law goes on this issue, perhaps the most decisive ruling was in *Lynch v. Clarke* (1843–1844), which examined the inheritance eligibility of Julia Lynch in the state of New York. The case set a resounding precedent in favor of the *jus soli* approach. Lynch's British parents had been resident in New York for four years at the time of the girl's birth, but very shortly afterward returned as a family to Ireland. The question before the court was Lynch's citizenship status with regard to the real estate inheritance of her father, Thomas Lunch, and the U.S. legal system had two broad options before it: to deem Julia eligible for the inheritance as a natural-born citizen because of her birth on U.S. soil or to deem her ineligible on the basis of blood because of the alien status of her parents. Ultimately, the New York Chancery Court decided in Lynch's favor, calling upon common law understanding and citing the Constitutional clause as unequivocally positive underpinnings for the plaintiff's argument. Vice Chancellor Lewis Sandford seemed willing to provide clarity for legal posterity:

Upon principle ... I entertain no doubt, but that by the law of the United States, every person born within the dominions and allegiance of the United States, whatever the situation of his parents, is a natural born citizen. It is surprising that there has been no judicial decision upon this question. (Owen 1845, 250)

Usefully, the Vice Chancellor went even further in his opinion, extrapolating the impact of his judgment on the interpretation of eligibility requirements for presidential office, directly underlining his absolute confidence in the precedent:

The only standard which then existed, of a natural born citizen, was the rule of common law, and no different standard has been adopted since. Suppose a person should be elected president who was native born, but of alien parents; could there be any reasonable doubt that he was eligible under the Constitution? I think not. The position would be decisive in his favour, that by the rule of common law, in force when the Constitution was adopted, he is a citizen. (246–247)

This prescient legal opinion, upholding Madison, Swift, Rawle, and others, could not be more explicit in its prioritization of birth location for determining American citizenship, even at the rarefied level of presidential legitimacy. It is clear that in the years and decades following the ratification of the Constitution, it was the common law understanding of citizenship, rather than some abstracted definition from Vattel or another source, that was accepted as legal provenance. And yet, this *jus soli* intellectual dominance is either deafeningly absent from the Birther movement's claims or, alternatively, relied upon as the basis for dubiously discrediting the Hawaiian location of Obama's birth.

The *Lynch* case was influential throughout the 19th century when the Civil War and the changing racial landscape roused further questions surrounding the definitions of citizenship. General Edward Bates, who served as President Abraham Lincoln's Attorney General, for example, received a letter from Treasury Secretary Salmon Chase in 1862 that questioned whether "colored men" might be considered to be United States citizens. The query was not theoretical, but practical. A sailing vessel under the command of a free black man claiming to be a U.S. citizen was detained by the Coast Guard, which faced the choice of releasing or seizing the vessel. Chase provided no extraneous detail of the man's identity or heritage. Bates's reply was a broad and lengthy consideration of the issue—so well respected that it was published as a pamphlet in its own right—in which he concluded that "the free man of color, mentioned in your letter, if born in the United States, is a citizen of the United States." Bates asserted that the Constitution "recognizes and reaffirms the universal principle, common to all nations, and as old as political society that the people born in a country do constitute the nation, and, as individuals, are *natural* members of the body politic," and that "every person born in the country is, at the moment of birth, prima facie a citizen ... without any reference to race or color, or any other accidental circumstance" (McPherson 1865, 384). Earlier that year, Bates provided the same opinion to a question as to the status of children born in the United States to alien parents:

Children born in the United States of alien parents, who have never been naturalized, are native-born citizens of the United States, and, of course, do not require the formality of naturalization to entitle them to the rights and privileges of such citizenship. I might sustain this opinion by a reference to the well settled principle of the common law of England on this subject; to the writings of many of the earlier and later commentators on our Constitution and laws; ... and lastly to the dicta and decisions of many of our national and state tribunals. But all of this has been well done by Assistant Vice Chancellor Sandford in the case of *Lynch vs. Clarke* ... (Ashton 1868, 328)

Even Representative John Bingham, whose words surrounding the 1866 Civil Rights Act are trotted out by the Birther movement as some sort of foundation for the rejection of Obama, has presented the question and answer on the issue: "Who are the natural born citizens but those born within the Republic? Those born within the Republic, whether black or white, are citizens by birth—natural born citizens" (*Congressional Globe* 37.2, 1639).

The 14th Amendment, while one of the most contentious Reconstruction amendments, emerged from the same line of thinking of the aforementioned legal perspectives. It formalized citizenship and equal legal protections for black and white Americans in the wake of increased racial violence and doubts surrounding the forward viability of the Civil Rights Act of 1866. Section One states:

All persons born or naturalized in the United States, and subject to the jurisdiction thereof, are citizens of the United States and of the State wherein they reside. No State shall make or enforce any law which shall abridge the privileges or immunities of citizens of the United States; nor shall any State deprive any person of life, liberty, or property, without due process of law; nor deny to any person within its jurisdiction the equal protection of the laws.

In overwriting the ambiguity of the natural-born citizenship clause, the 14th Amendment constitutionalized the equality principle evinced by the 1866 act and removed any real basis for a *jus sanguinis* interpretation of citizen eligibility. Senator Jacob Howard, author of the amendment's section on citizenship, wrote that his clause "will not, of course, include persons born in the United States who are foreigners, aliens, who belong to the families of ambassadors or foreign ministers accredited to the Government of the United States, but will include every other class of persons." While the Birthers continue to try to eke out slivers of ambiguity in the 14th Amendment for their purpose (even manipulating the grammar of the latter quotation), Howard and his colleagues were unequivocally specific in enumerating the minor exceptions to this natural and national law. In no feasible way might Obama's birth be considered to be in the "no-fly" zone of automatic natural citizenship.

The 14th Amendment clause, which serves as the line in the sand for citizenship definition, was tested and upheld by a legal case in 1898, *United States v. Wong Kim Ark*. Wong Kim Ark had been born in San Francisco in the early 1870s to Chinese parents, but upon returning from an overseas excursion was denied reentry into United States under Chinese immigration restrictions. In challenging the government over his status, Wong Kim Ark's claim relied heavily on the Supreme Court's interpretation of the 14th Amendment, and in particular the meaning of being "subject to the jurisdiction" of the United States. His challenge was ultimately successful, with a 6-2 majority holding that the 14th Amendment applied a *jus soli* principle that was almost universal in its application—even to the children of alien parents. Fuller and Harlan, in the minority dissenting opinion, argued that being subject to American jurisdiction required a *jus sanguinis* principle and that the United States had drifted from the expectations of English common law following the country's independence. The Supreme Court and lower courts have not in the proceeding century deviated from the centrality of the *jus soli* precedent. There is little genuine reprieve for the legal-minded Birther.

The argument that Obama's birth right is diminished because of the status, allegiance, or blood of his father finds little substantiation in the Constitution itself, corresponding writings, subsequent legal opinion, or the 14th Amendment. Vattel, though called upon as the primary witness of Obama's presidential ineligibility, has never been upheld in the majority legal opinion in defining a natural-born citizen within a *jus sanguinis* framework. One branch of Birtherism continues to pursue a *jus sanguinis* strategy in undoing the president's authority, whereas another (and sometimes connected) camp recognizes the *jus soli* precedent and focuses on "proving" that Obama was not born in this country or that his extant birth documentation was purposefully doctored to hide the truth of his origins.

PRESIDENT, SHOW YOUR PAPERS! RACE, CITIZENSHIP, AND DOCUMENTATION

While one branch of Birtherism continues to pursue a *jus sanguinis* strategy of undoing the president's authority on the basis of his father's bloodline, another has pursued a relentless *jus soli* approach, desirous of Obama's birth certification to prove his foreign nativity or doctored origins. The pretended revocation of Obama's eligibility via both of these means demonstrates the ongoing racialization of U.S. citizenship and lays bare the persistence of the "color line" (Du Bois 1903, 9) even at the most rarefied level of African American existence. Academics such as Eric Foner (1988), Yehudi Webster (1993), and Evelyn Glenn are unanimous in their belief that American citizenship has been from the nation's conception, and continues to be, organized by privileged whiteness, with "institutional mechanisms of racialization powerfully in operation in U.S. society" (Webster 1993, 26). As a consequence of the dominance and idealization of whiteness from the colonial era onward (including labor and property rights, for example), non-whites have been disproportionately and generationally barred from the normalcy of American citizenship (Haney-Lopez 2006). This disenfranchisement of the American minority, initially sustained by a shared and often unspoken understanding of inequality on the basis of skin color, physical stereotypes, and geographical location, has been supplemented by an evolving culture of racially restrictive citizenship documentation. In other words, the validity of black versus white personhood has been memorialized and assimilated into an American documentary psyche—from manumission papers, to freedom registration documents, to voting tests, to immigration paper requirements, to Obama's long-form birth certificate. As Matthew Hughey has persuasively argued, "The capricious demand for, and subjective scrutiny of, citizenship documentation is a point less emphasized" in the academic discourse on racialized belonging (Hughey 2012, 166). However, such an understanding is vital for understanding the context of Obama's 21st-century subjection to methods of othering via documentary inquisition.

Racialization and institutionalized certification have walked hand in hand throughout African American history. From the beginnings of slavery, documentation has been used to establish white hegemonic power over a predominantly powerless and less literate black people. Paper ball and chains. Treated as economically vital property, slaves were accounted for in a variety of ownership documents, such as bills of sale and tabular inventories of slave owners' stock. Until the emancipation of slaves with the ratification of the 13th Amendment (1864), fugitive slave laws (passed in 1793 and 1850, for example) endowed white persons with the power to requisition any person believed to be a potential "runaway" and to interrogate that individual's papers. The burden of proof to demonstrate a status other than slave was on the black detainee, who was expected to carry manumission papers (certificates of freedom) at all times.

Manumission began to be formalized in the late 17th century, to document the number of slaves released on the event of a slave owner's death or as a rare gift of compassion. Such legal documents, witnessed almost entirely by white owners and legal representatives, provided detached identity descriptions of the freed person, including height, skin color, notable body markings, and behavioral quirks—a passport, of sorts, to limited freedom. Runaway notices, with monetary rewards, were common, leading to the wrongful capture of many manumitted blacks or those who had been free from birth. Even if the correct identity papers had been obtained, such deeds could easily be destroyed or lost, unless logged with the relevant county offices—and even then there was no guarantee of fair play on the part of the white inquisitors. As John F. Campbell contends:

An immediate disincentive to their exhibiting a freedom to move around arose from the precarious nature of their "paper" freedom. In this sense a lost manu-mission paper, or one that was callously destroyed by a vindictive or labor-starved white manager, meant that the manumitted freedom was at an end unless it could be otherwise proven. (Campbell 2009, 150)

These papers were a vital, if vulnerable, security for freed black existence in a dominant white America. Without them, black people were in danger of (re)capture, conspiratorial challenge, oppression, forced labor, and punishment. The danger of this occurrence was more recently brought to public attention in the Oscar-winning cinematic adaptation of Solomon Northup's slave memoir of paperless-ness and kidnap, *Twelve Years a Slave* (2013).

During Reconstruction and the attendant enfranchisement and emanci-pation of the African American community, even greater documentary controls were placed upon black citizenship as fears grew over the loss of the ex-slave workforce. Despite this being the period in which a num-ber of oft-forgotten black men served in state and national legislatures (which were frequently in charge of authoring constitutional, legislative documentation), it was also an era of black codes, racial ostracism, and manifest prejudice to the benefit of white potency. Enhanced vagrancy laws and imperatives to sign annual labor contracts on pain of arrest maintained inequality by forcing the black community into debt and low-wage jobs. In Mississippi, an 1865 code required the black popula-tion to provide annual proof of year-long employment; if they could not do so, African Americans in the state were asked for forfeit previous wages and submit to incarceration. Louisiana was home to even greater restrictions, requiring blacks to present papers of dismissal to prospective employers and excluding them from living within certain cities or town-ships by means of local ordinance. In Opelousas, Louisiana, blacks required written statements from their employers to merely enter the town's limits; the statements had to detail the date, duration, and purpose of each visit. If a black person was found wandering the streets of Ope-lousas after dark, without the requisite papers on hand, or without an ameliorating white escort, imprisonment was to be expected. Such docu-mentary control was not unusual across the rural South.

More severe enforcement of *de jure* segregation as well as the congrega-tion of white supremacist groups created even greater interrogation of black documentation during the Jim Crow era. Literacy tests, which had been introduced earlier as a restriction to voting rights, were applied with renewed vigor, with readings of the Constitution and other comprehension tests introduced, requiring complete accuracy to pass the test. Often the documentation a person carried was not enough to avoid the corrupt and racist intimidation of some whites for whom no amount of paperwork could dissuade them from their false claims, violence, and lynchings. While this might seem like ancient history to some, the modernity of the Jim Crow era is often overlooked. In 1960 Kentucky, for example, the races of all candidates had to be included on electoral ballot papers, presenting a subversive racialized determination of the electability of non-white persons and reinforcing the political color line in written form. The Southern Strategy and Willie Horton era followed, with a loud volume of racial differentiation in the field of political campaigning.

More recently, with the continuous evolution of U.S. demographics and the persistence of immigration as a hot-button political issue, it is hard to avoid the phrase "*undocumented* aliens" in the more pejorative discourse; this descriptor is clearly a throwback to the language of the black codes. During Obama's presidency, a number of states, including Alabama, Arizona, and North Carolina, have considered legislation that explicitly targets racial groups to examine their legal American status through "Show me your papers" provisions. Arizona's Senate Bill 1070, which was passed into law in the spring of 2010, gained national attention for requiring any alien in Arizona to be in possession of the necessary documentation at all times, and obligating law enforcement agents to stop, detain, or arrest any individual where there is reasonable suspicion that a person might be an illegal immigrant. It created a state misdemeanor for failure to possess such documents at the time of inquiry, and provided that no such person could be released from detention without proven confirmation of legal immigration standing. There is more than an echo in this law of actions justified under the Fugitive Slave Laws of 18th- and 19th-century America.

In the age of Obama, it is clear that a renewed spirit of racialized documentation has arisen in the clamor for proof of Obama's foreign citizenship and the forensic examination of his documents in the public domain, derided by Birthers as fraudulent. From April 2008 to the present day, Obama has been asked to *show America his papers*. Whether it is the demand for certification from the *National Review*; the claims of a pro-Hillary Clinton campaign group in 2008; Orly Taitz's release of a fake Kenyan birth certificate; Sarah Palin's condoning of the Birther strategy as being in the public interest; Donald Trump's self-aggrandizing and bewildering claims that Obama has "conned the whole world" and his "investigators" in Hawaii can prove it (though they never did); Michele

Bachmann's claim that if she were running for president the first thing she would do would be to publish her own birth certificate (though she never did); Mitt Romney's less-than-subtle Michigan "joke" that "No one's ever asked to see my birth certificate" intended to bolster his extreme credentials; the conspiracy-laden propaganda from Corsi, D'Souza, and Gilbert; the endless innuendo emanating from right-wing media, such as Hannity, Dobbs, and Limbaugh; or the endless litigation of Obama's documentation—Obama's legitimacy and acceptance have been anchored to a predominantly white hegemonic standard of documentary control and interpretation.

To pose the same request to Obama to prove his citizenship by way of documentation, in the course of ordinary business, is to somehow suggest that he is a president less deserving of civil acceptance or equality with his white forebears. The Birther movement explicitly contends that one cannot accept Obama—his motivations, politics, and allegiance—at face value alone, that somehow he is in wont of white checkpoints of authentication, a president essentially less free.

Since Mark Penn suggested the strategy of de-Americanizing Obama for the purposes of political one-upmanship, Obama and his team have been frustrated by the attention devoted to scurrilous attacks on his identity documentation, with its associated detrimental impact upon the presidential office itself and the Democratic agenda. Obama sought to demythologize his own being by facing these undocumented claims with the force of his own birth evidence. In June 2008, he released the digital scanned image of his short-form birth certificate via the *Fight the Smears* website—the production of his own papers for access to the political arena, if you will. Independent sources and the state of Hawaii confirmed the efficacy of the released documentation, but because of the strength of the entrenched suspicion against an African American candidate who possessed an aura of unconventionality, the Birther movement marched on seemingly undeterred, with Taitz, Trump, Corsi, Limbaugh, Liddy, and Dobbs locked in an almost daily double-step of uninformed doubt.

Less than year into his presidency, Obama contended with questions raised by serious politicians, such as Senator Richard Shelby (Democrat-Alabama) and Representative Roy Blunt (Republican-Missouri), which cast doubt on the veracity of his birth documentation. There was no question now that Obama was being profiled on the national stage in an appeal to the irrational base in individual districts. In March 2009, Representative Bill Posey, from Florida's 15th Congressional district, introduced House Resolution 1503, which aimed to amend the Federal Election Campaign Act of 1971 to require future presidential aspirants to release "a copy of the candidate's birth certificate, together with such other documentation as may be necessary to establish that the candidate meets the qualifications for eligibility to the Office of President under the Constitution." Posey, it was reported, could not "swear on a stack of Bibles" that Obama was an American citizen, and he introduced H.R.1503 to prevent something like the Birther controversy from happening in future elections—though he was, by extension, knowingly keeping it alive. Although Posey introduced his bill without forewarning Republican leadership, he eventually gained the support of 12 GOP co-sponsors: Marsha Blackburn, Dan Burton, John Campbell, John R. Carter, Mike Conaway, John Culberson, Trent Franks, Louie Gohmert, Bob Goodlatte, Kenny Marchant, Randy Neugebauer, and Ted Poe. Posey's bill was widely disparaged, never making it out of committee to be voted upon in either legislative chamber. Chris Matthews, host of MSNBC's *Hardball* program, interviewed Representative John Campbell (California) with incredulity; holding Obama's certification in his hand, Matthews asked that if Campbell really wanted to put an end to the speculation, he should "mail this birth certificate to the wacko wing of your party." Stephen Colbert satirized the bill's intentions, comically turning the burden of proof upon Posey himself:

To quell the persistent rumors about Posey himself, I am demanding DNA tests to determine whether Florida congressmen are part alligator. I have had enough with the reckless whispering. But the rumor is that the morning after the great Okeechobee hurricane of 1928, Posey's grandmother got stranded with a 'gator, and fell in love. Now obviously I don't want to go into any details. But they say the swamp rang with her screams of ecstasy, mingled with insistent but gentle hissing of her reptilian Romeo. Well, I've done my part to make these terrible rumors go away.

In his typical manner, Colbert had struck at the heart of the tautologous argument of Posey and his co-sponsors. Although neither the House nor Senate has been successful in essentially legislating against Obama's identity, such efforts have legitimated the paranoia in accepting the president at his word.

April 27, 2011, is surely one of the more significant—if disheartening—days in the modern racial and presidential calendar. That morning, the White House had indicated that Obama would be making a statement in the Briefing Room shortly before 10 a.m. Jay Carney and Dan Pfeiffer assembled the press gaggle for a prebriefing an hour earlier, at which they distributed copies of President Obama's original long-form birth certificate. He had finally shown his papers. In the face of the ongoing Birther debacle, they explained, Obama had requested certified copies of the document—which was held within the vaults of the state's archives—to be released by Loretta Fuddy, Hawaii's Department of Health Director. Judith Corley had been dispatched to Honolulu to pay the necessary processing fees and to collect the requested copies for the sitting president of the United States, who had become infuriated with the distractive power of the accusations, to prove his origins. Obama spoke directly to the American people, to the Birther movement, and to the mainstream press, chastising the pursuit of this small and personal non-issue, in spite of the magnitude of the nation's challenges:

I have to say . . . that I have watched with bemusement. I have been puzzled at the degree to which this thing just kept on going. Now, normally, I would not comment on something like this because . . . I've got other things to do. But two weeks ago when the Republican House had put forward a budget that will have huge consequences potentially for the country, and when I gave a speech about my budget and how I felt we needed to invest in education and infrastructure, and making sure that we have a strong safety net for our seniors . . . during that entire week, the dominant news story wasn't about these huge monumental choices that we're going to have to make as a nation, it was about my birth certificate . . . .

We're not going to be able to do it if we spend time vilifying each other. We're not going to be able to do it if we just make stuff up and pretend that facts are not facts. We are not going to be able to solve our problems if we get distracted by sideshows and carnival barkers. We live in a serious time right now and we have the potential to deal with the issues we confront in a way that will make our kids, and our grandkids, and our great-grandkids proud . . . but we are going to have to get serious to do it. I know that there is going to be a segment of people that no matter what we put out that this issue will not be put to rest. But I am speaking to the vast majority of the American people, as well as to the press: we do not have time for this kind of silliness. We got better stuff to do. I've got better stuff to do. (Obama 2011)

Despite Obama's expressed "bemusement" and "puzzled" observation of the Birther demands, there is no doubt that the president was fully cognizant at that moment of his own role in an ongoing racialization of African American citizenship and the implicit and explicit resistance to non-white political representation. Obama also knew that despite his submission of documentation, of affidavits, of witness statements, of logical argument, to this abyss of prejudice, there would no abatement in the disqualification narrative due in part to of the stability of the conspiracy, the vitriol of modern partisan identity politics, and the history of white documentary control and black exclusion. Indeed, it was not long before Birthers regrouped to reject the certificate as an electronic forgery and the product of complicit political figures. Donald Trump would soon demand further documentation, including proof of Obama's college grades, resurrecting the prescriptive literacy-type interrogation of black Americans within the voting arena.

Finally, if there is a single crystalizing moment of contrast between the serious plotline of Obama's national government and the nonsensical, personal, dog-whistle, underworld of Birther politics, it perhaps occurred at the Washington Correspondents Dinner of 2011, held only three days after Obama's submission of his long-form birth certificate. Obama translated his exasperation surrounding this issue into a series of comic tableaus, extrapolating the Birther logic *ab absurdum*. "What a week!" he began, referencing the Birther conspiracy with some amount of understatement, before announcing, "Just in case there are any lingering questions tonight, I am releasing my official birth video." Scenes from the Disney film *The Lion King* played across large television screens in the ballroom, showing the birth of the African lion, Simba, in a generic desert setting. "That was a joke," he clarified for the Fox News table, teasing the potential for this animation to be taken as "proof" of Obama's Kenyan birth in the Tea Party universe. People laughed so heartily because the clarification was both ludicrous and necessary. Obama similarly used the speech to exact the Birther-style othering strategy upon a number of his Republican opponents, extrapolating the nonsensicality of the approach when applied to the WASP establishment.

Referring to Michele Bachmann, he said, "She is thinking about running for president, which is weird because I hear she was born in Canada." "Yes, Michele," he added, "this is how it starts."

About Tim Pawlenty, Obama joked, "He seems all American, but have you heard his real middle name? Tim *Hosni* Pawlenty. What a shame."

Regarding Jon Huntsman's potential foreignness, Obama proposed that the ambassador to China "didn't learn to speak Chinese to go there. Oh, no. He learned *English* to come *here.*"

Somehow such Birtherisms did not have the same sticking power when applied to the more traditional, white politician. Obama turned then to Donald Trump, the self-appointed leader of the Birthers sitting in the audience. "He can finally get back to focusing on the issues that matter," Obama derided, "like 'Did we fake the moon landing?', 'What really happened at Roswell?' and 'Where are Biggie and Tupac?' " Drawing a decisive contrast between Obama's presidential responsibilities and Trump's somewhat lesser dilemmas on *Celebrity Apprentice*, Obama joked, "These are the type of decisions that would keep me up at night."

The takedowns were deliberate and pregnant with irony. For what Obama could not relate to the audience that night in the Hilton ballroom was that while he was forced to make light of a national movement intent on destroying his presidency on the basis of false claims about his birth and allegiance, he had just moments previously instigated an audacious military action to locate and kill Osama bin Laden in Pakistan. As Obama was working behind the scenes to protect the American citizenry from its most illustrious foreign enemy—a patriotic action of astronomical proportions—he was, in parallel, confronting the manufactured and short-sighted political insinuation that he was some interloping, alien president, as sustained by an ever-expanding, inextinguishable, racialized Birther fantasy that shows no sign of going away while there is a black man in the White House.

REFERENCES

8 U.S. CODE § 1403: Persons Born in the Canal Zone or Republic of Panama on or after February 26, 1904.

Ashton, J. Hubley, ed. *Official Opinions of the Attorneys General of the United States,* Washington, DC: W. H. & O. H. Morrison, 1868.

"Barack Obama 1995 Interview on *Dreams from My Father* Part 1." YouTube video from a televised video with Connie Martinson on *Talks Books,* posted by "Andrew Kaczynski," November 20, 2011. http://www.youtube.com/watch?v=Rx_XS4s6aA4.

Blackstone, William, St. George Tucker, and Edward Christian. *Blackstone's Commentaries,* Philadelphia: William Young Birch and Abraham Small, 1803.

Campbell, John F. "How Free Is Free? The Limits of Manumission for Enslaved Africans in Eighteenth-Century British West Indian Sugar Society." In *Paths to Freedom,* edited by Rosemary Brana-Shute and Randy J. Sparks, 143–174, Columbia, SC: University of South Carolina Press, 2009.

Congressional Globe, House of Representatives, 37th Congress, 2nd Session, 1862.

Corsi, Jerome R. *Where's the Birth Certificate? The Case That Barack Obama Is Not Eligible to Be President.* Washington, DC: WND Books, 2011.

Costa, Robert. "Gingrich: Obama's 'Kenyan, Anti-colonial' Worldview." *The National Review Online* (September 11, 2010). http://www.nationalreview.com/corner/246302/gingrich-obama-s-kenyan-anti-colonial-worldview-robert-costa.

DailyKos.com. 2009. "Birthers are mostly Republican and Southern." July 31, 2009. http://www.dailykos.com/story/2009/07/31/760087/-Birthers-are-mostly-Republican-and-Southern.

Devos, Thierry, and Mahzarin R. Banaji. "American = White?" *Journal of Personality and Social Psychology* 88, no. 3 (March 2005): 447–466.

Devos, Thierry, Debbie S. Ma, and Travis Gaffud. "Is Barack Obama American Enough to Be the Next President? The Role of Ethnicity and National Identity in American Politics" Poster presented at the

IXth Annual Meeting of the Society for Personality and Social Psychology, Albuquerque, NM, 2008. http://www-rohan.sdsu.edu/~tdevos/thd/Devos_spsp2008.pdf

Du Bois, W. E. B. *The Souls of Black Folk*. New York, NY: New American Library, 1903.

Foner, Eric. *Reconstruction: America's Unfinished Revolution, 1863–1877*. New York, NY: Harper and Row, 1988.

Green, Joshua. "Penn Strategy Memo, March 19, 2008." *The Atlantic* (August 11, 2008). http://www.theatlantic.com/politics/archive/2008/08/penn-strategy-memo-march-19-2008/37952/.

Haney-Lopez, Ian. *White by Law: The Legal Construction of Race*. New York, NY: NYU Press, 2006.

Health.Hawaii.gov 2011. "Frequently Asked Questions about Vital Records of President Barack Hussein Obama II." April, 2011. http://health.hawaii.gov/vitalrecords/faq-obama/

Hinman, Arthur P. *How a British Subject Became President of the United States*. New York, NY: 1884.

Hughey, Matthew W. "Show me your papers! Obama's birth and the whiteness of belonging." *Qualitative sociology 35*, 2 (2012): 163–181.

Husle, Carl. "McCain's Canal Zone Birth Prompts Queries about Whether That Rules Him Out." *The New York Times* (February 28, 2008). http://www.nytimes.com/2008/02/28/us/politics/28mccain.html?pagewanted=print.

Jay, John, to George Washington, July 25, 1787. In *History of the Formation of the Constitution of the United States of America,* edited by George Bancroft. New Jersey: Lawbook Exchange Limited, 2000.

Kent, James. *Commentaries on American Law*. O. Halsted, 1826–1830.

Long, Breckenridge. "Is Mr. Charles Evans Hughes a 'Natural Born Citizen' within the Meaning of the Constitution?" *Chicago Legal News*, 146–148 (1916): 220–222. http://libertylegalfoundation.org/wp-content/uploads/2012/01/Breckinridge-Long.pdf.

Madison, James. 1789 statement. In *The Founders' Constitution,* edited by Philip B. Kurland and Ralph Lerner. Chicago, IL: University of Chicago Press, 1987.

McPherson, Edward. *The Political History of the United States of America, during the Great Rebellion, from November 6, 1860, to July 4, 1864.* Washington, DC: Philip and Solomons, 1865.

New York Times Archive. "Material for a Democratic Lie; St. Albans, Vt." *The New York Times* (December 22, 1880). http://query.nytimes.com/mem/archive-free/pdf?res=FA0C15F8395B1B7A93C0AB1789D95F448884F9.

Obama, Barack H. *Dreams from My Father*. New York, NY: Times Books, 1995.

Obama, Barack H. "Remarks by the President." Speech in Washington, DC, April 27, 2011. The White House. http://www.whitehouse.gov/the-press-office/2011/04/27/remarks-president.

Owen, Samuel. *The New-York Legal Observer: Containing Reports of Cases Decided in the Courts of Equity and Common Law, and Important Decisions in the English Courts.* S. Owen, 1845.

PublicMind.fdu.edu. 2013. "Conspiracy Theories Prosper: 25% of Americans are 'Truthers'." January 17, 2013. http://publicmind.fdu.edu/2013/outthere/

Ramsay, David. *Observations on the Decision of the House of Representatives of the United States, on the 22d Day of May, 1789: Respecting the Eligibility of the Hon. William Smith, of South-Carolina, to a Seat in That House.* Hodge, Allen and Campbell, 1789.

Rawle, William. *A View of the Constitution of the United States of America.* P. H. Nicklin, 1829.

S.Res.511: A Resolution Recognizing That John Sidney McCain, III, Is a Natural Born Citizen. http://www.opencongress.org/bill/110-sr511/text.

Swift, Zephaniah. *A System of the Laws of the State of Connecticut.* New Haven: John Byrne, 1795.

Taitz, Orly. "Demand for Emergency Hearing to NH Speaker of House Regarding Obama's Ballot Access." November 20, 2011. http://www.birtherreport.com/2011/11/demand-for-emergency-hearing-to-nh.html.

USAToday.com. 2011. "Poll: What Kind of President Would Donald Trump Make?" April 26, 2011. http://usatoday30.usatoday.com/news/politics/2011-04-25-trump-president-poll.htm

Vattel, Emer de. *The Law of Nations.* London: G. G. and J. Robinson, 1797.

Velasco, Eric. "Man Fighting Obama Candidacy Asks Black Jefferson County Judge to Step Aside due to Racial Bias." *The Birmingham News* (January 11, 2012). http://blog.al.com/spotnews/2012/01/man_challenging_obama_candidac.html.

Webster, Yehudi O. *The Racialization of America.* New York, NY: Palgrave Macmillan, 1993.

Chapter 3

Angry, Lazy, Stupid:
The Non-White President

Race can intrude in ugly ways. We can't escape the historical legacy
that this country has created, but that also affected my father back
in Kenya. We have this difficulty in understanding the Other, we live
as strangers, black and white . . . I still think it's a difficult struggle.

—*Barack Obama, interview, 1995*

Barack Obama's biracial skin is undoubtedly the canvas upon which his
opponents have drawn the (colored and colorful) narratives of his denigration as a person somehow inconsistent with the structures of white
belonging and political acceptance.

Indeed, this entire volume is a variation on that theme, of how
Obama's racial identity—from his cradle to his second term—has been
utilized as a lens through which to view his political, biographical, and
religious demonization as an anti-American other. As such, following a
brief discussion of Obama and post-racialism, the scope of this chapter
is narrowed to the analysis of three central racist caricatures that have
been applied to President Obama, and that revive negative associations
and expectations of the black character. The delegitimization of the first
African American president as angry, lazy, or stupid relies on a trifecta
of historically informed racial denigration types to embed a narrative of
WASP political superiority. The consequent revivification of the negative
caricatures of the African American male—the Coon, the Black Brute, the
Sambo, and the Uncle Tom—push Obama's presidency backward

through America's chronology to a place of total racial inequality, black disenfranchisement, political ridicule, and disrespect. If the language of racial progress is futuristic and positive—"Hope," "Change We Can Believe In," "Forward"—Obama's opponents' resurrection of old-fashioned racism has conceptually resituated Obama's identity within the epochs of American history in which his possibility as a political actor is read as an existential anathema.

THE MYTH OF POST-RACIALISM

In the minutes, hours, days, and weeks subsequent to Obama's historic election victory, which was heralded as a landmark of progress in the continuing struggle for racial equity, political commentators, pundits, and scholars suggested that the 2008 election represented the threshold gateway to a "post-racial" America (Curry 2008; Schneider 2008; Steele 2008; Thernstrom 2008). Indeed, a Gallup poll published on November 7, 2008, found that one third of all Americans surveyed viewed Obama's election as "the most important advance in the past 100 years" in terms of the progress for blacks in the United States.[1]

While increasing the Democratic share of white support by the standards of previous general election performances, however, Obama did not win the majority of that demographic. The 2008 election campaign had been one of the most fractious in recent times, with continuously personal and race-based suggestions being made that Obama was an unsuitable candidate because he was somehow "Other" to the American way. In response to his election, a predominantly white and right-wing grassroots organization, known as the Tea Party, energized its members to protest and discredit Obama's policies *and* identity as an ideological raison d'être. Arguably, in place of a post-racial America, Obama's election represented a hyper-racializing stimulus, provoking latent prejudicial sentiments and attachments in the American imagination. In the words of Myra Mendible, "Obama's election actually facilitated a counter discourse which obscures or downplays the persistence of inequality and racism, and which idealizes the current state of race relations in America" (2012, 4).

Numerous studies have found that racial attitudes have a substantive impact upon evaluations of President Barack Obama (Jackman and

[1]The same poll found that 67 percent of Americans believe that "relations between blacks and whites" would "eventually be worked out." Conversely, Gallup indicated that 56 percent of McCain voters expressed the view that they were afraid of Obama's presidency.

Vavreck 2010; Piston 2010). From their own research into partisan attachments, Tesler and Sears (2010) conclude that:

Obama activated older and more blatant forms of racial prejudice like old fashioned racism and anti-black affect even more powerfully. While both of these outdated attitudes were unrelated to party identification in the years and decades preceding the 2008 election, we show that they have become significantly linked to white partisanship in the age of Obama ... Obama substantially increased the black-white racial divide in both macro partisanship and in strength of Democratic identification.

That Obama's election has been racially divisive, in at least a rhetorical sense, is supported by Mendible. She understands the president's election as being essentially schismatic, rather than reparative, under the guise of post-racialism:

Obama's election exposed the fault lines of American society, evoking deep-seated apprehensions about race, immigration, and America's status in a post-9/11 world. Despite his attempts to bypass race as a factor and not alienate his white constituency, Obama's presidency has been to some degree hijacked by race. It can even be said that his election further obscured institutional racism and galvanized a racist backlash. (2012, 4)

Indeed, Obama's 2008 and 2012 electoral victories did not herald the genesis of a post-racial America or some halcyon color-blind society. Nor did they work to eviscerate racism. Arguably, Obama's ascendency revived the use of coding and subtle rhetorical gesture to undermine his candidacy, presidency, and any form of symbolic racial progress beyond white superiority he might represent.

Barack Obama, meanwhile, had understood, and cradled, his candidature and rhetoric as having the capacity to engender a perceived politics of post-racialism. In the wake of the divisions rendered by the George W. Bush administration, and calling upon the history of social and racial separatism, Obama framed his campaign as the enablement of a seismic "change we can believe in" toward a "more perfect union" that would move the country beyond tribal red and blue Americas, and indeed all divisive dichotomies. Obama extended his own iconicity—as a mixed-race symbol for multivariate change and racial, social, and geographical hybridity—through, for example, the deployment of his central slogan "Yes We Can," which signified a positive response to the status quo negative frames of institutional discrimination.

Yet, walking the tightrope of national electability, Obama's aura of post-racialism was often created by what he did *not* say. The president has, for example, has notably avoided the explicit discussion of racial, economic, and educational inequalities in the black community during his administration. Furthermore, the number of occasions on which Obama has delivered deliberative orations specifically on race and racism in America can be counted on one hand (with some fingers missing). His speech in the wake of the Jeremiah Wright controversy in March 2008, "A More Perfect Union," and his remarks made in the aftermath of the Trayvon Martin legal case, while both contemplative discourses on the African American experience, were both provoked by external events outside of Obama's control. In the latter address in 2013, Obama consciously delegated his role as a spokesperson on race:

There's been talk about whether we should convene a conversation on race. I haven't seen that be particularly productive. When politicians try to organize conversations, they end up being stilted and politicized and folks are locked into positions they already have. (Obama 2013)

That sentiment comported with Obama's earlier writings, such as the following passage from *The Audacity of Hope,* in which the future president cited the potentially alienating results of his personal instigation of racial discourse:

Rightly or wrongly, white guilt has largely exhausted itself in America; even the most fair-minded of whites, those who would genuinely like to see racial inequality ended and poverty relieved, tend to push back against suggestions of racial victimization—or race-specific claims based on the history of race discrimination in this country. (Obama 2007, 247)

   Obama's reticence to tackle issues of racial inequality and discrimination from the bully pulpit has both increased his cross-racial electoral appeal and, conversely, drawn criticism from representatives of civil rights organizations desirous of a potentially transformative presidential spokesperson. Darrel Enck-Wanzer has rightly recognized that dichotomy:

Obama is in a bit of a double bind and he probably knows it. On the one hand, failure to acknowledge race leaves him open to critiques like the one I advance here and criticism from African American leaders nationwide for failing to be proactive on policy issues relevant to racial minorities (Stolberg 2010; Thompson 2010). On the other hand, if he acknowledges race or claims racism, he (a) risks the charge of racism by violating the rhetorical norms of neoliberalism and (b) risks marking himself further as "different" in the eyes of many voters. (Enck-Wanzer 2011, 28)

This risk of seeming "different"—of othering himself as the son of a black African and, therefore, as outside the normative American experience—has been deftly avoided by Obama, even as his opponents on the Right have exaggerated that racial difference as a focus of partisan strategy.

The manifestation of Obama's situation outside of normative white belonging is often subtle and apparently nonracial. Let us take as an example the interruptive outburst of Representative Joe Wilson on September 9, 2009, during Barack Obama's presidential address to a joint session of Congress on his proposals for reforming American health care. Rebutting claims that his policy would "insure illegal immigrants" (itself a foreignizing accusation from the right wing), Obama stated, "The reforms I'm proposing would not apply to those who are here illegally." As Obama paused for breath and clarity, Wilson shouted uncontrollably from stage left, "You lie," gesturing toward the 44th president of the United States. The outburst was unprecedented. In the ceremonial largesse of presidential addresses to Congress, audience pleasure and displeasure are ordinarily symbolized by applauding ovation and keeping one's seat with quiet restraint, respectively. The traditional protest is silent, respectful, and non-interruptive. Wilson's paroxysm, by contrast, was an echo—and an unfortunate exemplar—of the colorful crowd interruptions at Tea Party rallies and right-wing protests enacted across the country. Wilson apologized for his behavior, which he characterized as "inappropriate and regrettable" and emblematic of a "lack of civility." The House agreed, passing a "resolution of disapproval" of the incident on September 15.

It was the noted incivility and rareness of the breach of conduct, tied with Obama's position as the first African American president, that drew many imputations of Wilson's potential racial motivation. Collective and individual instances of disrespecting Obama, in times when other presidents and candidates have enjoyed a veil of courtesy, might suggest that whiteness can be used as a discrete system of racial oppression and selective protection. Former President Jimmy Carter was one of the first to voice the opinion that Wilson's ejaculation was "based on racism" and "an inherent feeling among many in this country that an African American should not be president." Wilson's micro-objection to Obama's utterance spoke to a macro-objection of Obama's presidency. Maureen Dowd described the event as transformative in persuading her that the Right's campaign against the president was not color-blind:

[F]air or not, what I heard was an unspoken word in the air: You lie, boy! . . . I've been loath to admit that the shrieking lunacy of the summer—the frantic efforts to paint our first black president as the Other, a foreigner, socialist, fascist,

Marxist, racist, Commie, Nazi; a cad who would snuff old people; a snake who would indoctrinate kids—had much to do with race ... But Wilson's shocking disrespect for the office of the president—no Democrat ever shouted "liar" at W. when he was hawking a fake case for war in Iraq—convinced me: Some people just can't believe a black man is president and will never accept it. (Dowd 2009)

Wilson's shout, while consisting of only two syllables, revived the entire rhythmic history of white objection to black equality and representation. The behavior may not have been a conscious event of projected racism, but the accusation replicated and furthered the psychological system of black subjugation. As David Owen suggests,

In shouting during Obama's address, Wilson enacted a form of disrespect that was not deracialized. Wilson's action symbolically situated Obama as outside of what normal decorum demanded ... the racialized import of his action was to reproduce the historically embedded norm in the U.S. that blacks are not deserving of white respect. (Owen 2010, 116)

The words of Joe Wilson, whether conscious or not, legitimated Obama's demonization, on the nationally televised stage and with the weight of some level of congressional authority, through the implied equation of whiteness with belonging. To some, it was the primal cry of white protest against black authority—a 21st-century Negro-misrule narrative, reminiscent of the *Birth of a Nation* school of thought with regard to the virtues and value of African American leadership. In 2012, Bill O'Reilly invoked such sentiments by lamenting, "Obama wins because it's not the traditional America anymore. The white establishment is the minority. People want things."

The hyper-racialized and hyper-racializing rejection of Obama's presidency is, however, regularly more overt. Take, for example, the email sent by a Tennessee political aide featuring a collage of portraits of the 44 presidents of the United States. Whereas his predecessors are presented with traditional and stoic presidential portraiture, Obama's portrait is a jet-black background from which two white cartoon eyes peer from a relatively recent past of blackface and minstrelsy. Recall also the image created to portray Obama as a half-naked African tribal witch-doctor to undermine the Western acceptability of his healthcare reform legislation. Refer to the image circulated of Obama kneeling before Sarah Palin as a 1920s shoeshine boy. Peruse the pages of Darleen Click's comic, *Barack the Barbarian*, which present the axe-wielding Obama dominating cowering white females, in an echo of the Black Brute stereotypes of slavery and Reconstruction.

There has also been the subgenre of Obama's culinary racialization, through his association with watermelon and fried chicken, reviving the caricature of the Coon, who "is often portrayed as a lazy, easily frightened, inarticulate, good-for-nothing buffoon ... obsessed with stealing and eating chicken and watermelon" (Pilgrim 2012a). In 2009, Dean Grose, mayor of Los Alamitos, California, resigned after forwarding an email depicting the White House lawn as a watermelon patch, under the title "No Easter egg hunt this year"—further suggesting Obama's racial difference and anti-Christian administration. Meanwhile, a fast-food business owner in Brooklyn, New York, inspired widespread protests when he rebranded his restaurant as "Obama Fried Chicken." Daniel Hafley in Kentucky defended his life-size watermelon-eating Obama display as "freedom of speech," adding that the watermelon was not intended racially but was included because the faux Obama "might get hungry standing out here." The Internet is littered with innumerable crude photo-shopped images of Obama with the gastronomic props of Reconstruction-era racism, regenerating the "[a]dvertising trade cards [that] treated blacks as chicken-stealing, watermelon-eating brutes" (Jenkins 2012, 6).

Every criticism of Obama is axiomatically not a criticism founded in race. But where such criticisms coalesce around discrete themes that speak almost exclusively to the demonization and othering of the black American, and where there is evidence of a widespread terminological turn to describe the president using adjectives of traditional racial denigration such as angry, lazy, and stupid, it is both appropriate and a scholarly and moral duty to bring them to the light of scrutinizing discourse.

THE ANGRY BLACK PRESIDENT OR "NO DRAMA" OBAMA

I pointed out that it's not always easy for a black politician to gauge the right tone to take—too angry? Not angry enough?

—Barack Obama, *Audacity of Hope*, 2007

The denigration of Obama's personal temperament as either too angry or not angry enough reaches deep into the well of America's historical and racialized expectations of African American behavior. The Right's coded portrayal of Obama as the angry black president, despite most evidence to the contrary, consciously revives well-entrenched caricatures of black aggression stemming from the slave era, such as the Nat Turner trope (leader of slave rebellion), the Black Buck character (an untamable, violent black caricature), and the Brute stereotype. It does so in order to question Obama's ability to denude himself of such characteristics, either imagined or real, and to provide a moderate "finger on the trigger" as an American commander in chief.

Obama, meanwhile, has actively maneuvered his candidacy and presidency away from the tone and rhetoric of traditionally intemperate voices within the civil rights movement, such as those of Malcom X, Jesse Jackson, and the Reverend Al Sharpton, so as to avoid the pigeon holing of his electoral appeal. Nevertheless, Obama's persona of the calm, cool, collected, even professorial executive—the "No Drama Obama"—has led on occasion to seemingly contrary calls from the right (and the left) for the president to enthusiastically embrace the angry stereotype in his leadership. Down this rabbit hole of Obama's racial othering, then, his opponents can be found to claim simultaneously that Obama is too acrimonious *and* not acrimonious enough; meanwhile, his supporters decry the portrayal of the president as the angry black man, *but* later demand he adopt it as a mode of political being. This is hardly an endorsement of a post-racial political era, when America's first black president is forced into an unwinnable double bind of identity politics, in which he can never simultaneously deny, conform, satisfy, or disappoint the desired scale of "African American anger" as long as that caricatured expectation exists in the minds of his populace.

The elephant in the room of Obama's demonization on the grounds of harbored anger, of course, is the March 2008 controversy relating to the remarks made by Dr. Jeremiah Wright, Obama's pastor at Trinity United Church of Christ in Chicago. Following ABC News research, damaging excerpts from two of Wright's sermons, "The Day of Jerusalem's Fall" (2001) and "Confusing God and Government," were hurled like grenades into the minefield of the presidential campaign. The clipped videos of Wright's distinctively aggressive preaching style showed the Reverend straying into areas of social and political commentary. The edited segments presented Wright as an anti-patriot, preaching against the country's historical treatment of the black community in violently Biblical terms: "They wants [sic] us to sing *God Bless America*? No! No! No! Not *God Bless America*, God DAMN America!" Even more damaging was the climax of a sermon delivered only days after the terrorist attacks of September 11, 2001, in which Wright claimed:

We bombed Hiroshima. We bombed Nagasaki. And we nuked far more than the thousands in New York and the Pentagon, and we never batted an eye ... and now we are indignant? ... America's chickens are coming home to roost.

The edited videos, broadcast on an endless loop via traditional and social media, tied race relations, religion, heightened anger, and anti-Americanism into a startling series of images that presented Jeremiah Wright as the ultimate symbol of the angry black man involved in an aesthetic of unpatriotic revenge.

Unlike the previous attempts by the McCain campaign to tie Obama's own disposition to persons of questionable temperament—such as the 1960s radical, Bill Ayers—Obama's "guilt by association" with Wright was more convincing in light of the strength of the men's relationship. Wright had brought Obama into the Christian congregation, officiated at the marriage of Michelle and Barack Obama, and baptized their children. One of Wright's sermons had inspired the title of Obama's book, *The Audacity of Hope,* and had been used as the basis for a number of the candidate's oratorical themes. Wright had also been appointed to Obama's African American Religious Leadership Committee as part of the candidate's outreach efforts in 2007. The question, for many, was simple: had Obama, as a congregant, inherited the spirit of the angry black man merely by being in the presence of his pastor, another angry black man. Further, that the videos had emerged in the context of journalistic revelation created the sense that Obama might have been an angry black man behind closed doors.

Obama moved swiftly to disassociate himself from the pastor, who, in the words of Eric Deggans (2008), had "been reduced to an emotional image—the Willie Horton of 2008—a boogeyman of black nationalism and aggression." In response to the controversy, on March 18, 2008, Obama delivered his most wide-ranging, conciliatory, and personal oration on America's racial history, titled "A More Perfect Union," at the National Constitution Center in Philadelphia. By its visual rhetoric alone, Obama's speech was intended to supplant the image of Wright's pulpit with the candidate's podium. Obama delivered an opposing homily of reparative union, surrounded by American flags, in a calm and restrained rhetorical style, quoting the founding documents as American scripture. At the macro level, Obama's 37 minutes behind his political lectern helped to vanish the notion that he was a disciple in Wright's image. At the micro level, Obama used the content of his speech to first extricate himself from his pastor's comments:

I have already condemned, in unequivocal terms, the statements of Reverend Wright that have caused such controversy. For some, nagging questions remain. Did I know him to be an occasionally fierce critic of American domestic and foreign policy? Of course. Did I ever hear him make remarks that could be considered controversial while I sat in church? Yes. Did I strongly disagree with many of his political views? Absolutely—just as I'm sure many of you have heard remarks from your pastors, priests, or rabbis with which you strongly disagreed.

But the remarks that have caused this recent firestorm weren't simply controversial. They weren't simply a religious leader's effort to speak out against perceived injustice. Instead, they expressed a profoundly distorted view of this country—a view that sees white racism as endemic, and that elevates what is wrong with America above all that we know is right with America. (Obama 2008)

Obama also moved to humanize Wright out of the two-dimensional "angry black" stereotype of racial history into the model black and patriotic citizen:

But the truth is, that isn't all that I know of the man. The man I met more than twenty years ago is a man who helped introduce me to my Christian faith, a man who spoke to me about our obligations to love one another, to care for the sick and lift up the poor. He is a man who served his country as a U.S. Marine, who has studied and lectured at some of the finest universities and seminaries in the country, and who for over thirty years led a church that serves the community by doing God's work here on Earth—by housing the homeless, ministering to the needy, providing day care services and scholarships and prison ministries, and reaching out to those suffering from HIV/AIDS. (Obama 2008)

Later in the speech, Obama seemed to neutralize the one-sidedness of African American anger, by paralleling Wright's remarks with the racist utterances of Obama's own white grandmother:

I can no more disown him than I can disown the black community. I can no more disown him than I can my white grandmother—a woman who helped raise me, a woman who sacrificed again and again for me, a woman who loves me as much as she loves anything in this world, but a woman who once confessed her fear of black men who passed by her on the street, and who on more than one occasion has uttered racial or ethnic stereotypes that made me cringe.

These people are a part of me. And they are a part of America, this country that I love. (Obama 2008)

Overall, the speech mentions the word "anger" a total of 11 times (by comparison, the word "America," for example, is used 6 times), exemplifying Obama's understanding of the caricature of black acrimony being proliferated in the public discourse. He parallels black anger with white anger as a means of balance and unification, but also makes clear that

that emotion is a complex and key component of the African American psychology:

The fact that so many people are surprised to hear that anger in some of Reverend Wright's sermons simply reminds us of the old truism that the most segregated hour in American life occurs on Sunday morning. That anger is not always productive; indeed, all too often it distracts attention from solving real problems; it keeps us from squarely facing our own complicity in our condition, and prevents the African American community from forging the alliances it needs to bring about real change. But the anger is real; it is powerful; and to simply wish it away, to condemn it without understanding its roots, only serves to widen the chasm of misunderstanding that exists between the races. (Obama 2008)

Obama transformed the image of an angry black man through the personification of his theme of the *more perfect union*. Although anger was the theme forced upon him, he criticized, humanized, contextualized, and neutralized it, in an oratorical tour de force that emphasized the three-dimensional nature of the black emotional spectrum.

As far back as February 2007, Obama's potential candidacy was tinged with the suggestion that he lacked emotional control. In her column for *The New York Times,* Maureen Dowd provided a portrait of Senator Obama days after his announcement of candidacy, in which she seemed to provide a number of judgments on his state of agitation:

Barack Obama looked as if he needed a smoke and he needed it bad. [...]
    He was a tad testy. Traipsing around desolate stretches of snowy—and extremely white—Iowa [...]
    The Illinois senator didn't have on an implacable mask of amiability, as Hillary did in Iowa. He didn't look happily in his element, like Bill Clinton. [...]
    Beyond his smooth-jazz façade, the reassuring baritone and that ensorcelling smile, the 45-year-old had moments of looking conflicted. (Dowd 2007)

Undergoing cigarette withdrawal, seemingly "testy" without an "implacable mask of amiability": Dowd seemed to be hinting that this Democratic candidate was noticeably irate. He was not as happy as the Clintons, for example, and seemingly out of sorts—even contrasting—with his white surroundings.

As the campaign got into full swing, Ben Stein appeared on Fox News less than 24 hours after the announcement of Sarah Palin's vice presidential nomination. Asked if he thought Obama's populist campaign stood a chance, Stein became the first to verbalize that he did not think America was prepared for a "black angry candidate." The euphemistic language suggesting Obama's anger problem, from Dowd onward, had found its clarion horn in Stein's televised admission. Stein would later return to the theory in October 2010, talking about Obama's antithesis to the rich: "I think he's a very angry guy. And he's angry at businessmen, he's jealous of their success . . . I don't blame him for being angry . . . Mr. Obama grew up in very difficult circumstances. He's not a very happy guy." Even Glenn Beck, a media touch-point for the president's denigration, nervously disagreed and cut to a commercial break.

The electoral strategy of depicting Obama's candidacy as one of antagonism was seemingly endorsed by President George W. Bush, who appeared by satellite at the Republican National Convention on September 2, 2008. "If the Hanoi Hilton could not break John McCain's resolve to do what is best for his country," Bush said, "you can be sure the angry Left never will" (Bush 2008). His comment precipitated a standing ovation and rapid applause. Yet, while the remark reminded voters of McCain's military sacrifice, it also compared the angry Left, under Obama's leadership, to a group of North Vietnamese torturers.

In October 2008, Rush Limbaugh, in his inimitable style, went beyond merely asserting that Obama betrayed an inner anger, by stating that Obama and a whole host of associate "angry blacks" were engaged in a decades-long plot to train African American children to become a generation of malcontented, anti-American militants:

We know that the standard of living has risen. We know that technological advancement is going along at light speed. And yet during this period of time, whether it be the last 57 years or be it the last 20 years, it seems that a majority of the black population has remained angry, frustrated, and behind. They've been left behind. They are acting like they've been left behind, and of course we've heard that this is because of racism, natural systemic institutional racism in America, that we are unfair, that this country is just horrible and rotten . . . We thought that it was just liberal welfare policies and all that that kept blacks from progressing while other minorities grew and prospered, but no, it is these wackos from Bill Ayers to Jeremiah Wright to other anti-American Afrocentric black liberation theologists with ACORN, and Barack Obama is smack dab in the middle of it, they have been training young black kids to hate, hate, hate this country, and they trained their parents before that to hate, hate, hate this country. It was a movement. It was a Bill Ayers, anti-capitalist, anti-American educational movement. ACORN is how it was implemented, right under our noses. (Limbaugh 2008)

Limbaugh's diatribe of an imagined child anger program implored voters to understand that Obama's fury had almost eugenic consequences and was aligned with the right-wing indicators of the Democrat's terroristic launch pad (Bill Ayers) and Christian radicalization (Jeremiah Wright).

During the 2012 campaign, Fox News revived the "angry Obama" trope during a discussion of Romney's momentum in recent polling. Playing a clip from a campaign rally speech during which Obama diagnosed Romney's flip-flopping positions as "Romnesia," the panel dwelled upon the president's supposed emotional instability and guttural acrimony toward his challenger. During the segment on the *Journal Editorial Report*, Dorothy Rabinowitz summarized the point:

What are we looking at here? We have to acknowledge, the president is a very angry man. That has been there evidently in the past, since that debate, all along . . . If you took a look at Mitt Romney's immense crowds, that evoked the same, tremendous passion that Obama had, only it was Mitt Romney winning. So you have this enraged president and it comes out he can't stop, just as Biden could not stop, he cannot stop behaving inappropriately. (*Journal Editorial Report* 2012)

Daniel Henninger, Rabinowitz's colleague and fellow panelist, supplemented the pop psychological assessment with a personal pathology:

I honestly think that Barack Obama harbors some deep, personal animosity towards Mitt Romney. He can't stop doing that even as his advisers say, "You've got to go in another direction." (*Journal Editorial Report* 2012)

This was not the first time the president had been characterized as a man of deeply situated fury hidden behind a public mask. Dinesh D'Souza devoted a *New York Times* best-selling book, *The Roots of Obama's Rage* (2011), to the extrapolation of the idea of Obama's fulfillment of the angry black man stereotype. His theories were subsequently turned into a documentary, *2016: Obama's America*, which posited a dystopian future for the United States should the president gain a second turn to enact his agenda of rage. The premise of both the book and the film is the pseudo-Freudian claim that the only way to unlock the secrets of the president's mystifying world is to understand that Obama is haunted by the rueful spirit of his Kenyan father, intent on using his administration to exact revenge on his behalf:

President [Obama] is trapped in his father's time machine. Incredibly, the U.S. is being ruled according to the dreams of a Luo tribesman of the 1950s. This philandering, inebriated African socialist, who raged against the world for denying him the realization of his anticolonial ambitions, is now setting the nation's agenda through the reincarnation of his dreams in his son. The son makes it happen, but he candidly admits he is only living out his father's dream. The invisible father provides the inspiration, and the son dutifully gets the job done. America today is governed by a ghost. (D'Souza 2011, 198)

The conspiracy theory consciously equates Obama's racial heritage with a hereditary Afro-centric motive to architect America's decline as revenge for colonial crimes. D'Souza's central theory, which was read and watched by millions, reinforces the historical association of black skin and internal anger. In other words, D'Souza frames Obama's political psychology as inextricably linked to the history of colonialism, code-wording the president's anger as the racialized echo of a slave insurrection impulse—a 21st-century Nat Turner, if you will—revolting against the villainy of white America. Obama's presidency, under D'Souza's treatment, is the stuff of racialized gothic fiction.

MICHELLE OBAMA AND THE ANGRY BLACK WOMAN

While characterizing President Obama as some Black Brute stereotype, the right-wing press have presented Michelle Obama, since the primaries of 2008, as the marital manifestation of the "angry black woman." The attack on the First Lady as some sort of dominant black Sapphire figure is a proxy for situating her husband within a personal, political, and domestic network of African American hostility. The implication was that President Obama's acrimony was kindled and sustained not only by some inner perversion, but also by the overbearing "kitchen table" influence of a militant and perpetually angry African American spouse. In other words, Michelle Obama became the feminine and exterior signifier to the implied, internalized, and often imperceptible wrath of the black aggressor in chief.

The entire theory of Michelle Obama's anti-American rage stems, of course, from her infamously misjudged utterance during a campaign speech in Milwaukee, Wisconsin. At that event, she said, "For the first time in my adult life I am proud of my country because it feels like hope is finally making a comeback." Although Michelle Obama later clarified the remarks as a misstatement of her pride in the new wave of engagement in the political process, "cable news programs replayed those 15 words in an endless loop of outrage" (Powell & Kantor 2008). Cindy McCain contrasted herself with the caricatured Mrs. Obama, stating, "I have and always will be proud of my country." An article in *Commentary* magazine pondered whether Michelle Obama could find a single thing in America to be proud of: "How about the passage of the Civil Rights Act of 1991? Or Ruth Bader Ginsburg's elevation to the Supreme Court?" (Abcarian 2008). On Fox News, Bill Kristol described the remarks as "revealing" of a "narrative of despair." Michelle Malkin originally described her as a Lady Macbeth figure and later as Obama's "bitter half." Joe Scarborough said it was the "type of phrase that makes so many Americans just jolt up," while Rush Limbaugh described her comments as "unhinged." Mychal Massie, chairman of a conservative black leadership think tank, claimed, "Compared to the eloquent grace of Jackie Kennedy, Nancy Reagan, Barbara Bush, and yes, even Rosalind Carter, she portrays herself as just another angry black harridan who spits in the face of the nation that made her rich, famous, and prestigious."

The First Lady's negative public image transformation over subsequent months could be traced through the visual semantic of national magazine cover pages. In February 2008, the same month of the Milwaukee comments, Michelle Obama appeared on the front cover of *Newsweek* in a pastellized sheen and approachable portrait complete with conventional pearls, an open smile, and a sort of "naked arm" vulnerability. The headline: "He Calls Her His Rock." Two months later, in April 2008, and the influence of Michelle Obama had been transmogrified into the overbearing image found on the front cover of the conservative *National Review*. Here she was dressed in an angry red, cast in the stance of a scolding and unapproachable matriarch, replete with a pointed finger, and an open-mouthed, furrowed grimace. The headline: "Mrs. Grievance: Michelle Obama and Her Discontent." The accompanying article, written by Mark Steyn, described an angry woman motivated by "narcissism and self-absorption," embodying a "peculiar mix of privilege and victimology which is not where most Americans live" (Steyn 2008). Three months later, Michelle Obama would appear on the controversial front cover of *The New Yorker* magazine in combat gear and armed with an assault rifle, as some sort of weaponized Sapphire.

On Fox News in June 2008, in response to remarks made by Jane Hall of American University ("I think one way that people who are going to try to defeat Obama is to somehow prove ... his wife is an angry black woman"), Cal Thomas justified the strategy because there was no alternative interpretive lens for the interpretation of an African American in politics:

I want to pick up on something that Jane said about the angry black woman. Look at the image of angry black women on television. Politically you have Maxine Waters of California, liberal Democrat. She's always angry every time she gets on television. Cynthia McKinney, another angry black woman. And who are the black women you see on the local news at night in cities all over the country. They're usually angry about something. They've had a son who has been shot in a drive-by shooting. They are angry at Bush. So you don't really have a profile of non-angry black women. (Scott 2008)

In September 2008, Bill O'Reilly introduced Michelle Obama as the candidate's "controversial wife." He explained, "I have a lot of people who call me on the radio and say she looks angry. And I have to say there's some validity to that. She looks like an angry woman." Using curiously racialized language on his radio show, O'Reilly responded to a caller by saying, "I don't want to go on a lynching party against Michelle Obama unless there's evidence, hard facts, that say this is how the woman really feels. If that's how she really feels . . . then that's legit. We'll track it down."

Sean Hannity examined Michelle Obama's senior thesis, finding potential evidence of black separatism or militancy. Many criticisms surrounding the first lady's childhood obesity initiative, the Let's Move campaign, have been framed to suggest her combative approach to achieving her political end. Glenn Beck implied that the program would lead to people being put in jail for serving French fries instead of carrots; on *Hannity,* Tucker Carlson asked, "Why would you want to raise your own kids when Michelle Obama will do it for you . . . at gunpoint?" Meanwhile, Jason Mattera, on the Fox Business Network, described the first lady as a "dietary dominatrix." So popular had this narrative become that Obama himself toyed with the "Angry Michelle" meme at the 2011 White House Correspondents Dinner speech. "We made a terrific team at the Easter egg roll this week," Obama said, "I'd give out bags of candy to the kids and she'd snatch them right back out of their little hands. [Laughter] Snatched them!"

Even during Nelson Mandela's memorial service in South Africa in 2013, when the president was pictured taking a controversial "selfie" with the Danish Prime Minister, Helle Thorning-Schmidt, Michelle Obama's sedate and serious pose was taken as evidence of the fury of a woman scorned. Subsequent rumors of marital divorce (e.g., *The National Enquirer*'s "Furious Michelle Obama's Had Enough!!!") were attended by the images of an enraged, finger-pointing, and powerful First Lady.

In 2012, the stereotypes of Michelle Obama as the "angry black woman" or the militant Sapphire, were given new life by Jodi Kantor's book *The Obamas,* in which the president's wife is portrayed as a domineering and obstructionist political operative, embroiled in heated conflicts with President Obama's political coterie. In recognition of the attention that Kantor's publication was receiving in Obama's reelection year, Michelle Obama appeared on CBS *This Morning* with Gayle King to refute the negative stereotyping of her White House role:

I guess it's more interesting to imagine this conflicted situation here and a strong woman . . . you know, but that's been an image that people have tried to paint of me since the day Barack announced, that I'm some angry black woman.

This characterization of the First Lady is undoubtedly more continuous, varied, and overt than anything President Obama himself has faced through the application of the "angry black man" stereotype.

As Michelle Obama recognized in her interview with King, her other-ing demonization is achieved through the racial revival of stock black female caricatures of aggression. She is an active black woman in the White House, reviving the tropes and history of passive black women housed within *white households*. Unlike the slavery-era Mammy carica-ture (of contented female enslavement and servitude) and the Jezebel ster-eotype (of predatory promiscuity and low morals), however, the Sapphire figure of the emasculating, mean, and militantly angry black woman is resurrected in the portrayal of America's first African American First Lady. The definition of the Sapphire caricature reads as though it might have been the campaign playbook for Michelle Obama's political deni-gration:

She is tart-tongued and emasculating, one hand on a hip and the other pointing and jabbing (or arms akimbo), violently and rhythmically rocking her head, mocking African American men . . . She is a shrill nagger with irrational states of anger and indignation and is often mean-spirited and abusive. Although Afri-can American men are her primary targets, she has venom for anyone who insults or disrespects her. The Sapphire's desire to dominate and her hyper-sensitivity to injustices make her a perpetual complainer, but she does not criticize to improve things; rather, she criticizes because she is unendingly bitter and wishes that unhappiness on others. The Sapphire Caricature is a harsh portrayal of African American women, but it is more than that; it is a social control mechanism that is employed to punish black women who violate the societal norms that encour-age them to be passive, servile, non-threatening, and unseen. (Pilgrim, 2012b)

To understand Michelle Obama's widely promoted caricature, then, is to comprehend that her critics are subconsciously pushing her to enact the antifeminist and traditional white frame of reference for the modern First Lady, as passive, servile, nonthreatening, and unseen. Yet when Michelle Obama steps onto a political stage or indicates an active involvement in her husband's candidacy and presidency, she oversteps the institutional expectation of chastened whiteness and leaps into the abyss of female racialization of anti-white bellicosity. Journalist Erin Aubry Kaplan elaborates:

[A]s soon as she began revealing herself as a person and airing her views a bit, she began shape-shifting in the public eye into another kind of black woman altogether: angry, obstinate, mouthy—a stereotypical harpy lurking in all black women that a friend of mine calls "Serpentina." The consternation about Michelle suggested an old racist sentiment that you can take the girl out of the ghetto, but you can never take the ghetto out of the girl. (Kaplan 2008)

As a female proxy for Obama's demonization, Michelle Obama's rendering as a woman predisposed to the possession of black anger implies that the conventional presidential disposition of judicious, even temper is not to found in the soul of her husband, the Angry Black Man.

NOT ANGRY ENOUGH?

Despite the racialized denigration of both husband and wife as the angry couple of modern politics, the conceptualization of Obama's burning acrimony simply does not comport with any objective characterization of the Democrat's observable temperament. Instead of being a President of Rage, many have interpreted his natural propensity to embody the President of Cool as one of the central aspects of his electoral appeal, particularly in the era of a post-Bush presidency. Obama's image oscillates between the racialized expectation of anti-white anger and the observed post-racialist character of conciliatory black moderation. Such paradoxical concern over Obama's black temper can be understood through the lens of the phenomenon of "bipolar black masculinity," as described by Frank Rudy Cooper. "The media tends to represent black men as either the completely threatening and race-affirming Bad Black Man or the completely comforting and assimilationist Good Black Man," Cooper writes, claiming that, "for Obama, this meant he had to avoid the stereotype of the angry black man" (Cooper 2008).

Since 2008, Obama has been characterized by many as a candidate and a president of serene disposition, betraying an inner composure, deliberateness, and professorial air. David Gergen, a first-hand witness to many presidencies over the last half century, has observed that Obama exudes an "Aloha Zen" of "comfortable calm" reflective of a president who "seems easygoing, not so full of himself." Upon the president's 2008 victory, Chris Dodd, former U.S. senator and Democratic primary contender, was thankful that "Obama has a wonderful temperament." Julia Whitty, writing for *Mother Jones,* asked, "Just How Unflappable is

Barack Obama?"; he concluded that "the man's a rock. He doesn't twitch. He doesn't sway. The wattage of his smile doesn't waver. Is this a good thing? Is it supernatural?" In March 2008, General Tony McPeak, retired Air Force Chief of Staff, neologized the much-proliferated memes of "no shock Barack" and "no drama Obama." So calm, so unflappable, and so unlike any previous civil rights leader and Chicago-style politician is Obama that even before the election, Patrick Healy in *The New York Times* mused, "In a Time of Crisis, Is Obama *Too* Cool?" Throughout the campaign, Obama maintained the line that "both by training and disposition I understand where we need to take the country." While his public slogan might have been "Yes We Can," David Plouffe revealed that for his campaign staff, Obama's motto was simply "No Drama."

For Obama, this was not a new strategy for building positive electoral support, but rather something of a learned behavior. In *Dreams from My Father,* Obama recounts his ability to reassure his mother that he would not get into trouble, like his friend, through the projection of black tranquility:

It was usually an effective tactic, another one of those tricks I had learned: People were satisfied so long as you were courteous and smiled and made no sudden moves. They were more than satisfied; they were relieved to find a well-mannered young black man who didn't seem angry all the time. (Obama 1995)

The caricature of Obama as the angry black man was in many respects a right-wing invention that played into white Americans' racialized expectations of the credible African American presidential candidate, even when such characterizations seemed contrary to all observable evidence. Yet in 2008, there was a political advantage, too, in the right wing's widespread claim of Obama's acrimony, in that it pre-empted and neutralized the expected attacks on Republican candidate John McCain as *the* candidate of known and proven irascibility. John McCain's "anger management problem," as it was described in the press, would be somehow less sensational in the wake of the comparative resurgence of the angry black man stereotype.

McCain had an impressive list of references for his history of bad temper. Senator Thad Cochrane (Republican-Mississippi) said that "the thought of his being president sends a cold chill down my spine," because "[h]e is erratic. He is hotheaded. He loses his temper and he worries me." Former Senator Bob Smith from New Hampshire went further to debunk McCain's suitability as a candidate, claiming that "his temper would place this country at risk in international affairs, and the world perhaps in danger. In my mind, it should disqualify him." Rick Santorum was quoted as remembering that "John was very rough in the sandbox," adding that "Everybody has a McCain story." As far back as 1999, the *Washington Post* reported, "In a front page article and separate editorial Sunday, *The Arizona Republic* said it wanted the nation to know about the 'volcanic' temper McCain has unleashed on several top state officials." Even the oft-quoted description of the Republican candidate as a maverick was a conceptual "cover" for any behavior that seemed out of line with ordinary civility. Moreover, while Obama remembered his ability to remain the calm black man in his autobiography, McCain wrote of his own struggles with temperament in his 2002 memoir *Worth the Fighting For*: "My temper has often been both a matter of public speculation and personal concern ... I have a temper, to state the obvious, which I have tried to control with varying degrees of success because it does not always serve my interest or the public's" (McCain and Salter 2002).

In light of the converse realities and proofs of each man's temperament, the concentration on Obama's potential anger as a racial characteristic, despite McCain's long reputation of potentially damaging ire, is an astonishing indictment of the continuing power and social affinity of race-based caricature.

One key moment in Obama's presidency serves as an example of the bipolarity, on the right and the left, of expectations surrounding Obama's emotional responses as a nation's leader. On April 20, 2010, a lethal explosion at the *Deepwater Horizon* offshore drilling rig 40 miles off the coast of Louisiana set in motion the largest ever accidental marine-based oil spill, which created a national environmental disaster in the United States. Obama's administration was roundly criticized for its response to the spill, which was, according to *The New York Times,* "bedeviled by a lack of preparation, organization, urgency and clear lines of authority among federal, state and local officials" (Brooks 2010, June 17). BP was condemned for its slow and ineffective attempts to plug the spill in a timely manner, whereas Obama was criticized for not asserting greater control over the clean-up efforts and for taking too long to communicate effectively with the public in a time of national disaster. For many, however, the primary complaint was not Obama's organizational response, but rather his seeming lack of emotional reaction. Unlike President Bill Clinton, Obama did not seem to be *feeling their pain.*

In spite of his more spirited news conferences throughout May and June 2010, Obama still was not quite angry enough. Maureen Dowd began her column by announcing that "President Spock's behavior is illogical," before continuing to say that "once more, he has wilfully and inexplicably resisted fulfilling a signal part of his job: being a prism in moments of fear and pride, reflecting what Americans feel so they know he gets it" (Dowd 2010). Bill O'Reilly also described Obama's emotional attachment as alien, suggesting that he "looks a little cold-blooded ... He looks a little like, Alright, I'm here—you know, if that pelican is full of oil, hey, that's just the way it goes" (O'Reilly 2010). David Brooks explained that Obama's critics were looking for at least a performative expression of interpreted public outrage: "They demand that he hold press conferences, show leadership, announce that buck stops here and do something. They want him to emote and perform the proper theatrical gestures so they can see their emotions enacted on the public stage" (Brooks 2010, May 31). James Carville, a resident of New Orleans, was craving for Obama to deliver some lines of paternalistic fury: "This president needs to tell BP, 'I'm your daddy.'" Some urged Obama to explicitly take up the mantle of the black, angry stereotype, such as the existentially controversial late-night host Bill Maher:

I thought when we elected a black president, we were going to get a black president. You know, this [BP oil spill] is where I want a real black president. I want him in a meeting with the BP CEOs, you know, where he lifts up his shirt where you can see the gun in his pants. That's—[in black man voice] "We've got a motherfu**ing problem here?" Shoot somebody in the foot. (Chen 2010)

Maher seemed to verbalize the seeming desire from the American citizenry for Obama to embrace the uber-racial caricatures of black, weaponized cinematic villains. In fact, the African American filmmaker, Spike Lee—who knows something about narrative-emotional timing—said that the time was right for Obama to "go off." Saladin Ambar explained, "Folks are waiting for a Samuel Jackson *Snakes on a Plane* moment from this president, as in: 'We gotta' get this $#@!!* oil back in the $#@!!* rig!' But that's just not who Obama is." It became indistinguishable as to when Obama's detractors were asking him to be more presidentially animated and when they were merely demanding that he "be" black.

Obama and his administration responded to the seeming demand for explicit, even dramatic, anger by ramping up the tenor of rhetoric relating to the oil spill's management. On June 1, Obama's press secretary, Robin Gibbs, told the denizens of the press room that the ongoing crisis and BP's efforts "enraged the president," leading CBS's Chip Reid to ask, "Have we really seen rage from the president?" Gibbs said that behind closed doors he approached his meetings with a "clenched jaw" and used such language as "plug the damn hole" (Gibbs 2010). But back-room reporting of the president's wrath remained unconvincing for his critics. Consequently, Obama chose to enact his irritation on Matt Lauer's NBC *Today*

Show. Denuding himself of previous characterizations as a detached academic, Obama told Lauer that his relationship with BP management was not *entente cordiale.* "I don't sit around just talking to experts because this is a college seminar," Obama brooded. "We talk to these folks because they potentially have the best answers—so I know whose ass to kick." Was that enough rage?

It turns out, in fact, that Obama's single statement of restrained aggression was *too much.* In a single utterance, Obama's image shifted from an emotionally stoic Vulcan to the Black Brute stereotype. Matt Drudge's headline described Obama's statement as "Street," a sentiment echoed by the *Washington Times'* Jeffrey Kuhner, who said the comment was "street gangster language more befitting a community organizer in the South Side of Chicago." Kuhner continued:

Presidents historically have used salty, even profane language in private discussions—Andrew Jackson, Harry Truman and Richard Nixon being the most notable. Yet in public statements, they understood the need to respect the dignity and decorum of the Oval Office. Every president has—until Mr. Obama. (June 10, 2010)

CNBC host Becky Quick said, "When you are president of the United States ... I would expect a different choice of words." Appearing on *Morning Joe,* Mark Halperin parsed the spasmodic public expectation of, and disdain for, Obama's embodiment of ire. "One of the problems Barack Obama faces in public life ... is he cannot get angry and be an effective communicator as an African American," Halperin identified, later using his iPad to show the Drudge headline: "so Matt Drudge takes the Matt Lauer quote, and he casts it as 'Obama Goes Street.' And it includes this photo of an angry-looking Barack Obama. I think it's all pretty clear. It's pretty clear to all of us what's going on there." Conservative voice Joe Scarborough emphatically agreed: "There's no doubt that race plays a factor here."

Indeed, to many political observers and racial scholars, it was exceptionally clear that Obama had tried to walk the liminal line between his strategic and innate state of presidential calm on one side and the abyss of prejudicial expectations of the angry black man on the other side. The event exemplified that Obama's emotional mode of being required expert positioning in a world of fragile racial frameworks, and that the president's initial reluctance to convey a sentiment of rage was, in retrospect, well judged. In this political landscape of "bipolar black masculinities," any slight deviation from his role as "Mr. Equanimity and Mr. Consolation" (Blake 2010) reminded his audiences that he was a black man with the imagined propensity for a Jekyll-and-Hyde reversion to stereotypical choleric temperament. Alternatively, if Obama became too detached from the emotional state of his populace, his very sensibility of black calm became somehow offensive and inappropriate.

If Obama had conducted his presidential campaign with the firebrand "kicking ass" rhetoric of the Gulf of Mexico oil disaster, it would have "fed deeply into a pre-existing set of narratives about the angry black man," according to William Cobb, author of *The Substance of Hope*.

The anger would have gotten in the way. He would have frightened off white voters who were interested in him because he seemed to be like the black guy they worked with or went to graduate school with—not a black guy who is threatening. (Blake 2010)

Conversely, the Jeremiah Wright scandal had almost derailed Obama's candidacy because it had suggested that he was indoctrinated by a stereotypical anti-white, anti-American revenge mythology. According to Ta-Nehisi Coates, it is Obama's "remarkable ability to soothe race consciousness among whites," rather than stoke it, which is the definition of Obama's "genius":

Any black person who's worked in the professional world is well acquainted with this trick. But never has it been practiced at such a high level, and never have its limits been so obviously exposed. This need to talk in dulcet tones, to never be angry regardless of the offense, bespeaks a strange and compromised integration indeed, revealing a country so infantile that it can countenance white acceptance of blacks only when they meet an Al Roker standard. (Coates 2012)

Paul Street, an American journalist and author of *Barack Obama and the Future of American Politics*, agrees that Obama's emotional acceptability has been the central tenet of his broad melting-pot appeal: "That's how he negotiated his way through multiple worlds, and reached out across bridges" (Blake 2010).

In the 2012 election, the issue of Obama's emotional triangulation was brought to the fore by Obama's unexpectedly poor, even emotionally staid, first debate performance against the Republican nominee, Mitt Romney. Even with Jeremiah Wright and the Gulf of Mexico oil spill disaster in the rear-view mirror, many of Obama's supporters urged a more combative, firebrand style of discourse. Others, however, suggested that a recent incident had left Obama sensitive to the avoidance of the black man stereotype. Michael Moore hypothesized that the distribution of a tape showing Obama speaking passionately to a black audience in New

Orleans, with more pronounced black inflection, had spooked the president's campaign from conveying any signs of acrimony. Bill Maher seconded the race theory as an explanation for Obama's low-key demeanor, saying, "Maybe what is in his mind is, 'Look, I can never look like the angry black man.' " Georgetown professor Eric Dyson issued a warning: "Lest we forget this, lest we pretend this doesn't make a difference, the specter hanging over him is: 'I can't come off as too vigorous because then it looks like I'm being an angry black man' " (Cassidy 2012).

Obama himself knows the racial history better than most, and he knows that his coded presentation as an angry black man—as well as the calls for him to momentarily inhabit the stereotype—are echoes of entrenched themes of African American othering and foreignization that have consistently played upon white fears. This stereotype reaches back to the earliest justifications of black subjugation, to the portrayal of black men as animalistic, savage, and wrathful, in need of the taming influence of the white slave owner. It revives the images of the Black Brute, Black Beast, and Black Buck as racial slurs against the unpredictable and dangerous African American temperament. It recalls, for example, the revolt of the Virginian slave Nat Turner, whose "attempt to overturn the South's 'peculiar institution' by precipitating a slave revolution fuelled southern white nightmares for decades to come, visions of angry black men hell bent on exacting revenge disturbing the thoughts of both slave-owning and non-slave-owning whites alike" (James 2010). It revives the racialized historiography surrounding the Reconstruction era that presented free black political participation as "Negro misrule" and a vehicle for violent black revenge over what D. W. Griffith termed "the helpless white minority" (Griffith 1915). It recalls the white fear of aggressive black men, recounted in the words of George Winston:

When a knock is heard at the door [a white woman] shudders with nameless horror. The black brute is lurking in the dark, a monstrous beast, crazed with lust. His ferocity is almost demoniacal. A mad bull or tiger could scarcely be more brutal. A whole community is frenzied with horror, with the blind and furious rage for vengeance. (Winston 1901)

Further, that fear is informed by the description of black peoples in Thomas Dixon's *The Clansman*:

Half child, half animal, the sport of impulse, whim, and conceit ... a being who, left to his will, roams at night and sleeps in the day, whose speech knows no word of love, whose passions, once aroused, are as the fury of the tiger. (Dixon 2002)

This view reinforced the perception of black leaders such as Malcom X, Stokely Carmichael, and Jesse Jackson as intemperate civil rights activists. It revived the televised altercation between Roy Innis and Al Sharpton. It reminded Americans of the Willie Horton political advertisement distributed by the George H. W. Bush campaign in 1988 to impute the record of Michael Dukakis by way of his association with an African American murderer. And, of course, it appealed to the 20 percent of Americans polled in 2008, who when given a choice of numerous positive and negative adjectives to describe African Americans, chose the word "violent."

BELOW PAR AND SHOOTING HOOPS: THE HOMO OTURIS PRESIDENT

That Obama has been the victim of an angry black man stereotype, depicted as a vengeful and militant Mulatto, has not precluded him from sometimes being cast as the contrary caricature of African American apathy and dilatoriness, leading to his presentation as the "lazy Negro" in the White House. This terminological prism of Obama's ineffectiveness, disengagement, or hedonism revives patterns of accusations leveled at black communities in America from slavery, Reconstruction to more recent debates over welfare dependency and electoral disenfranchisement. Despite the on-its-face incompatibility of slave labor with the concept of laziness or black Reconstruction political representation with the notion of lethargy, Obama's highly active candidacy and presidency revived the typecast criticism of African American dormancy. While Dwight Eisenhower and George W. Bush garnered some criticism for their perceived leisureliness during their own presidencies, and most presidents are known for poor timekeeping, it never became a defining trope. By contrast, there is something peculiarly othering, unmistakably racial, about the presentation of the nation's premier African American president—with an unenviable schedule and range of challenges—as a golf-playing, slam-dunking, indolent, and disinterested slacker in chief.

Perhaps the first time this caricature was brought to mainstream public attention in the form of a partisan critique was in 2012, in the wake of the first presidential debate between Governor Mitt Romney and President Obama. Romney unquestionably won that debate, garnering universal praise for his superlative and dominant performance. Meanwhile, commentators mused that the event was one of Obama's weaker performances, with the president appearing more timid and passive than in previous outings. During an interview with Andrea Mitchell on MSNBC, Romney surrogate and former governor of New Hampshire John H.

Sununu deliberately asserted that the specific cause of the sitting president's lackluster disputation was his personal slothfulness:

What people saw last night I think was a president that revealed his incompetence, how *lazy and detached* he is, and how he has absolutely no idea how serious the economic problems of the country are.

Mitchell, puzzled at the assessment and concerned that she had misunderstood his comments, gave Sununu some wiggle room to walk back the remarks:

Governor, I want to give you a chance to maybe take it back. Did you really mean to call Barack Obama, the President of the United States, lazy?

Without pausing, Sununu doubled down on the critique, referencing the president's recent public appearance:

Yes. I think you saw him admit it the night before when he delivered the pizzas. He said, you know, "They're making me do this work." He didn't want to prepare for this debate. He is lazy and disengaged. (Real Clear Politics 2012)

Along with Mitchell, listeners across America no doubt questioned the motivation of Sununu's repeated concentration on Obama's personal lethargy. The suggestion that Obama was unwilling to put in the minimum amount of preparation or effort for a presidential debate crucial to his political future, or that he was happier delivering fast food than engaging in serious research, was indicative of a purposeful racialization. Journalism expert Frank Harris, writing for the *Hartford Courant,* described Sununu's statement as "a blow way below the belt and far across the racial line." He continued:

Sununu clearly knew what it meant to call someone black—the president, no less—lazy. It is one of those racial stereotypes so often used over the years for Americans of African descent ... Sununu's enmity toward Obama continues a nasty trend of disrespect for the president that has more than a few racial overtones. This particular stereotype of black people being lazy needs to die a quick and decisive death. But stereotypes die hard. No amount of exemplary work will change it. (Harris 2012)

This was not the first time that the right wing used the characterization of laziness as the lens for interpreting Obama's failures. Rewinding to January 2008, Karl Rove deployed the very same argument for explaining Hillary Clinton's surprise victory over Obama in the New Hampshire primary. In the ABC debate, Rove spliced the difference between the Democratic contenders:

Her remarks helped wash away the memory of her angry replies to attacks at the debate's start. His trash talking was an unattractive carryover from his days playing pickup basketball at Harvard, and capped a mediocre night. (Rove 2008)

Beyond the extraordinary racialized trash talk and preoccupation with basketball tactics, Obama also lacked the expected energy and willingness to engage in the minutia of policy and decision making, according to Rove's triangulation:

Mr. Obama has failed to rise to leadership on a single major issue in the Senate. In the Illinois legislature, he had a habit of ducking major issues, voting "present" on bills important to many Democratic interest groups, like abortion-rights and gun-control advocates. He is often lazy, given to misstatements and exaggerations, and, when he doesn't know the answer, too ready to try to bluff his way through. (Rove 2008)

Richard Wolffe, discussing Rove's claims with Keith Olbermann, said that the Obama campaign (usually restrained when it came to discussing issues of race politics) was interpreting the comments as a deliberately crafted resurrection of African American stereotyping, teetering on the precipice of explicit discrimination:

Talking to some of Obama's aides, I think they detected a pretty ugly undertone in Rove's op-ed there. The "trash-talking." The "basketball." The "lazy" thing. Is he suggesting that there's some sort of color aspect to Barack Obama's behavior that he's getting at? It was uncomfortably close to the edge of being plain-out racist. (Edwards and Kane 2008)

When Obama failed to deliver a victory or a Herculean performance, there was no shortage of "old white guys" ready to ascribe a stereotypical black languor as the cause. In his 2007 book *The Evangelical President,* Bill Sammon, for example, reports a conversation he had with a Bush White House official on Obama's early candidacy, tracing the early Republican strategy of underlining the Illinois senator's sluggish acumen:

"I like the guy," he told me. "A very likable, approachable guy. And he's very smart and incredibly charismatic—and knows it." He added that while Obama was "capable" of the intellectual exactitude required to win the presidency, he instead relied too heavily on his easy charm. "It's sort of like, 'That's all I need to get by,' which bespeaks sort of a condescending attitude towards the voters," the official told me. "And a laziness, an intellectual laziness." (Sammon 2007)

The Republican machine knew that there was electoral advantage to both subtle and overt denigration of Obama's personal vitality, as it chimed with a significant portion of the white voting bloc that harbored latent prejudice against black candidates. A poll conducted in early September 2008, by AP-Yahoo News in connection with Stanford University, found that one third of white Democrats and Independents harbored "negative views towards blacks" and would choose to describe the African American community with at least one pejorative adjective. While 20 percent of the 2,227 adult respondents would describe black people as "violent" (showing the lasting ripples of the angry black man trope), 13 percent associated the African American community with the adjective "lazy." In the same survey, more than one fourth of white Democrats agreed with the statement, "If blacks would only try harder, they could be just as well off as whites." Respondents who agreed with this sentiment that laziness was the only barrier to racial inequality were significantly less likely to support Obama in a general election. Paul Sniderman, in analyzing the data, said, "There are a lot fewer bigots than there were 50 years ago, but that doesn't mean there's only a few bigots." The existence of a constituency of voters already aligned with the stereotype of black idleness provides some indication as to why Obama's detractors have strived to categorize him as the president of Lazy for electoral advantage.

A few months after the *Deepwater Horizon* oil spill and during BP's largely derided recovery efforts, Obama's opponents took aim at the president for having too much leisure time during Father's Day weekend. The chairman of the Republican Party, Michael Steele, cited Obama's attendance at baseball games, his presence at White House music events, and his proclivity for golfing as evidence of a lackluster executive philosophy. "Until this problem is fixed," Steele challenged, "no more golf outings, no more baseball games, no more Beatle concerts, Mr. President" (Jackson 2010). Steele compared Obama's "lackadaisical approach" and golf game to the out-of-touch yachting excursion recently taken by the BP chairman, Tony Hayward. Rudy Giuliani agreed. Other conservative thinkers, including John Podhoretz, have warned of the dangers of subscribing to "the comforting delusion that he's a golf-mad dilettante"—that Obama is some kind of *Homo otiosus* (man of leisure)—as a detriment to properly estimating Obama's acumen (Drum 2013).

During Obama's 2012 reelection campaign, potential Republican contenders and right-wing media outlets dwelled on the increased number of recipients of Supplemental Nutrition Assistance Program benefits to attack Obama as "the drug dealer of welfare," as someone demotivating an entire generation of Americans from hard work. Gingrich deplored him consistently as the "finest food stamp president in American history," whereas Dick Morris claimed, "Obama has basically put everybody in the country on welfare" (Kessler 2011). In August 2012, Romney released a campaign advertisement, called "Right Choice," claiming that Obama was planning to remove all work requirements from the welfare system. The video ad began with Bill Clinton signing the much-debated 1996 welfare reform act, before launching into the central claim that PolitiFact has since rated as "Pants on Fire" wrong:

On July 12, President Obama quietly announced a plan to gut welfare reform by dropping work requirements. Under Obama's plan, you wouldn't have to work and wouldn't have to train for a job. They just send you your welfare check, and "welfare to work" goes back to being plain old welfare. (PolitiFact.com 2012)

The 30-second advertisement is a jam-packed celebration of the white Protestant worker ethic, flashing between a white male wiping the sweat from his brow, a white man seemingly in a boardroom setting, a white woman operating heavy machinery, and the white candidate talking to a room of white workers. There's even an appearance of the alabaster columns of the *White* House portico. Apart from Obama, who is cast in a suspicious, darkened side-profile pose, there are no discernable faces of racial minority, no hint of association between *them* and the frenetic activity of American productivity. The president himself becomes the metonymic representative of those lazy demographic segments most likely to receive welfare support, in a video that might be more appropriately titled "White Choice."

Then, in September 2012, explosive videotape leaked of Mitt Romney delivering his now-infamous "47 percent speech" at a fundraiser in May of that year. In his remarks, Romney neatly divided the electorate into indolent natural Obama supporters and those energetically striving for the Romney-esque American dream:

There are 47 percent of the people who will vote for the president no matter what. All right, there are 47 percent who are with him, who are dependent upon government, who believe that they are victims, who believe the government has a responsibility to care for them, who believe that they are entitled to health care, to food, to housing, to you-name-it. . . . My job is not to worry about those people. I'll never convince them they should take personal responsibility and care for their lives. (Corn 2012)

For Romney, Obama was fully aligned with, and inseparable from, a culture of deep dependency, of Americans luxuriating in their own feigned victimhood. The exact phrasing was not there, but the diametric calculation was clear: Obama supporters were lazy and Romney supporters were not. Although eventually renouncing those behind-closed-doors comments, after the election Romney claimed that he had lost the election because Obama had given "gifts" to the dependency bloc—blacks, Hispanics, and young voters (Berman 2012). Assessing Romney's failure, Sununu told a political forum that "they [the Obama campaign] aggressively got out the base of their base ... that's dependent, to a great extent economically, on government policy and government programs."

During the same election, Newt Gingrich proposed that there was something almost biologically discrete about Obama's supposed weariness and his inability to perform the job of president with the same zeal as his predecessors. Like a welfare recipient, he had been given so much, but did not have the inclination to *do* anything with it:

[Obama] really is like the substitute [National Football League] referees in the sense that he's not a real president. He doesn't do anything that presidents do, he doesn't worry about any of the things the presidents do, but he has the White House, he has enormous power, and he'll go down in history as the president, and I suspect that he's pretty contemptuous of the rest of us. . . . You have to wonder what he's doing. I'm assuming that there's some rhythm to Barack Obama that the rest of us don't understand. Whether he needs large amounts of rest, whether he needs to go play basketball for a while or watch ESPN, I mean, I don't quite know what his rhythm is, but this is a guy that is a brilliant performer as an orator, who may very well get reelected at the present date, and who, frankly, he happens to be a partial, part-time president. . . . This is a man who in an age of false celebrity-hood is sort of the perfect president, because he's a false president. He's a guy that doesn't do the president's job. (Cirilli 2012)

The terminology alone—"substitute," "not a real president," "some rhythm," "rest," "play basketball," "watch ESPN," "partial, part time," and "false celebrity-hood"—is a masterful and acrobatic linguistic display of sheer dog-whistle rhetoric against the first African American president. The concession to his talents—in sports, performance, celebrity, and oratory—are the traditional pigeon holes of acceptable black societal representation and achievement. Gingrich, calling upon the support of those racial tendencies revealed by the white Democratic poll, implies that the political arena remains too exhausting for a person of Obama's complexion, forcing his historical position into one of the very stereotypes a post-racializing society aims to strive against.

In 2013, the association between Obama, African Americans, and some form of languor remained part of the political currency of the day. In that year, the Buncombe County Republican precinct chairman, Don Yelton, made national headlines when he appeared on the *Daily Show* to discuss New Jersey's introduction of new voter restriction legislation. Prefacing his remarks by stating "The law is not racist," Yelton continued to say, "The law is going to kick the Democrats in the butt ... If it hurts a bunch of lazy blacks that wants the government to give them everything, so be it." Although Yelton's words, and subsequent resignation, were arguably local quirks, they spoke to the Obama-era phenomenon of simultaneously calling the president and African Americans lazy, while putting in place the very stymying obstacles to prevent their respective agendas' advancement and participation. Similarly, House Majority Whip Kevin McCarthy, in an interview with Greta Van Susteren, cited presidential laziness and athletic distraction as the cause of Obama's inability to produce an agreed budget: "I bet you he spends more time filling out his March Madness brackets than he does writing a budget," McCarthy mused. That President Obama was not familiar with hard-working employment seemed to be the sentiment underlying Sarah Palin's Fox News appearance in June 2013, during which she suggested Obama's history as a community organizer somehow affected his response to the leaks of Edward Snowden:

But with Obama deciding to just, oh, I guess, lead from behind on this issue, too, that's the community organizer in our president. That's a bit of that lackadaisical, eh, you know, don't have to take responsibility. His résumé proves he hasn't had to responsibility for much in all these years. This is just another issue, another example that falls in line with a community organizer. (Feldman 2013)

Teamed with the term "lackadaisical," which has a rich history of utilization in the South against African American slaves and workers,[2] Palin's repeated identification of the president as a lazy community organizer seems to be coding something deeper than mere decision-making abilities with regard to National Security Agency leaks. The

---

[2]Regan, Mariann S. *Into the Briar Patch*. AuthorHouse, 2011. "[T]his stereotype was born during slavery and Jim Crow. Growing up, I learned that the South's rich vocabulary for laziness was often applied to African-Americans: shiftless, no-account, trifling, good-for-nothing, lackadaisical, half-hearted, slow as molasses. In the South, slaves labored in the fields from sunup to sundown. Yet somehow the blacks were the ones who got called lazy."

dissonance, even for Palin, communicates a racial insinuation of almost genetic torpidity. The founder of Fox News and Palin's employer, Roger Ailes, included the Obama-as-lazy trope in a series of disparaging personal assessments in his controversial biography *Roger Ailes: Off Camera*:

Obama's the one who never worked a day in his life. He never earned a penny that wasn't public money. How many fundraisers does he attend every week? How often does he play basketball and golf? I wish I had that kind of time. He's lazy, but the media won't report that.

Ailes knows that the accusation of Obama's lifelong government employment dependence is not accurate, but is also cognizant that it perpetuates and validates the conceptual currency of the welfare presidency slur. The reference to fundraising embellishes that same idea of Obama relying on financial hand-outs for his own political "survival," and the mention of basketball and golf reinforces the racialized image of a president more at home on the courts than within the corridors of power. Cultural critic Touré recognized Ailes's remarks as related to the long history of the racist portrayal of African American apathy:

This sort of "lazy" term is something we heard flung at us as black people going back to slavery . . . we perceive them as being guilty of not wanting to work. Of course they didn't want to work. They were slaves! (Newby 2013)

Unquestionably, the historical black experience undoubtedly acts as genesis and catalyst in Obama's forced and false political prostration by the conservative right.

Slavery, and the perpetuated subjugation of black peoples in the United States, has relied upon various arguments for African American inferiority and white American superiority. Pseudoscience, early ethnography, and armchair anthropology—all lumped together under the broad umbrella of scientific racism—provided the basic hypotheses for racial differentiation and the suitability of black peoples to the slave labor. While stating that African Americans were uniquely and physically built for long stretches of manual labor, one key conception of such scientific racism was that black people harbored an innate laziness (leading to dependence and theft) that was monitored, corrected and controlled by the institution of slavery.

The French Enlightenment thinker Montesquieu, even while writing against the immorality of slavery, outlined the perceived physiological racial differences in energy levels caused by the conditions of one's geographical habitat:

[P]hysiologically, colder climates breed courageous and hardworking people who lack physical sensitivity; in contrast, warm climates encourage laziness but also heighten the senses and therefore the passions ... There are countries where the excess of heat enervates the body and renders men so slothful and dispirited, that nothing but the fear of chastisement can oblige them to perform any laborious duty: slavery is there more reconcilable to reason. (Rodriguez 1997)

An American physician, Samuel Cartwright (of Drapetomania fame), went one step further in 1851 when he proposed that black persons were prone to a psychiatric disease known as "dysaesthesia aethiopica," which accounted for the widespread and symptomatic laziness observed in black populations. This condition was exclusive to the black physiology, "called by overseers 'rascality' " and related to the body's insensitivity to external stimuli; it caused "so great a hebetude of the intellectual faculties, as to be like a person half asleep" (Cartwright 2004). Cartwright further stated that his research revealed the malady to be most concentrated in populations of freed slaves, and he claimed that he had a simple cure: re-enslavement and bodily whippings. "The best means to stimulate the skin is," Cartwright wrote, "first, to have the patient well washed with warm water and soap; then, to anoint it all over in oil, and to slap the oil in with a broad leather strap; then to put the patient to some hard kind of work in the sunshine." The result of such pseudo-medical contrivance has created a fundamental white versus black dialectic of innate energies, Susan Tracy writes:

The master emerges as a commanding and resolute, but benevolent, figure who always has the slave's true interest in mind. In contrast, both male and females slaves are represented as ignorant and improvident, lazy and playful, submissive and loyal. The institution of slavery is thus redeemed as being protective and beneficial for blacks, introducing them to Christianity and teaching them the discipline of work. The implication throughout is that black men and women have neither the intelligence, self-discipline, or morality to work their own land as independent farmers. (Tracy 2009)

Such a dialectic is clearly invoked when the suggestion is made that the first and only black president in U.S. history is incapable of possessing the same intellectual capacity and Protestant work ethic as his white forebears and redeeming challengers.

In the lead-up to the Reconstruction period, the trope of black somnolence was aestheticized in artistic representations of the sleeping African

American. In William Mount's 1836 painting, *Farmers Nooning* for example, four adult farmers break under a tree in the late summer afternoon. While the white farmers remain awake under the shade, the eye is drawn to the sleeping black worker, reclined upon a haystack in the romantic posture of a Correggio nude goddess. The sun blazes upon his prostrate body, reinforcing the aligned stereotypes of both black fatigue and a heightened tolerance for heat. The boy trickster, representing a sort of perpetual white control and about to wake the man by tickling his face with a blade of corn, is a benign form of Cartwright's invigoration of the skin's sensitivity for laziness's cure.

James Goodwyn Clonney (1912–1867) produced a number of scenes featuring the slumbering black man, often surrounded by white characters contrarily employed in sport or occupation. In a similar scene to *Farmers Nooning,* Clonney's *Waking Up* shows two young boys attempting to wake a reclined black fisherman by clambering upon the rocks to poke his nose. Meanwhile, the boy overhead, holding the rod, seems reminiscent of a white hand applying the whipping cane to a slacking worker. Similarly, Clonney's *Fishing Party on Long Island*

Farmers Nooning, **William Sidney Mount, 1836. (Library of Congress)**

Sound off New Rochelle and *A Negro Boy Asleep* depict the African American body romantically prostrate in the environments of marine and agricultural occupation.

Melissa Renn interprets such art as contributing to the pre-Reconstruction-era proliferation of the racialized trope of black laziness:

Another caricature that appeared in both 19th century popular prints and genre paintings was the sleeping black man, reclining in a sleeping faun pose drawn from classical antiquity. This image of the sleeping African American has been interpreted in various ways, but it contributed to the stereotyping of black people as lazy and idle. (Rice and Katz-Hyman 2010)

There is at least some political aestheticization of the sleeping black president applied to Barack Obama. The Clinton campaign questioned who would be ready to take that 3 a.m. phone call and others have suggested that Obama failed to prevent the attack on the Benghazi embassy because he was sleeping. One Tweet, sent shortly after Ted Cruz's marathon Senate speech against the Affordable Care Act, contrasted the Republican senator and the president as alert and fatigued, respectively: "Ted Cruz stayed awake for at least 21 hours to debate Obamacare," it read. "Obama couldn't even stay awake to find out what happened in #Benghazi." Dana Milbank and others have similar used the metaphor of Obama being "asleep at the wheel" or "asleep on the job" for the vehicle of their policy critiques.

Reconstruction-era black politicians and enfranchised voters were cast as unworthy, idle demagogues in much of the contemporary and subsequent assessments of the period. *The New York Daily Tribune*, for example, reported that in South Carolina the white population resented the new powers given to the state's black citizens, who "are extremely indolent, and will make no exertion beyond what is necessary to obtain food enough to satisfy their hunger" (May 1, 1871). In the 1915 film *Birth of a Nation*, D. W. Griffith provided an overt visual caricature of lazy and militant "Negro rule" during the late 19th century. In one scene inside the state legislature prior to the climactic riot, Griffith presents a series of heavy-handed visual clues to the black representative's leisurely approach to public service; one eats food throughout the proceedings, another sneakily drinks alcohol from a flask, and another puts his feet up on the desk and takes his boots off, leading to the Speaker of the House reactively ruling that "All members must wear shoes."

Reparative historiography has gone some way to provide balance to such presentations of the first wave of elected black representatives in America. Indeed, in my own biographical case study of the industrious

Reconstruction politician Richard Harvey Cain, I directly oppose previous characterizations of his supposed disengagement and apathy:

His [Cain's] exclusion from the nineteenth-century conversation is not for want
of accomplishment or merit. As an inimitable preacher, state senator, activist,
orator, churchman, congressional representative twice over, educational advocate, writer, debater, fundraiser, and editor of the *South Carolina Leader* and
the *Missionary Record* newspapers, few men of any color can lay claim to such
a breadth of influence or capability, against the backdrop of a mercurial post-
bellum South Carolina. (Parlett 2012)

In the subsequent Jim Crow era, *de jure* segregation revived black caricatures with zeal. The Coon and Sambo characters, in particular,
depicted black Americans as acutely idle, unintelligent, and unable to
muster the energy to improve their fortunes and sustained the stereotypes
of the slave era. The Coon caricature (whose name is taken from the rac-
coon animal) was a central component of racial comedy skits and a key
character in minstrelsy entertainment. White audiences were regaled by
the slow-talking, lethargic jester-type figure, whose ultimate life goal
was leisurely repose, but never high office. "Coon music" translated the
visual caricature into a genre of racially offensive song.

When it comes to the presentation of Barack Obama as lazy, lethargic,
or unwilling to work as a *real* president should by Gingrich, Ailes,
Sununu, Romney, Palin, Steele and others, examination of the racialized
incidence of such stereotypes for the black slave and Reconstruction citizen, for example, is instructive. This is not to say that each criticism of
Obama's ineffectiveness or lack of passion is a calculated racial slur,
intended to blow old dog whistles and revive the aesthetic of reclined
black men. Yet in many cases, the sheer collocation of terminology, the
triangulation of remnant prejudicial sentiment, and the seemingly *non
sequitur* deployment of the lethargy critique is convincing evidence of
the purposeful demonization of the 44th president as the political
incarnation of the lazy black man.

By contrast, while the public interprets the House of Representatives as
a Do-Nothing Congress, intent on making Obama a one-term and (ironically) legislatively inactive president, the Democratic community has not
caricatured the House using white stereotypes, such as redneck cowboys
or dumb blondes. Instead, in his 2014 State of the Union Address, referencing the stymying consequence of rigid partisanship and no doubt
aware of the Republicans' simultaneous critique of presidential inaction
and constant obstructionism, Obama called for a dynamic, White
House-led, "Year of Action." Committing to act alone through executive

power in his second term, Obama challenged the very caricature of presidential inertia and the racialized lens through which it has been proliferated. In turn, Obama has since been accused of becoming the activist, or even Imperial, President, demonstrating the Cornelian dilemma of satisfactorily situating Obama's personal energies.

THE STUPID PRESIDENT: A MODERN TEST OF LITERACY

A less well-established claim, though one still rooted in racial stereotypes of the black American experience, is that Obama simply does not have the intellectual capacity to fulfill the requirements of presidential office. Questions surrounding Obama's college records, his intellectual capacity, and student status descended rapidly into an extension of the Birther movement, with a "show your papers" standard being applied in the realm of Obama's education. Although President Obama's academic qualifications and achievements are significant, his opponents' pursuit of some sort of disqualifying educational aberration in his "deceptive" biography suggests the existence of a white intelligentsia, from whose ranks a mixed-race candidate might be successfully barred. It revives, in the 21st century, an ethic of highly racialized educational exclusion and mental denigration stemming from forced slave illiteracy, generations of scientific racism that pathologized black mental inferiority, the collapse of Reconstruction-era freedoms, school segregation, and the affirmative action debate.

Barack Obama attended overseas schools until the age of 10, before he returned to Hawaii as a student at the private preparatory Punahou School in 1971. Upon graduating from high school, he moved to California in 1979, enrolling as a student at Occidental College in Los Angeles. In 1981, Obama transferred to the prestigious Columbia University in New York, as a junior majoring in political science. Three years after his graduation from Columbia, and with some experience as a community organizer under his belt, Obama was admitted to Harvard Law School in 1988. By his second year, Obama had become the first African American president of the *Harvard Law Review*, drawing national media interest. He later graduated with a J.D. *magna cum laude* in 1991 before taking up the position as a visiting fellow at the University of Chicago. Here, he lectured in constitutional law for a total of 12 years, completed his memoir, and became involved with Chicago political and legal organizations. Although Obama's educational path is unconventional, it bears the hallmarks of a meteoric rise by a generationally significant intellect. Lest it be forgotten, Obama's mother obtained a Ph.D. in anthropology and his father won a prestigious Kenyan scholarship to study economics at the University of Hawaii, before later attending his son's alma mater, Harvard.

Obama's educational othering was initiated in the mainstream media by a 2008 editorial in the *Wall Street Journal*, which suggested that Obama was dissembling about key landmarks in his academic progression:

The Columbia years are a hole in the sprawling Obama hagiography. In his two published memoirs, the 47-year-old Democratic nominee barely mentions his experience there ... Why not release his Columbia transcript? Why has his senior essay gone missing?
... Fox News contacted some 400 of his classmates and found no one who remembered him. ("Obama's Lost Years" 2008)

Although Obama was engaged in an electoral contest against John McCain, who had graduated as 894th out of 899 students at the Naval Academy, the conservative press became obsessed with documentary evidence of the candidate's intellectual mediocrity. Orly Taitz (of Birther infamy) pursued the conspiracy with zeal, in the belief that it supported her ultimate end of Obama's foreignization. As with the demand for Obama's original birth certificate, Taitz theorized the reluctance to publish Obama's college records was because they indicated an allegiance to a nation other than the United States. "Sometimes students with poor grades from other countries who have citizenship in other countries can get into top universities," Taitz explained, "[t]hat might be one of the reasons why his records are not unsealed. If his records show he got into Columbia University as a foreign exchange student, then we have a serious issue with his citizenship" (Goldberg 2011). Questioning Obama's education was firmly in the tradition of Obama's delegitimization on the basis of identity.

In the latter stages of the 2012 campaign and a year after Obama released his long-form birth certificate, the issue of Obama's educational certification gained greater currency in the right-wing universe. Sean Hannity invited Wayne Allyn Root onto his program in August of that year to broadcast the theory that because Root never met Obama at Columbia University, Obama was never admitted:

If anyone should have questions about Obama's record at Columbia University, it's me. We both graduated (according to Obama) Columbia University, Class of '83. We were both (according to Obama) pre-law and political science majors. And I thought I knew most everyone at Columbia. I certainly thought I'd *heard* of all of my fellow political science majors. But not Obama (or as he was known then, Barry Soetoro). I never met him. Never saw him. Never even heard of him. And none of the classmates that I knew at Columbia have ever met him, saw him, or heard of him. (Moon 2012)

In the same month, Rush Limbaugh reported the uncorroborated story of an unnamed member of Obama's Harvard cohort who claimed that Obama's grades were memorably poor, and by implication inadequate for ascent to the highest political office:

I got on the phone with somebody who said they went to school with Barack Obama at Harvard. And the guy told me that Obama got the lowest grades that any Harvard graduate ever got and that a bunch of professors gave him B's and C's when he didn't even show up to class. And then he hung up. Now, this guy from Harvard said that Obama had the lowest grades anybody ever got at Harvard, had professors that covered for him and he wasn't even there. (Limbaugh 2012)

Pat Buchanan announced on MSNBC's *Hardball with Chris Matthews,* "He's probably affirmative action all the way." Donald Trump, taking credit for the release of Obama's birth certificate, questioned how Obama, as a "terrible student," could possibly rise to the rank of *Harvard Law Review* president. Trump, with a combination of directness and self-promotion, issued a personal challenge to President Obama to unseal and deliver his college (and passport) records and applications in exchange for financial remuneration. Setting the president a strict one-week deadline, he claimed, "If Barack Obama opens up and gives his college records and applications, and if he gives his passport applications and records, I will give to a charity of his choice ... a check, immediately, for $5 million."

Meanwhile, named and reliable witnesses to Obama's academic achievements refuted the conspiracy surrounding his supposed intellectual inadequacy. Laurence Tribe, for example, said, "The allegation is absurd. Obama earned every one of his enormously high grades. 'Affirmative action' had nothing to do with his success there. He was the most impressive student and research assistant I have taught in my 40 years at Harvard" (Wilson 2012).

Similarly, the downgrading of Obama's intellectual capacity has been implied equally by the claim that he cannot speak without the use of a teleprompter and by the claim that he is functionally incapable of being the author of his own memoir *Dreams from My Father* (1995). Both claims purport to be based on some sense of Obama's rhetorical illiteracy and, consequently, his intertwined legitimacy.

The issue of Obama's teleprompter over-reliance is one that has been deployed by opponents to underline Obama's dependence upon empty rhetoric, to allege his ignorance, or to insinuate his general ineptitude to fulfill even the simplest speaking task without the safety net of the campaign accessory. In 2010, Governor Tim Pawlenty claimed that "the next era of hope and change" was more the age of "hope and change and teleprompters." Michele Bachmann poked fun at Obama's use of the accessory, promising that "President Bachmann will not have teleprompters in the White House." In 2011, when thieves pilfered a truck containing the president's audio equipment and podiums, the *Drudge Report* quipped "SPEECHLESS: OBAMA'S TELEPROMPTER STOLEN!" At the 2011 White House Correspondents Dinner, Obama poked fun at the characterization of his dependency on the teleprompter in a video called "The President's Speech"—a parody of the historical drama *The King's Speech* and King George VI's struggle with a severe speech impediment. Proving that the criticism had entered the political zeitgeist, the satirical news source *The Onion* reported "Obama's Home Teleprompter Malfunctions During Family Dinner," claiming that despite the glitch, Obama had further *increased* his reliance on the machine, sending "it alone on low priority diplomatic meetings and photo ops." In his mocked association with electronic scripting, there is an implication that Obama cannot satisfactorily enact the bully pulpit unaided.

In keeping with the theme of Obama's academic fraudulence comes the accusation that Obama used a ghost writer for the composition of his best-selling autobiography, *Dreams from My Father* because he was unable to conjure up even satisfactory prose. The primary conspiracy theory—which fueled Obama's demonization through guilt by association—claimed that William Ayers, cofounder of the Weather Underground, secretly penned Obama's personal tome. Since 2008, Jake Cashill has argued that Obama simply does not have the style or capacity to write a memoir of such literary merit. As evidence, Cashill marshals extant samples of Obama's previous writings, such as an article titled "Breaking the War Mentality," to contrast and ridicule the gulf of sophistication:

Though thematically it's no sillier than the average paper written by a Columbia undergraduate in 1983, stylistically it's a disaster. It's an utter total disaster. This might be excusable if, for instance, a year before this they had found Barack Obama in an Indonesian cave being raised being raised by wolves, but to this point he had just spent the last 4 years in America's best colleges . . . In this one essay . . . he has five sentences in which the noun does not agree with the verb . . . My children were writing better than this in grade school. ("Jack Cashill: Deconstructing Obama" 2011)

Cashill's substantive theory was that "after failing to finish his book on time, and after forfeiting his advance from Simon & Schuster, Obama brought his sprawling, messy, sophomoric manuscript to the famed dining room table of Bill Ayers and supplicated, 'Help.'"

Christopher Anderson, appearing on the Fox News program *Hannity*, claimed that he "found the literary devices and themes [of *Dreams*] bear a jarring similarity to Ayers' own writings." Donald Trump did not soften his unique literary assessment when he alleged, "The man that wrote the second book didn't write the first book ... The difference was like chicken salad and chicken s**t." Indeed, it was further reported in the days leading up to the 2008 election that Oxford University professor Dr. Peter Millican, an expert in computational linguistics, was contacted by Californian businessman Robert Fox to undertake an analysis of markers of linguistic similarity found in Obama's autobiography and William Ayers's *Fugitive Days*. Millican, who "thought it was extremely unlikely that we would get a positive result," later concluded that cross examination of these works had demonstrated that "the allegations were completely untrue" (Criddle 2008).

The extent, volume, and tenacity of Obama's othering on the basis of unfounded educational doubts recalls the senseless subjugation and exclusion of the black thinker from political and societal participation throughout African American history. The centuries-long institution of white superiority over the black body and mind was enabled by "craniologists, eugenicists, phrenologists, and Social Darwinists, at every educational level, [who] buttressed the belief that blacks were innately intellectually and culturally inferior to whites" (Pilgrim 2012c). Even Thomas Jefferson (1787) advanced "as a suspicion only, that the blacks ... are inferior to the whites in the endowment of body and mind."

Historically, a prejudiced application of the natural sciences to infer black stupidity gave rise to the systematic and self-serving denigration of the African American cerebral capacity through, for example, the suggested correlation of brain size and intelligence. German philosopher Chistoph Meiners claimed that while the skull of a black person is often larger, the brain itself is the smallest, and least effective, of any in the human race. Franz Pruner concurred with the prejudicial cranial theory, stating that the Negro brain was a corollary to that found in apes.

It was perhaps Samuel Morton's extensive examination of the craniological theory of racial intellectual inequality, however, that most greatly influenced early 19th-century thought. In *Crania Americana*, Morton reported the results of his years-long collection and study of human skulls from across the globe, including his finding—ultimately challenged on the basis of evidentiary bias—that Africans possessed the smallest cranial capacity and, therefore, represented the lowest form of human intellectual potential. According to Morton, there was an average of 9 cubic inches' difference between the Caucasian and Negro brain. To explain his differentiation of the white and black mind, Morton proposed the theory of polygenesis: the notion that the two races are entirely unrelated and incompatible.

Morton's work was influential in the perpetuation of racialized considerations of American intelligence. Early American psychological thought gravitated toward racialized differentiation between the white and black brain. In 1905, for example, Granville Stanley Hall wrote, "No two races in history, taken as a whole, differ so much in their traits, both physical and psychic, as the Caucasian and the African. The color of the skin and the crookedness of the hair are only the outward signs of many far deeper differences, including cranial and thoracic capacity. ..." In 1916, Lewis Terman, excluding black people from the realm of citizenship and political engagement, wrote that African American children "are ineducable beyond the nearest rudiments of training. No amount of school instruction will ever make them intelligent voters or capable citizens in the sense of the world."

The narrative of Frederick Douglass provides an insight into the quotidian application of this psychological inequality in the life of an American slave kept at bay through forced ignorance. Having found that Douglass was learning the alphabet, Mr. Auld proclaimed:

A nigger should know nothing but to obey his master—to as he is told to do. Learning would spoil the best nigger in the world. Now if you teach that nigger how to read, there would be no keeping him. It would forever unfit him to be a slave. He would at once become unmanageable, and of no value to his master. As to himself, it could do him no good, but a great deal of harm. It would make him discontented and unhappy. (Douglass and Jacobs 2007)

The fear that mental emancipation would lead to physical unrest was one of the motivating principles behind maintaining the educational suppression of the black American mind.

Following the collapse of Reconstruction-era freedoms, and despite growing levels of black literacy across the nation, black Americans were excluded from societal and electoral participation, often on the grounds of intelligence or literacy. Throughout the Jim Crow era, the denial of male suffrage was facilitated by the introduction of disenfranchising obstacles to the ballot box. The literacy test was introduced as a requirement for voting in the late 19th century. Because of the introduction of the Grandfather Clause, which allowed anyone to vote who could prove that they had an ancestor who could vote prior to 1867 (i.e., white men), the literacy test was administered predominantly to black populations and poor whites. Conducted by, and at the total discretion of, white electoral officials, the tests were regularly administered unfairly or included impossible questions such as "How many seeds are there in a watermelon?" or "Name every county judge in the state." Even in the rare cases of a successful test result, poll taxes and anti-black intimidation made engagement in the electoral process virtually impossible.

Accusations that Obama's inferior intellect cannot coexist with political or presidential office is a subtle reinvigoration of the tropes of black societal segregation or exclusion based on prejudicial scientific racism. Obama's dependency on teleprompters, his inability to write his own books, and the suspicions that he has faked or exaggerated his academic credentials—requiring checking by white officials—are startling echoes of racial denigration from centuries past. Arguably, there is a direct correlation of *intent* between the Jim Crow era literacy tests, which, teamed with other strategies of marginalization and intimidation, were put in place to limit African American suffrage and the 21st-century coded requirement for Barack Obama, the first black president, to prove his educational credentials prior to engaging further in the political process.

REFERENCES

Abcarian, Robin. "Michelle Obama Criticized for Remarks." Los Angeles Times (February 20, 2008). http://articles.latimes.com/2008/feb/20/nation/na-michelle20.

"Barack Obama 1995 Interview on *Dreams from My Father* Part 1." YouTube video from a televised video with Connie Martinson on *Talks Books,* posted by "Andrew Kaczynski," November 20, 2011. http://www.youtube.com/watch?v=Rx_XS4s6aA4.

Berman, Dan. "Mitt Romney: President Obama Won Because of 'Gifts.' " *Politico* (November 14, 2012). http://www.politico.com/news/stories/1112/83878.html.

Blake, John. "Why Obama Doesn't Dare Become the 'Angry Black Man.' " *CNN* (June 10, 2010). http://edition.cnn.com/2010/POLITICS/06/08/rage.obama/.

Brooks, David. "The Oil Plume." *The New York Times* (May 31, 2010). http://www.nytimes.com/2010/06/01/opinion/01brooks.html?gwh=C5C9CAEA2BF3952237EE3CBBF91E9E90&gwt=pay.

Brooks, David. "Trim the 'Experts,' Trust the Locals." *The New York Times* (June 17, 2010). http://www.nytimes.com/2010/06/18/opinion/18brooks.html.

Bush, George W. "Address to the Republican National Convention." Speech in Saint Paul, MN, September 2, 2008. http://elections.nytimes.com/2008/president/conventions/videos/transcripts/20080902_BUSH_SPEECH.html.

Chafets, Zev. *Roger Ailes: Off Camera*. Penguin, 2013.

Cartwright, Samuel A. "'Report on the Diseases and Physical Peculiarities of the Negro Race." *Health, Disease, and Illness: Concepts in Medicine* (2004): 28–39.

Cassidy, John. "Obama and the 'Angry Black Man' Factor." *The New Yorker* (October 17, 2012). http://www.newyorker.com/online/blogs/johncassidy/2012/10/obama-and-the-angry-black-man-factor.html.

Chen, Adrian. "Maher Wants Obama to Act like a Real Black President with Guns and Stuff." *Gawker* (May 30, 2010). http://gawker.com/5551249/bill-maher-wants-obama-to-act-like-a-real-black-president-with-guns-and-stuff.

Cirilli, Kevin. "Newt Gingrich: Like NFL Refs, President Obama 'Not Real.' " *Politico* (September 26, 2012). http://www.politico.com/news/stories/0912/81688.html.

Coates, Ta-Nehisi. "Fear of a Black President." *The Atlantic* (August 22, 2012). http://www.theatlantic.com/magazine/archive/2012/09/fear-of-a-black-president/309064/?single_page=true.

Cooper, Frank Rudy. "Our First Unisex President: Black Masculinity and Obama's Feminine Side." *Denver University Law Review* 86 (2008): 633.

Corn, David. "Secret Video: Romney Tells Millionaire Donors What He Really Thinks of Obama Voters." *Mother Jones* (September 17, 2012). http://www.motherjones.com/politics/2012/09/secret-video-romney-private-fundraiser.

Criddle, Laura. "Oxford Don Embroiled in Obama Smear." *The Cherwell* (November 6, 2008). http://www.cherwell.org/news/2008/11/06/oxford-don-embroiled-in-obama-smear.

Curry, Tom. "How Obama Won the White House." *MSNBC.com* (November 5, 2008). http://www.nbcnews.com/id/27540321/ns/politics-decision_08/t/how-obama-won-white-house/

Deggans, Eric. "Rev. Jeremiah Wright's Media Blitz Forces Barack Obama to Face the Angry Black Man Test—Again." *The Huffington Post* (April 28, 2008). http://www.huffingtonpost.com/eric-deggans/rev-jeremiah-wrights-medi_b_98957.html.

Dixon, Thomas. *The Clansman: An Historical Romance of the Ku Klux Klan*. Lexington, Kentucky: Pelican, 2002.

Douglass, Frederick, and Harriet Jacobs. *Narrative of the Life of Frederick Douglass, an American Slave & Incidents in the Life of a Slave Girl*. Random House Digital, 2007.

Dowd, Maureen. "Obama, Legally Blonde?" *The New York Times* (February 14, 2007).

Dowd, Maureen. "Boy, oh, Boy." *The New York Times* (September 12, 2009). http://www.nytimes.com/2009/09/13/opinion/13dowd.html.

Dowd, Maureen. "Once More, with Feeling." *The New York Times* (May 29, 2010). http://www.nytimes.com/2010/05/30/opinion/30dowd.html.

Drum, Kevin. "Barack Obama Is Dumb and Lazy." *Mother Jones* (March 29, 2013). http://www.motherjones.com/kevin-drum/2013/03/barack-obama-dumb-and-lazy.

D'Souza, Dinesh. *The Roots of Obama's Rage.* Washington, DC: Regnery, 2011.

Edwards, David, and Muriel Kane. 2008. "MSNBC Analyst: Rove Obama Attack close to 'Outright Racist.' " *The Raw Story* (January 11, 2008). http://rawstory.com/news/2007/MSNBC_Analyst_Rove_Obama_attack_almost_0111.html.

Enck-Wanzer, Darrel. "Barack Obama, the Tea Party, and the Threat of Race: On Racial Neoliberalism and Born Again Racism." *Communication, Culture & Critique* 4, no. 1 (2011): 23–30.

Feldman, Josh. "Palin Bashes Obama over Snowden Manhunt: 'The Community Organizer In Our President' Leading from Behind." *Mediaite* (June 29, 2013). http://www.mediaite.com/tv/palin-bashes-obama-over-snowden-manhunt-the-community-organizer-in-our-president-leading-from-behind/.

Gibbs, Robert. "Press Briefing by Press Secretary Robert Gibbs." The White House, June 1, 2010. http://www.whitehouse.gov/the-press-office/press-briefing-press-secretary-robert-gibbs-6110.

Goldberg, Michelle. "Donald Trump's New Obama Conspiracy Theory." *The Daily Beast* (April 26, 2011). http://www.thedailybeast.com/articles/2011/04/26/donald-trump-takes-up-birthers-obama-college-conspiracy-theory.html.

Griffith, D. W. *Birth of a Nation.* Epoch Producing Co. 1915.

Hall, G. Stanley. "The Negro in Africa and America." *The Pedagogical Seminary* 12, no. 3 (1905): 350–368.

Harris, Frank III. "Calling Obama Lazy Crosses Racial Line." *The Courant* (October 10, 2012). http://articles.courant.com/2012-10-10/news/hc-op-harris-obama-weak-in-debated-not-lazy-1011-20121010_1_lazy-person-republican-challenger-mitt-romney-president-barack-obama.

"Jack Cashill: Deconstructing Obama." YouTube video clip, March 21, 2011. http://www.Youtube.com, http://www.youtube.com/watch?v=xxPhnhQ7Tr0.

Jackman, Simon, and Lynn Vavreck. "Obama's Advantage? Race, Partisanship and Racial Attitudes in Context." Annual Meeting of the Midwest Political Science Association, 2010.

Jackson, David. "Obama: No Moratorium on Golf." *USA Today* (June 21, 2010). http://content.usatoday.com/communities/theoval/post/2010/06/obama-no-moratorium-on-golf/1#.UvQQHfl_vX8.

James, Frank. "Can a President Be an Angry Black Man?" *NPR* (June 8, 2010). http://www.npr.org/blogs/thetwo-way/2010/06/could_america_handle_an_angry.html.

Jefferson, Thomas. *Notes on the State of Virginia.* 1787.

Jenkins, Lynnette R. "Politics as Usual: Black Stereotypes and President Obama's Racialization." 2012. http://works.bepress.com/lynnette_jenkins/1/.

Journal Editorial Report. "Is Romney's Lead the Real Deal?" Video, 7:23, October 27, 2012. http://www.foxnews.com/on-air/journal-editorial-report/2012/10/29/romneys-lead-real-deal.

Kaplan, E. A. "Who's Afraid of Michelle Obama?" *Salon* (April 20, 2008). http://www.salon.com/mwt/feature/2008/06/24/michelle_obama/index.html.

Kessler, Glenn. "Barack Obama: The 'Food-Stamp President'?" *The Washington Post: The Fact Checker* (December 8, 2011). http://www.washingtonpost.com/blogs/fact-checker/post/barack-obama-the-food-stamp-president/2011/12/07/gIQAzTdQdO_blog.html.

Limbaugh, Rush. "ACORN's Aim: Chaos at the Polls." *The Rush Limbaugh Show* (October 14, 2008). http://www.rushlimbaugh.com/daily/2008/10/14/acorn_s_aim_chaos_at_the_polls.

Limbaugh, Rush. "Obama Got Worst Grades in Harvard History—and It's Up to Him to Prove He Didn't." *The Rush Limbaugh Show* (August 2, 2012). http://www.rushlimbaugh.com/daily/2012/08/02/obama_got_worst_grades_in_harvard_history_and_it_s_up_to_him_to_prove_he_didn_t.

McCain, John, and Mark Salter. *Worth the Fighting for: A Memoir.* New York: Random House, 2002.

Mendible, Myra. "The Politics of Race and Class in the Age of Obama." *Revue de recherche en civilisation américaine* 3 (March 2012). http://rrca.revues.org/489.

Moon, Robert. "Obama Classmate: There Is a Reason Obama Refuses to Release His College Records." *The Examiner* (August 7, 2012). http://www.examiner.com/article/obama-classmate-there-is-a-reason-obama-refuses-to-release-his-college-records.

Newby, Joe. "Al Sharpton, Touré: Ailes Used Racist 'Dog Whistle' in Calling Obama 'Lazy.'" *The Examiner* (March 8, 2013). http://www.examiner.com/article/al-sharpton-tour-ailes-used-racist-dog-whistle-calling-obama-lazy.

Obama, Barack H. *Dreams from My Father.* New York: Times Books, 1995.

Obama, Barack H. *The Audacity of Hope: Thoughts on Reclaiming the American Dream.* New York: Canongate Books, 2007.

Obama, Barack H. "A More Perfect Union." Speech in Philadelphia, PA, March 18, 2008. http://blogs.wsj.com/washwire/2008/03/18/text-of-obamas-speech-a-more-perfect-union/.

Obama, Barack H. "Remarks by the President on Trayvon Martin." Speech in the White House, Washington, DC, July 19, 2013. http://www.whitehouse.gov/the-press-office/2013/07/19/remarks-president-trayvon-martin.

"Obama's Lost Years." September 11, 2008. *The Wall Street Journal.* http://online.wsj.com/news/articles/SB122108881386721289.

O'Reilly, Bill. "Is Obama Not Emotional enough?" *The O'Reilly Factor* (June 2, 2010). http://www.billoreilly.com/show?action=viewTVShow&showID=2615.

Owen, David. "Othering Obama: How Whiteness Is Used to Undermine Authority." *Altre Modernità* 3 (March 2010): 112–119. doi: 10.13130/2035-7680/517.

Parlett, Martin. "Like a Lion Bound, Hear Him Roar: Richard Harvey Cain and a Rhetoric of Reconstruction." In *Before Obama: A Reappraisal of Black Reconstruction Era Politicians*, edited by Matthew Lynch, 285–316. Santa Barbara, California: ABC-CLIO, 2012.

Pilgrim, David. "The Coon Caricature." Jim Crow Museum of Racist Memorabilia, 2012a. http://www.ferris.edu/jimcrow/coon/.

Pilgrim, David. "The Sapphire Caricature." Jim Crow Museum of Racist Memorabilia, 2012b. http://www.ferris.edu/jimcrow/sapphire/.

Pilgrim, David. "What Was Jim Crow?" Jim Crow Museum of Racist Memorabilia, 2012c. http://www.ferris.edu/jimcrow/what.

Piston, Spencer. "How Explicit Racial Prejudice Hurt Obama in the 2008 Election." *Political Behavior* 32 (2010): 431–451.

PolitiFact.com. "Mitt Romney Says Barack Obama's Plan for Welfare Reform: 'They Just Send You Your Check.' " August 7, 2012. http://www.politifact.com/truth-o-meter/statements/2012/aug/07/mitt-romney/mitt-romney-says-barack-obamas-plan-abandons-tenet/.

Powell, Michael, and Jodi Kantor. "After Attacks, Michelle Obama Looks for a New Introduction." *The New York Times* (Jun 18, 2008). http://www.nytimes.com/2008/06/18/us/politics/18michelle.html?pagewanted=all

Real Clear Politics. "Andrea Mitchell Asks Sununu to Apologize for Calling Obama 'Lazy.' " October 4, 2012. http://www.realclearpolitics.com/video/2012/10/04/andrea_mitchell_asks_sununu_to_apologize_for_calling_obama_lazy.html.

Rice, Kym S., and Martha B. Katz-Hyman. *World of a Slave: Encyclopedia of the Material Life of Slaves in the United States*. Westport, CT: ABC-CLIO, 2010.

Rodriguez, Junius P., ed. *The Historical Encyclopedia of World Slavery: AK; Vol. II, LZ*. Vol. 1. Santa Barbara, California: ABC-CLIO, 1997.

Rove, Karl. "Why Hillary Won." *The Wall Street Journal* (January 10, 2008). http://online.wsj.com/news/articles/SB119992615845679531.

Sammon, Bill. *The Evangelical President: George Bush's Struggle to Spread a Moral Democracy throughout the World*. Washington, DC: Regnery, 2007.

Schneider, William. "What Racial Divide?" *National Journal Magazine* (November 8, 2008). http://www.nationaljournal.com/columns/political-pulse/what-racial-divide—20081108.

Scott, J. "Transcript: 'FOX News Watch." June 14, 2008. http://www.foxnews.com/story/2008/06/16/transcript-fox-news-watch-june-14-2008/.

Steele, Shelby. "Obama's Post-Racial Promise." *The Los Angeles Times* (November 5, 2008). http://www.latimes.com/news/opinion/opinionla/la-oe-steele5-2008nov05-story.html#page=1.

Steyn, Mark. "Mrs Grievance ..." *National Review* (April 21, 2008). http://www.freerepublic.com/focus/news/2006753/posts.

Terman, Lewis Madison. *The Measurement of Intelligence c. 2.* Boston, MA: Houghton Mifflin, 1916.

Tesler, Michael, and David Sears. "President Obama and the Growing Polarization of Partisan Attachments by Racial Attitudes and Race." Presentation at Annual Meeting of the American Political Science Association, Washington, DC, 2010.

Thernstrom, Abigail. "Great Black Hope? The Reality of President-Elect Obama." *National Review Online* (November 6, 2008). http://www.nationalreview.com/articles/226264/great-black-hope/nro-symposium

Tracy, Susan J. *In the Master's Eye: Representations of Women, Blacks, and Poor Whites in Antebellum Southern Literature.* Amherst, MA: University of Massachusetts Press, 2009.

Wilson, John K. "Limbaugh Falsely Smears Obama's Harvard Record." *The Daily Kos* (August 2, 2012). http://www.dailykos.com/story/2012/08/02/1116174/-Limbaugh-Falsely-Smears-Obama-s-Harvard-Record.

Winston, George T. "The Relation of the Whites to the Negroes." *Annals of the American Academy of Political and Social Science* 18 (1901): 105–118.

Chapter 4

His Name Is Hussein: The Muslim Terrorist President

The front cover of *The New Yorker* magazine said it all.

Obama stood in the center of the Oval Office, clothed in the trappings of Islamic garb. He wore a white turban-esque headdress and brown open sandals, symbolically placing his left foot upon the neck of the American eagle on the presidential carpet beneath. The portrait of George Washington had been discarded and replaced with a visual homage to Osama bin Laden, who stared out from his gilded frame with pride as Obama threw the American flag into the crackling fire. Michelle Obama was there, too, celebrating in the terroristic dissent. She stood opposite her husband, adorned in a paramilitary ensemble, with steel-toe boots, camouflage pants, and an AK-47 slung over her shoulder with ample ammunition. Michelle was now a member of the Black Panther movement or the Weather Underground, with her hair liberated into a full, rounded Afro. A silent fist bump transacted between the couple communicated a mutual approval of spousal extremism.

You might be forgiven for thinking that we have stumbled into the recesses of the right wing's florid imagination or a scene found upon a discarded Tea Party banner, but in fact this was the July 2008 frontispiece to one of the most liberal magazines in the United States. The intent of Barry Blitt's illustration, entitled "The Politics of Fear," the magazine later clarified, was to satirize the numerous conservative rumors about Obama's Muslim origins and jihadi intentions. The magazine had assumed that the extreme presentation of Obama's religious identity had become so well established in the political zeitgeist that it was possible to lampoon such gossip by its mere cartoon depiction. As a result, the tropes of Obama's Islamification, de-Christianization, and clandestine extremism were fused into a single caricature stacked high upon newsstands across the nation for public consumption.

Ultimately, the satirical indictment was an editorial miscalculation that revealed the fissures of religious identity politics at play in the 2008 campaign. Many readers got the joke, recognizing the magazine's poking finger at the farcicality of the Obama-as-Muslim conspiracy. But others, quite understandably, questioned whether the cover might merely enhance the currency of Obama's scandalizers. This was the nightmare projection of what the Right expected behind closed doors in a potential Obama White House—an ultimate alien infiltration, where two terrorisms (domestic and international) collide with catastrophic effect. Through Barack Obama's portrayal, the image reinforced the Orientalizing and Islamifying memes of his opponents, the Birther crowd's contention that Obama is un-American, the "palling around with terrorists" rhetoric of the McCain campaign, and the racial unease surrounding the candidate's soft patriotism. Through Michelle Obama, the image channeled the interpretation of the Obamas as hyper-racialized, tied to the most radical elements of American society, proponents of the "angry black man" strategy, and intent on the destruction of order, or of government itself. Indeed, the absence of the true object of the satire (the conspiratorial Right) from the image led to the potential danger of a literalist interpretation of the Obamas as the "browned" political equivalents of Bonnie and Clyde. For some, it was a gift—and a mainstream concession—to the dog-whistle agenda of the far Right extremists.

The image was critiqued as such by Rachel Sklar of the *Huffington Post*, who wrote, "Anyone who's tried to paint Obama as a Muslim, anyone who's tried to portray Michelle as angry or a secret revolutionary out to get Whitey, anyone who has questioned their patriotism—well, here's your image" (Sklar 2008). John Aravoisis, a Democratic strategist, agreed that the satire failed because the image did not challenge the religious othering of candidate Obama, but rather gave it a succinct and vividly memorable representation:

A liberal publication like *The New Yorker* thinks it's funny to make Mrs. Obama some radical Black Panther, Barack Obama basically a terrorist (you'll note that he looks just like Osama bin Laden on the wall), and they're even burning the American flag in the Oval Office . . . Is *The New Yorker* so out of touch that they don't realize that much of America, or at least too much of America, harbors these very same concerns about Obama and his wife? . . . [T]ell us how this pokes fun at the stereotype? It reinforces it. (Aravoisis 2008)

The editor of *The New Yorker* defended the cover, claiming that further clarification would be contrary to comedic intent. "Satire doesn't run with subtitles," David Remnick said, and "a satirical cartoon would not be any good if it came with a set of instructions" (NPR.org 2008). He was right, of course, but the issue for many was that this image did not lampoon Obama's opponents, but rather seemed to further the innuendos against Obama's spiritual identity. Kevin Drum cited the confused perspective as the artwork's ultimate failing:

If artist Barry Blitt had some real cojones, he would have drawn the same cover but shown it as a gigantic word bubble coming out of John McCain's mouth—implying, you see, that this is how McCain wants the world to view Obama. But he didn't. Because that would have been unfair. And McCain would have complained about it. And for some reason, the risk that a failed satire would unfairly defame McCain is somehow seen as worse than the risk that a failed satire would unfairly defame Obama. (Drum 2008)

The magazine cover walked a liminal tightrope between being interpreted as left-wing satire and simultaneously as right-wing anti-Obama literalism. With fear of the latter, Obama campaign spokesperson, Bill Burton, released a statement of firm disapproval:

The New Yorker may think, as one of their staff explained to us, that their cover is a satirical lampoon of the caricature Senator Obama's right wing critics have tried to create. But most readers will see it as tasteless and offensive. And we agree. (Allen 2008)

Tucker Bounds, spokesperson for the McCain campaign, echoed the sentiment, despite the fact that this campaign would ultimately propagate the allegation that Obama launched his campaign in the living room of a domestic terrorist. When asked directly by Maria Gavrilovic of CBS News for an immediate reaction to the illustration, Obama shrugged his shoulders with disbelief and without comment. Significantly, that the candidate did not laugh off the illustration as immaterial portended a political concern that the misrepresentation of his religious identity was no jesting matter.

Indeed, in this single antonymic presidential portrait from the cover of *The New Yorker* magazine one finds all of the elements of Obama's religious demonization discussed in this chapter. Primarily, Obama's religious othering has been tied to a specific Orientalizing foreignization—namely, that Obama's background, parentage, schooling, and name denote an Islamic theology. This accusation aims to situate the president outside the Judeo-Christian normalcy of presidential politics in an era of heightened Islamic fear and terroristic association. Raw anxieties surrounding foreign religion and the post-9/11 equation of Islam with anti-American extremism resulted in a potent and intemperate form of partisan othering of the Illinois senator: Obama was not simply a clandestine Muslim; he was a dangerous and unpatriotic jihadi, hiding within the gray suit of the political establishment. The contention that Obama is an Islamic extremist behind closed doors is to say that (1) Obama's true religious identity has been purposefully hidden because it is theologically dubious or politically inconvenient; (2) this subterfuge speaks to a broader character flaw of evasiveness and dishonesty; (3) Obama is actively deleterious to America's national security; and (4) he is spiritually out of line with the Judeo-Christian status quo expectation of presidential religiosity. Thus, with one volley of the Obama-as-Muslim slur, Obama's opponents are able to serve a number of demonizing religious claims under the umbrella of a single adjective of dogma.

The secondary, but associated, theme of Obama's religious othering is to portray his professed Christianity as extremely immoderate, to the point that it is practically alien to a mainstream American theology. Through his associations with the controversial pastor Dr. Jeremiah Wright of Chicago's Trinity United Church of Christ, Obama's religious observance became a nationally televised controversy. In 2008, disquieting snippets of Wright's radical sermons and aggressive preaching style streamed across network news without interruption and were marshaled as evidence by some of Obama's associated dangerous and racialized zeal. Further, many claimed that the Obamas were disciples of Wright's hyper-racialized doctrine of black liberation theology. By such means, Barack Obama's Christian faith has been transfigured as a sort of browned theological extremism bearing the anti-American hallmarks of fanatic Islam. On the opposite side of the Christian spectrum—and demonstrating once more the sheer variety of perspectives from which Obama is othered—the president has been simultaneously cast as an atheist. Militantly so. Godless. Beyond the reforming power of Christian faith. Taking this perspective to its illogical extreme, some have interpreted Obama as the Antichrist incarnate, with the utter enemization of Obama casting him as a satanic demagogue and the political herald of the end-times. Reinforcing this perception of Obama as a radical atheist, Muslim, apostate, jihadi, demonic, and theological charlatan, the *New Yorker* image touched upon the kaleidoscopic presentation of Obama's distance from the "standard" religious identity.

As with the many frames of Obama's foreignization, his religious othering has been sustained by a willful misinterpretation of the president's biography and the power of guilt by (oftentimes fabricated) association.

From the supposed genetic inheritance of his mother's agnosticism and his father's Islam to his temporary residency in Indonesia; from his sometimes education at a predominantly Muslim school to his unusual (and oftentimes stressed) middle name; from the one consonant separating "Obama" from "Osama" to his Indonesian wedding ring; from his Cairo speech to his bowing to foreign leaders; from his conciliatory foreign policy approach to engaging the Middle East to his support of the Ground Zero mosque, the political views of his pastor, and the claimed infiltration of government by the Muslim Brotherhood—Obama's enemies have drawn from a wide range of source material to create numerous profiles of an anti-American theocrat. Obama's pursuit of sustained Bush-era military operations in the Middle East and his ordained execution of Osama bin Laden have done little to dispel the charge.

A significant number of Americans have been encouraged to believe, and continue to believe, that Obama is a Muslim, an atheist, or a Christian of a more perverse kind. These religious identity politics were initially circulated by an obscure Illinois challenger to Obama in 2004, but judging from public polling they reached national-level saturation from 2008 onward. In March 2008, in the wake of the Reverend Wright controversy, a Pew Research poll found 79 percent of public had heard the Obama-as-Muslim rumors and an average of 10 percent of respondents believed that candidate practiced Islam. Digging beneath this statistic, the Pew researchers found that this interpretation was almost bipartisan, with 14 percent of Republicans, 10 percent of Democrats, and 8 percent of independents subscribing to the Obama-as-Muslim narrative. In this poll, voters who did not attend college were three times more likely to believe the Muslim allegation as compared to respondents with a college degree. Furthermore, voters in the South and Midwest and white evangelical Protestants demonstrated a greater proclivity for accepting the characterization. Just over half accepted that Obama was a Christian, while 34 percent did not know his true affiliation. Despite the poll being taken in the weeks following the Jeremiah Wright controversy and Obama's problematic alignment with a controversial Christian congregation, the poll showed no logical abandonment of the Muslim allegation. The Pew results were virtually unchanged in a July 2008 poll and a March 2009 survey after Obama's inauguration, demonstrating the stability of the othering narrative and its seeming ability to withstand Obama's legitimization as America's popularly elected political leader.

Similarly, a study during the latter stages of the 2008 campaign conducted by the University of Georgia found that despite the efforts of the Obama campaign to dispel the myth of the de-Christianization of the candidate, a persistent 20 percent of respondents (as measured from

September through November 2008) firmly believed that Obama took his religious instruction from the Quran rather than the Bible. Notably, the poll found that a number of Americans who had initially accepted Obama as a Christian candidate had subsequently changed their minds to believe the false Obama-as-Muslim charge. Such respondents tended to be less educated, more right-wing, Biblical literalists who were predisposed to disbelieve mainstream media, "so therefore journalists telling them that this is not true could actually have the opposite effect."

In Obama's second year as president, and during the contentious midterm elections that became a referendum on Obama's administration, a Pew Research survey showed a significant rise in the number of Americans who believed that Obama is Muslim. Whereas 18 percent now held this view, a massive 43 percent were entirely uncertain about Obama's religious affiliation. The number of Americans who identified Obama as a Christian fell 14 percentage points, to just one third of respondents. A Harris Interactive poll taken in the same year showed even greater detachment from the facts: 57 percent of conservatives contacted asserted that Obama was a Muslim, while another 25 percent (one logically presumes there is no overlap) contended that Obama is the Antichrist, the enemy of Christian faith.

Even during Obama's reelection campaign, polls showed that the president's religious identification was fluid in the eye of the American public. An October 2012 Associated Press survey threw up a number of interesting replies to the question, "Do you happen to know the religion of Barack Obama?" While slightly more than one fourth believed that Obama was Protestant and 18 percent contended that he was Muslim, 5 percent claimed that he was Catholic and 10 percent claimed that he followed "some other religion" (but not Mormonism of Judaism).[1] Conversely, 67 percent of those polled recognized Romney—a candidate without the longevity of Obama's national profile—correctly as Mormon.

The literature (though it might be painful to describe it as such) sustaining Obama's religiously themed alienation is also wide ranging and ever growing. Michael Ledeen's *Obama's Betrayal of Israel* (2010) suggests that the president's pursuit of a two-state solution for the Middle East crisis is disloyal to the Jewish nation. Obama displays a policy bias

---

[1]This poll initially displayed results incorrectly, showing that 18 percent of the American public thought Obama was Jewish. That such a metric was initially accepted is testament to the seeming acceptance of Obama's varietal religious identification. http://surveys.ap.org/data/GfK/AP_Racial_Attitudes_Topline_09182012.pdf.

toward the Palestinian effort despite public assertions to the contrary, Ledeen claims, positioning Obama as an enemy of Jewish peoples and, by default, a sympathizer to the Muslim cause. From a political perspective, Ledeen's tome takes aim at the Jewish lobby's support of Obama and attempts to introduce a schism between the president and America's closest ally. If Obama's religious identity is problematic to America's friends, then surely it is also poisonous to America and her own people, is the claim.

Stephen Kirby's *Islam and Barack Hussein Obama: A Handbook on Islam* (2010) is little more than an excuse to use Obama's name (Hussein included) in the same title as the word Islam (twice). The author, a former police officer, juxtaposes his interpretation of Islam's "ugliness" against Obama's pro-Islamic statements during major addresses, including his famous Cairo speech in 2009, to indict the president's religious identity by association. A supplementary section accuses Obama as exhibiting a "telling" indifference to the killing of two U.S. Army privates in Arkansas by a Muslim convert in June 2009.

Others opined that Obama's secretive Muslim identity weakened the foreign policy and security of the United States, especially in preventing future Islamic extremist attacks. Turn the pages of Jed Babbin's *How Obama Is Transforming America's Military from Superpower to Paper Tiger* (2010), Michael Mukasey's *How Obama Has Mishandled the War on Terror* (2011), Marc Thiessen's *Courting Disaster: How the CIA Kept America Safe and How Barack Obama Is Inviting the Next Attack* (2010), Andrew McCarthy's *How Obama Embraces Islam's Sharia Agenda* (2011), or Michael Coffman's *Radical Islam in the House: The Plan to Take America for the Global Islamic State* (2013), and you will find arguments—some outrageous, all maligning—that Obama's very presence, including his religious being and biography, is a potential source of terror and national hazard. If found in the unfortunate position of reading Martin and Patricia Reott's *Unauthorized Diary of a Muslim President* (2012), you will be invited to reinterpret real world and national events through the perspective of a clandestine Islamic commander in chief. The husband-and-wife authors, self-described as "proud parents and patriots," take a "hard look at how Barack Hussein Obama is helping Islamic Supremacists to 'destroy America from within, by our own hands' and reveals the lie behind the phrase 'Islam is a religion of peace.'" If guilt by tangential association is more your groove, then Frank Gaffney's *The Muslim Brotherhood in the Obama Administration* (2012) purports that some radical Muslims have been invited to infiltrate government mainly through then-Secretary of State Hillary Clinton's advisers. Gaffney, in support of Michele Bachmann and others, supports the resurrection of a McCarthyite religious investigation, claiming that the "rise of these Muslim Brotherhood sympathizers in elite American policy circles tells the story of the success of the Brotherhood in its stealth jihad."

Even political critiques are framed within exaggerative religious terms. David Harsanyi uses the print media to suggest that debt, dependency, surrender, and death are the apocalyptic representations of America's Obama-era downfall. In *Obama's Four Horsemen: The Disasters Unleashed by Obama's Reelection* (2013), Harsanyi argues that the president's handling of domestic and foreign crises will precipitate a disaster of Biblical proportions, maligning Obama's presidency within the framework of Christian end-times. Alternatively, you could turn to the blogosphere, the cache of articles from *World Net Daily*, the greatest hits of Glenn Beck, and the more than 500,000 YouTube videos on the subject, to find a representative sample of the extent, tone, and fallacies of the Obama-as-Muslim misinformation campaign.

FROM THE FOUNDING FATHERS TO OBAMA: FEAR OF THE RELIGIOUS OTHER

As well as requiring a negative reimagining of Obama's personal biography, Obama's religious foreignization involves a resurrection of latent and institutionalized theological-political anxieties that stretch back to the cradle of America's founding.

From George Washington (accused of being a Mason) to Barack Obama (smeared as a Muslim, atheist, and terrorist), presidential disputation has continuously involved the use of religion as a basis for partisan attack. Electoral contests, increasingly dichotomous as partisanship increases, follow strategies of binary representation, hovering between ideological beatification and demonization, and the unsophisticated oppositional dialectic of candidate-saints versus candidate-sinners. Meanwhile, partisan labels become synonymous with absolute denominations. Depending on one's political persuasion and encouraged by the evolution of negative campaigning, candidates are cast as exclusively good or evil in a two-dimensional moral space where working across the "aisle" is increasingly electorally disadvantageous.

The specific demonization of presidential candidates' individual theologies, however, seems to be most pointed during times of acute national tension, uncertainty, or fear. Specific political religious othering also follows the waxing and waning of particular American attitudes toward discrete theologies. This point is illustrated through a brief examination of Jefferson, Lincoln, Roosevelt, and Obama as presidents elected to lead within periods of distinct national anxiety. When such tensions collide with contemporary or religious prejudices, potent presidential religious identity politics are made manifest.

The 1800 presidential campaign undoubtedly remains one of the most significant and contentious in America's electoral history—an epic, revolutionary political battle between Thomas Jefferson, representing the pro-French and decentralist party of Democratic Republicans, and John Adams, representing the Federalist platform of pro-British and centralist policies. Pursuit of such high idealism, however, was offset by campaigns characterized for their unprecedented level of unscrupulous, slanderous, and personal attacks. The assaults upon Jefferson were influenced, in no small measure, by the conduct and aftermath of the French Revolution (1789–1799) and specifically Jefferson's alleged Francophile sympathies with the revolutionary radicals. Despite Jefferson being the man who introduced the very concept of a "wall of separation between Church and State" as a constitutionally enshrined principle, he endured potent political critique in the form of religious identity slurs. Jefferson's religious character was sullied in a variety of ways: opponents claimed that he promoted a unhealthy questioning attitude toward God, rejected organized religion, was a follower of loose deism, was a radical atheist, and was utterly hostile to the Christian faith. Famously in 1800, the *New England Palladium* gave voice to the Federalist attack that Jefferson was a dangerous heretic:

Should the infidel Jefferson be elected to the Presidency, the seal of death is that moment set on our holy religion, our churches will be prostrated, and some infamous prostitute, under the title of goddess of reason, will preside in the sanctuaries now devoted to the worship of the most High. (Kaplan 1998)

Such vitriol seems almost familiar. Here, too, fears of foreign ideology energized religious attacks upon a presidential candidate based on biography, implied sympathies, and unabashed identity politics. Jefferson certainly possessed unorthodox religious views, was antagonistic toward the supernatural elements of religious doctrine, and was vehemently anti-clerical (influenced by his observations of the Catholic clergy's political interference in pre-Revolutionary France). His record as the prime mover in the disestablishment of religion in Virginia also contributed to the characterization of him as advocating religious intolerance. Jefferson was perhaps most accurately described as an anti-institutional deist, regularly expressing a belief in the divine, but aligned with the British Empiricism tradition. Jefferson used the concept of divine justice to support the project of abolishment and emancipation, and concluded his second inaugural with the following peroration:

I shall need, too, the favor of that Being in whose hands we are, who led our fathers, as Israel of old, from their native land and planted them in a country flowing with all the necessaries and comforts of life; who has covered our infancy with His providence and our riper years with His wisdom and power, and to whose goodness I ask you to join in supplications with me that He will so enlighten the minds of your servants, guide their councils, and prosper their measures that whatsoever they do shall result in your good, and shall secure to you the peace, friendship, and approbation of all nations. (Jefferson 1805)

Thomas Jefferson's preference for a form of Christianity without the vestments of the supernatural and supranatural was eventually encapsulated by the so-called Jefferson Bible. In this 1813 volume, formally known as *The Life and Morals of Jesus of Nazareth*, Jefferson handpicked certain sections from the New Testament, consciously excising passages relating to Christ's divinity, the event of miracles, and the resurrection claims to create a purely natural compass for human probity. Jefferson implored that "[i]n extracting the pure principles which he taught, we should have to strip off the artificial vestments in which they have been muffled by priests ... [so that] there will be found remaining the most sublime and benevolent code of morals which has ever been offered to man" (Jefferson 1829).

Throughout his life and his political campaigns, many opposed what they interpreted as Jefferson's cavalier attitude toward Christian teaching. In 1800, voting for Jefferson was, according to the Federalist press, a ballot for a "French infidel" who did not practice religious observation, equal to a "rebellion against God." In September of that year, the Federalist *Gazette of the United States* wrote that the election turned upon a single moral question: "Shall I continue in allegiance to God—and a Religious President; Or impiously declare for Jefferson—and No God!!!" As with Obama, the terminology of Jefferson's theological rejection was varied, but as Sanford maintains in *The Religious Life of Thomas Jefferson*, "To most religious people, including Jefferson's enemies, there was little difference between being atheist, deist, or infidel" (Sanford 1987 [1829]). In other words, such terms were merely the cue words for Jefferson's general religious othering, expressed in a period of post-revolutionary anxiety about European radical influence upon national integrity and the future of the Federalist Party (which, upon Jefferson's election, would never return to power).

Lincoln, too, was a transformational president in a period of American moral exigency, whose personal religiosity became the basis for political and oppositional attack. Like Jefferson, Lincoln's belief system did not fit neatly into an establishment Christian paradigm, and he consciously refused to publicize his religious beliefs. While Lincoln appealed to God in public addresses and his emancipation rhetoric, and professed a belief in an omnipotent force, he had been a free-thinking youth, disassociated from his parents' Baptist place of worship and never joined a formal congregation. This theological vacuum created a space for contemporary detractors to construct various pejorative characterizations of Lincoln as an atheist, deist, and, later, a Catholic. His colleagues remarked that he admired the works of deists, including Thomas Paine and Voltaire, and was an early follower of Darwin. A fellow Illinois lawyer, James Adams, engaged in a particularly acerbic newspaper squabble during which Adams labeled the future president as a "deist."

Lincoln subsequently earned the Whig Party's nomination for the 1846 congressional campaign in Illinois's 7th District and his opponent, Peter Cartwright—a Methodist evangelical—put religious belief front and center in the election. Cartwright's campaign began to circulate the rumor that Lincoln was an "open scoffer at Christianity," and Lincoln's associates demanded that he publish a handbill to publicly refute the potentially damaging claims. In July of that year, Lincoln published a handbill "replying to charges of infidelity" addressed to the "voters of the Seventh Congressional District":

That I am not a member of any Christian Church, is true; but I have never denied the truth of the Scriptures; and I have never spoken with intentional disrespect of religion in general, or any denomination of Christians in particular . . . I do not think I could myself, be brought to support a man for office, whom I knew to be an open enemy of, and scoffer at, religion. Leaving the higher matter of eternal consequences, between him and his Maker, I still do not think any man has the right thus to insult the feelings, and injure the morals, or the community in which he may live. If, then, I was guilty of such conduct, I should blame no man who should condemn me for it; but I do blame those, whoever they may be, who falsely put such a charge in circulation against me. (Lincoln 1953, 382)

His response was hardly a direct profession of Christian faith. Perhaps fearing the success of the eloquent preacher in garnering a large portion of the "spiritual" vote, Lincoln decided to attend one of Cartwright's regular religious meetings to put the issue to bed. Paul F. Boller provides one of the better anecdotes of the event:

After his sermon, Cartwright declared, "All who desire to lead a new life, to give their hearts to God, and go to Heaven, will stand." A sprinkling of men, women and children stood up. Then Cartwright cried: "All who do not wish to go to hell will stand!" At this point everyone stood up except Lincoln. Then said Cartwright in his gravest voice: "I observe that many responded to the first invitation to give their hearts to God and go to heaven. And I further observe that all of you save one indicated that you did not wish to go to hell. The sole exception is Mr. Lincoln, who did not respond to either invitation. May I inquire of you, Mr. Lincoln, where are you going?" Lincoln got up slowly and said quietly: "I came here as a respectful listener. I did not know I was to be singled out by Brother Cartwright. I believe in treating religious matters with due solemnity. I admit that the questions propounded by Brother Cartwright are of great importance. I did not feel called upon to answer as the rest did. Brother Cartwright asks me directly where I am going. I desire to reply with equal directness. I am going to Congress." The meeting quickly broke up. (Boller 1996, 29)

The election results showed that in certain areas Cartwright's religious-baiting had succeeded in denting Lincoln's overall majority.

During Lincoln's entry into the national political arena in 1860, the Republican's deist identity was opened to even greater scrutiny by an American public cautious of a candidate critical of Christian doctrine or the clergy. It was during this period, and in the midst of pre-Civil War tensions, that Lincoln was maligned as a clandestine Catholic, with childhood ties to the Jesuit community. Joseph Nightingale wrote:

Lincoln's early Catholic associations, if brought to light by a heightened interest in his beginnings, could be turned against him. Although any accusations that he was a "secret Catholic" could be refuted, they would be credited by the many who believed that Catholics were engaged in a conspiracy against protestant and republican America ... Many of the family's neighbors and acquaintances were Catholic ... His uncle ... married a devout Catholic from a prominent Catholic family ... Lincoln, if previous events were a harbinger, faced the possibility of charges that he came from a Catholic family, that he was a secret Catholic himself, and a tool of the Pope for the defeat of democracy. (Nightingale 1999)

Later, in 1864, the San Francisco and New Zealand press published claims that Lincoln had been baptized as a Catholic in later life (at the age of 43) by Father Raho.

The Catholic accusation, though often overlooked, represented widespread anxieties surrounding Lincoln's Christian identity and reflected a national anti-Catholic movement that reached significant proportions during Lincoln's ascendancy and the 1856 campaign. Catholic immigration was criticized as detrimental to labor markets, wage expectations, and national Protestant unity. Pamphlets, poetry, sermons, and novels proliferated the anti-Catholic sentiments of the period. The contemporary experience of Catholic nuns, for example, is illustrative of the religious tensions that Lincoln's candidacy had the potential to rouse:

Before the Civil War, nuns often didn't wear habits in public or when traveling, because of anti-Catholic hostility. In Indiana, children threw rocks at them. In New England, anti-Catholic mobs threatened to burn down their convents (and sometimes actually did). And in New York, a man walked up to a Sister in habit, called her a "damned papist bitch," and slapped her face. (McNamara 2011)

Lincoln's potential Catholicism was interpreted, like Obama's alleged Islamism, as a potential omen of national collapse—the former initiating papal infiltration, the latter marking the inauguration of an American caliphate. John F. Kennedy was also compelled to address the acceptability of his Catholic religion for presidential office, in a 1960 speech to concerned Protestant ministers.

The presidency of Franklin Delano Roosevelt, bookended as it was by the Great Depression and World War II, was an administration that oversaw an era of national anxiety and moral divarication. The rumor that Roosevelt was a closeted Jew gathered steam throughout the 1940s, propelled by decades of anti-Semitic sentiment. As with Lincoln and Obama, Roosevelt's religious attacks were based on tangential associations or early biographical details including, for example, the possibility that Roosevelt's Dutch immigrant great-great-great-great-great grandfather, Claes Martenzsen von Rosenvelt, had Jewish blood running through his veins. In each of his four electoral victories, Roosevelt consistently received more than 80 percent of the Jewish vote; in his administration, he appointed a significant number of Jewish advisers, recruited thousands of Jews as public servants, prepared the ground for Jewish representatives, and, of course, intervened in the European conflict to prevent the onslaught of Nazism. Opponents of Roosevelt's administration and the rapid societal changes ushered in by the New Deal agenda often substituted sound political debate for an accusation of Jewish infiltration, suggesting that somehow Roosevelt's political actions were contrary to the Protestant way.

Roosevelt's religious othering as a covert Jew had domestic and overseas loci. Domestically, regular criticism was leveled against Roosevelt's appointment of Jewish Americans to the top echelons of government, including Felix Frankfurter to the U.S. Supreme Court, and his selection of Henry Morgenthau as the first Jewish Treasury Secretary. Literature that criticized the president through the lens of anti-Semitism was widespread, including the pamphlet distributed by the Pelley Publishers in

1937, known as *What Every Congressman Should Know!* The front cover of this pamphlet featured the dome of the Capitol building anointed by the glowing Star of David, suggesting that Jewish influence upon government had reached its zenith. The back cover provided a blurb for the anti-Semite, anti-Roosevelt argument within its pages: "The American people are a bit fed up on being considered guinea pigs for the Zionistic experimentings of an American Kingdom of Israel" (Pelley 1936).

Three years into Roosevelt's presidency during the 1936 campaign, the anti-Semite propaganda decrying the government's religious affiliation was highly virulent. The New Deal agenda was uninspiringly caricatured as the "Jew Deal" in an article that appeared in *The White Knight,* while a pamphlet written by Robert Edmondson referenced Roosevelt's "supreme council" and administration of "Jewish revolutionary socialistic radicals" conducting business in accordance with the "seal of Solomon" (Feingold 1995). Roosevelt's prominent wartime adviser, Bernard Baruch, who had been born in the United States to German Jewish immigrant parents, was described as the "unofficial president" due to his perceived (and malign) influence on FDR. Polls commissioned toward the end of Roosevelt's administration showed that almost two thirds of the American public expressed concern regarding the influence of Jews in policymaking.

Outside the United States, Hitler reveled in the characterization of Roosevelt as a clandestine Jew, as it furthered his general enemization of the United States. In 1939, Hitler had gleefully conveyed to General Friedrich von Boetticher, the German military envoy in Washington, D.C., that he was sitting on evidentiary documents revealing Roosevelt's Jewish genealogy. Later, in 1941, he would tell a Spanish attaché the same thing, elaborating that "the arch culprit for this war is Roosevelt, with his freemasons, Jews, and the general Jewish bolshevism" (Plaud 2007). In December of the same year, Hitler informed the Finnish foreign minister that "the whole of World Jewry is on the side of the Bolsheviks" (Irving 1977). At home and abroad, Roosevelt was denigrated by anti-Semitic critics as President "Rosenfeld." Ironically, and demonstrating the fickleness of these religious identity politics, Roosevelt has subsequently been recast as an *anti*-Semite because of his perceived lack of action throughout the revisionist history of World War II and the Holocaust. Roosevelt initially resisted mass Jewish immigration—undoubtedly in part because of his fear that political opponents would use it as a tangible symbol of the president's anti-American Jewish sympathies.

Jefferson—during a post-revolutionary era characterized by fear of European-style radical atheism; Lincoln—during a period of national schism and anti-Catholicism; and Roosevelt—in an era of economic tension and internationally epic scales of anti-Semitism: each was tarnished in his respective political sphere as the religious enemy, betraying the latent fears and animosities of his contextual America. Obama's demonization as a Muslim and anti-Christian is manifest in an era of post-9/11 anxieties surrounding Islamic extremism and its orientation against American virtue.

OBAMA: ISLAM, RACE, BROWNED TERROR, AND POST-9/11 FEARS

Obama's demonization on religious grounds is both similar to, and markedly different from, that of previous administrations. The religious identity politics surrounding Obama rely upon an intersection of three key elements: (1) extant political and economic anxieties, (2) remnant anti-Islamic sentiments in the wake of the September 11, 2001, terrorist attacks, and (3) the racialized body and Orientalized biography of the president, proliferated by his opponents. These elements—some happenstance and others purposeful—are the triumvirate of undoubtedly the most pernicious religious othering ever to reach the realm of presidential office.

Like his aforementioned white forebears, Obama's presidency arrived in a period of significant national anxieties, including the Great Recession and its economic aftermath of inequality, military operations in Afghanistan and Iraq, and a transformational overhaul and expansion of health-care insurance coverage. Economics, foreign policy, and health care have accordingly been the battlegrounds for the nearly complete cleavage between the two main political parties in the United States, whereby government shutdowns, filibusters, reduced bipartisanship, and increased misinformation have engendered one of the least active, and most angry, legislative periods in U.S. history. Threats of repeal, overturnings, stalemates, blocked appointments, and Tea Party revolutions, teamed with the inability for Democrats and Republicans to work together on a single major legislative issue, have given rise to some of the lowest government approval ratings since measurement of such ratings began, ultimately creating a political space of seeming irrationality based on divisiveness, personal attack, and the hyperarousal of latent fears.

Unlike Jefferson, Lincoln, and Roosevelt, Obama inherited an America that was energized against a specific form of religiosity—namely, anti-American Islamic extremism in the wake of the 9/11 attacks. As Sue Veres Royal (2011), co-director of the U.S. in the World Initiative, has written, "The events of September 11, 2001 struck an unexpecting, yet already weary American public whose view of the rest of the world was that of a world filled with problems, disorder and dangerous people." The worldview paradigm of global complexity, danger, and mayhem was reduced to a simple binary of friend and enemy, same and other, pro-American and un-American. This linguistic strategy reconciled the public's interpretation of international chaos in the wake of the attack into a fundamentally crude fairytale narrative that "fell directly in line with precarious stereotypes—dehumanizing entire populations." In *Containing (Un)American Bodies* (2010), Mary Bloodsworth-Lugo and Carmen Lugo-Lugo contended that President George W. Bush's response to the 9/11 events throughout his administration "reinvigorated a series of oppositional pairs through rhetorical means" (1). Obama, then, inherited a bully pulpit that had systematically implemented a rhetoric of post-9/11 opposites between moral forces of native goodness and foreign evils:

Rhetorically, this effort was initiated through former President Bush's well-rehearsed statement, "Either you are with us, or you are with the terrorists" (2001), which conveyed to both the American public and the international community that support for the United States was expected—and that failure to demonstrate that support would relegate non-supporters to the category "them" (which is to say, "terrorists"). (Bloodsworth-Lugo and Lugo-Lugo 2011, 261)

It was a classic and continuous othering process between those within and outside of the United States' geographical and moral borders, which had the potential to direct the discourse far beyond the immediate historical instant. The narrative was so easily established as a mental organizational structure because it reverted to latent stereotypes of foreign, Arab and Muslim worlds—"browned" geographies now collectively termed the "axis of evil." Furthermore, through its "fluid and expansive construction, otherwise unrelated individuals and groups have been easily merged within the category 'terrorist.' "

With the dearth of any standard enemy locus—no state, no dictator, no defined territory—the Bush administration moved to endow terrorism with a certain corporeality to establish the abstract "war on terror" as a legitimate binary opposition between the American armed forces and a particular religious psychology *physically* present in the Middle East. This provided the abstract of terror with a recognizable body: that of the young Arab man, in the pose of the mythic and antithetical oriental figure, fanatical, suspicious, dangerous, and religiously alien.

This rhetorical effort to give the concept of terror a physical form has enabled Obama's opponents in the post-9/11 world to present Obama's own body as one of threatening alterity: an anti-patriot with an Islamic middle name, who was fathered by an African of Muslim ancestry, removed to Indonesia to live with his Muslim stepfather, and schooled alongside practicing Muslim children. As a result, Obama's religious foreignization has been uniquely tied to his own racial identity and biography, whereby detractors have elided his mixed-race status and Muslim associations with the "browned" concept of Islamic terrorism.

The concept of "browning," as suggested by Bloodsworth-Lugo and Lugo-Lugo, supports this interpretation. According to these writers, "browning"

marks a cyclical process through which bodies are rendered threatening (i.e., "browned") via their constructed association with post-9/11 renderings of terrorists or terrorism. Once "browned," these same bodies are offered as threats in need of containment. Thus, "browning" marks a dialectical and self-supporting process through which the same bodies marked as threats are rendered in need of constraint given their very construction as threatening (or "browned") bodies. (Bloodsworth-Lugo and Lugo-Lugo 2011, 265)

Obama's presidency collided with a period of excited Muslim fear—an acute anxiety surrounding "browned" bodies that were prepared to implode themselves through airplane hijackings and suicide bombings so as to endanger America and her citizens. Through the expansion of the "browning" project, Obama's literal body of difference, by virtue of his being of mixed race, was subsequently and powerfully aligned with his unconventional "global" biography, to create a president of dangerous alterity. When this theory is expanded to the electoral landscape, to ensure that Obama is not elected, or is impeached, or is overthrown becomes part of that impulse to contain and neutralize the browned or terroristic body.

Tied regularly with Obama's mixed-race background, parentage, name, and identity, the president's browning is undoubtedly a racial as well as religious project of demonization:

In the case of Obama, "browning" occurred via questions regarding his patriotism, his name (and thus, his ethnic background) and his religious affiliations ... in the presidential primaries, Obama was routinely positioned as a Black man, with a Muslim name—effectively placing him at the intersection of historical significances places on Black, male bodies within the United States and "newer" renderings of threatening bodies as "brown." (Bloodsworth-Lugo and Lugo-Lugo 2011, 266)

The racial and religious prejudice against black and brown bodies found its unique culmination in the Right's caricature of Obama as a radical Muslim or Black Panther revivalist. Inheriting the rhetorical and psychological framework of the Bush administration, Obama walked into a White House that had inadvertently created the conditions for Obama's religiously themed demonization. Where Bush's position in this dichotomy of good and evil was secured and protected by the othering impulse at 9/11's epicenter, Obama—as a mixed-race young man, with a Kenyan father and an Arabic middle name, with a conciliatory approach to the resolution of Middle Eastern disputes—perversely revived the primordial fears of an America under threat. The level of terror personification created the space for the identity politics that formed the basis of the hard Right's anti-Obama attack. As Veres Royal (2011) maintains, "In times of heightened fear and anxiety, stereotypes are exacerbated, identity with one's own group increases, suspicion of other groups is heightened, and we hold tightly to familiar/default scenarios." The corporealization of terror in the aftermath of the September 11 attacks meant that terrorism could now technically inhabit any potential host body, like some anti-American epidemic ready to destroy the *body politic*, even if that body is the president of the United States. Obama has inherited and largely maintained a Middle East policy from the Bush administration, which in turn has maintained the rhetorical binary of American good versus Islamic evil. In other, well-expressed words,

without the clear articulation of an enemy *by* Obama (or his administration), recent anxieties have found their location *in* Obama (or his administration). Within many contexts, Obama himself has emerged as the paradigmatic enemy "other." (Bloodsworth-Lugo and Lugo-Lugo 2011, 274)

THE OBAMA-AS-MUSLIM CONSPIRACY: A DECADE OF HIJACKED IDENTITY

In March 2004, while he was still an Illinois state senator, Obama sat down with journalist Cathleen Falsani in a Chicago café to talk about God. In response to Falsani's first question, "What do you believe," Obama gave a seemingly uncontroversial four word responsorial: "I am a Christian" (Falsani 2004). We have come to expect little else from potential presidential candidates.

Now fast-forward a decade to 2014, and PolitiFact.com is once again assessing the validity of the latest conspiracy theory alleging Obama's Islamic fanaticism and its impact on U.S. policy. On this occasion, the fact-checking platform is analyzing an accusation, distributed on social media and in chain emails, that Obama has established a "nationwide Muslim outreach program for children" so that children can earn higher grades upon completion of Islamic theological study. The online story reported that Obama had held a news conference in which he had said, "I encourage every student in America to participate in your school's Muslim outreach program. Learn about the Muslim community, the beauty of the Sunnah and the magic of the Qur'an." Under scrutiny, the website gave it the rating "Pants on Fire" on its infamous truth-o-meter. In fact, the claim bore linguistic similarities to a previous (and also entirely false) claim made in October 2013 that Obama was creating National Muslim Appreciation Month in November.

The story of what had transpired during those intervening years to create the gulf of perception between Obama's avowed Christianity and his disparaged religious persona is the process of Obama's demonization and de-Christianization for the political purposes of the Right. As with each of the frames of Obama's othering, these systematic mistruths have been sustained by a pejorative and often racialized interpretation of Obama's biography and life influences.

Admittedly, Obama religious background, which is tied to his international identity, defies conventional definition. Obama's mother was, according to Obama, "one of the most spiritual people I knew," but did not foster a "religious household." Her own parents were practicing Christians, Baptist and Methodist, and ultimately joined a Universalist congregation, but Obama's mother "wasn't a church lady." Although Dunham rejected organized religion, she had, according to her son, "as much influence on my values as anybody," though she did not wear "her religion on her sleeve." Obama explains the philosophy of his early spiritual guidance:

I don't think as a child I had a structured religious education. But my mother was deeply spiritual person, and would spend a lot of time talking about values and give me books about the world's religions, and talk to me about them. And I think always, her view always was that underlying these religions were a common set of beliefs about how you treat other people and how you aspire to act, not just for yourself but also for the greater good. (Falsani 2004)

His African father (and namesake) was born to a Muslim family and tradition in Kenya, yet Barack Obama, Sr., identified as an agnostic or atheist during his adulthood. Regardless, his father was largely absent from Obama's entire life, returning to Kenya when the future president was only two years old and having spent much of his time at Harvard University in Massachusetts during the younger Obama's infancy. Obama later spent some of his formative childhood in Indonesia, a Muslim-majority country, with a Muslim stepfather—"a man who saw religion as not particularly useful." While there, he was educated at a

school with a significant Muslim cohort. Obama also attended a Catholic
school, which in Indonesia provided a patchwork of theological expo-
sure: "I went to a Catholic school in a Muslim country. So I was studying
the Bible and catechisms by day, and at night you'd hear the prayer call."
    Like his mother, Obama has regularly expressed his inheritance of a
tolerance for, and sensitivity to, religious heterogeneity:

I draw from the Christian faith. On the other hand, I was born in Hawaii where
obviously there are a lot of Eastern influences. I lived in Indonesia, the largest
Muslim country in the world, between the ages of six and 10. My father was from
Kenya, and although he was probably most accurately labeled an agnostic, his
father was Muslim. And I'd say, probably, intellectually I've drawn as much from
Judaism as any other faith. So, I'm rooted in the Christian tradition. I believe that
there are many paths to the same place, and that is a belief that there is a higher
power, a belief that we are connected as a people. That there are values that tran-
scend race or culture, that move us forward, and there's an obligation for all of us
individually as well as collectively to take responsibility to make those values
lived. (Falsani 2004)

    Obama's journey to becoming an official congregant of the Trinity
United Church of Christ grew out of his work alongside church and
Christian groups as a young community organizer in Chicago. In a
2006 speech on faith and public service, the future president described
that he viewed religious devotion as an integral and contributory force
for positive social change in America, citing the African American religious tradition in the history of the black struggle. While in Chicago in
the 1980s, Obama "came to realize that something was missing" and
was "drawn not just to work with the church, but to be in the church,"
understanding faith as "an active, palpable agent in the world ... a source
of hope" for the community around him. Eventually, after building a
friendship with pastor Jeremiah Wright, he formalized his commitment
to Christianity:

I was finally able to walk down the aisle of Trinity United Church of Christ on
95th Street in the Southside of Chicago one day and affirm my Christian faith.
It came about as a choice, and not an epiphany. I didn't fall out in church. The
questions I had didn't magically disappear. But kneeling beneath that cross on
the South Side, I felt that I heard God's spirit beckoning me. I submitted myself
to His will, and dedicated myself to discovering His truth. (Harrison and Gilbert
2007, 102)

    Since then, Obama has recognized the importance of understanding a
person's faith as a codex for harnessing individual beliefs and values,

particularly in progressive politics. "If we truly hope to speak to people where they're at," Obama said, "to communicate our hopes and values in a way that's relevant to their own—then as progressives, we cannot abandon the field of religious discourse" (Harrison and Gilbert 2007, 102). If we bleach the religious lexicon from the language of political conversation, he argues, we would lose something of the prism through which Americans come to understand social justice and morality:

> Imagine Lincoln's *Second Inaugural Address* without reference to "the judgments of the Lord." Or King's *I Have a Dream* speech without references to "all of God's children." Their summoning of a higher truth helped inspire what had seemed impossible, and move the nation to embrace a common destiny. (Harrison and Gilbert 2007, 103)

For Obama, his faith—and what that faith guided him to do for his common man—was a personal belief, with a public (or even political) dimension. In so stating, Obama could have little imagined the ensuing transmogrification of his personal belief system, through partisan demonization, into a form of theological fanaticism that presented a public evil of some sort. When Obama expressed the important interaction between private faith and political action, he could not have predicted the accusation from the extreme Right that he has used his own Christianity as a public and calculated façade, hiding a private, and politically inconvenient, Islamic extremism or radical atheism beneath.

Obama's de-Christianization and Islamification by political opponents for electoral gain began in 2004, during his campaign for the U.S. Senate. The state senator from Illinois had just been catapulted to a position of national prominence following his keynote address ("We Are One People") to the Democratic National Convention when, only days later, the perennial candidate and litigator, Andy Martin, initiated the slur that Obama is a secret Muslim. "I feel sad having to expose Barack Obama," Martin wrote, "but the man is a complete fraud." Selectively drawing upon elements of Obama's genealogy, Martin concluded that Obama "is a Muslim who has concealed his religion" with a name that is both "Arabic and Koranic" in association, placing him beyond the border limits of the "Land of Lincoln" (Martin 2004). The overall implication was that the Illinois senator was a significant pro-Islamic threat to American values and the Jewish state, as an unknown entity surrounded by (manufactured) whispered associations.

During that same campaign, Obama's Republican opponent, Alan Keyes, who was drafted to run late in the race after the original nominee became ensnared in a sex scandal, assaulted Obama's religious identity from another angle. Keyes, who also called Obama a socialist and a liar, is famed for his intemperate rhetorical style. In this campaign, he focused on social issues, including abortion. Keyes contrasted his supposedly divinely inspired pro-life position with Obama's pro-choice stance and deduced that if God had a vote, he would not be casting it for the Democratic candidate:

Jesus Christ would not vote for Barack Obama. Christ would not vote for Barack Obama because Barack Obama has behaved in a way that is inconceivable for Christ to have behaved. (Harrison and Gilbert 2007, 98)

That theological-cum-political assertion is a stunning utterance from any potential U.S. senator, but here its intent was to follow Martin's Muslim aspersion and to denude Obama of all Christian support. In so doing, Keyes, taking the stance of a prophet, tried to construct a crude binary in which a vote for the Democratic candidate was a vote against the Christian savior. (It also reinforced President George W. Bush's born-again rhetoric, which had become commonplace in the justifying discourse of his Middle East policy.) Obama knew that this was the vitriol of an opponent "well-versed in the Jerry Falwell–Pat Robertson style of rhetoric that often labels progressives as both immoral and godless" (Harrison and Gilbert 2007, 98). Nevertheless. it deeply affected him. Even though he was 40 points up in the polls, Obama later said, "I had to take Mr. Keyes seriously, for he claimed to speak for my religion, and my God. He claimed knowledge of certain truths ... I was running to be the U.S. Senator of Illinois and not the Minister of Illinois" (98).

Following his election to the Senate, the de-Christianization and Islamification of Obama temporarily died down. Then, as rumors emerged that the junior senator was a potential candidate in the upcoming presidential contest, those looking for negative campaign materials turned to Andy Martin's claims of religious suspicion and revived them. In a *U.S. Veteran Dispatch* piece in December 2006, titled "Barack Hussein Obama: Who Is He?," Ted Sampley revived the original claims and embellished them with a cartoon depiction of Obama wearing a blue fez that bore both Christian and Muslim emblems, communicating Obama's implied religious murkiness. Mixing metaphors, the email called Obama the "messiah in the Democratic party" who has "been walking on water toward the White House" while being "a threat to the Jewish people because he is a closet Muslim." The evidence? His "Arabic Koranic" name, of course. The blogosphere began to reflexively substantiate further claims by relying upon Martin's and Sampley's false remarks as authoritative source material, embellishing the claims for Obama's religious status with a catalogue of new demonizing features.

At the end of 2006, Debbie Schlussel—an attorney, political commentator, and all-round conservative controversy-chaser—claimed to have been initially unconvinced at the Muslim rumors, but upon the strength of her own "research" became an advocate for the Islamic conspiracy. On her own website, she provided a mainly accurate biography of the president but with an Islamic bias, before lurching to the fantastical:

> While Obama may not identify as a Muslim, that's not how the Arab and Muslim streets see it. In Arab culture and Islamic law, if your father is a Muslim, so are you. And once a Muslim, always a Muslim. You cannot go back. In Islamic eyes, Obama is certainly a Muslim. He may think he is a Christian, but they do not. (Schlussel 2006)

According to Schlussel, Obama could no longer lay claim to his own religious identity; instead, the issue was settled by overseas Islamic forces to which Obama and his faith belonged. In the binary rhetoric of the post-9/11 world, Schlussel maintained that no matter what Obama said publicly, the potential election of a covert Muslim would place American patriotic interests in immediate peril, because the president would be directly and theologically aligned with U.S. enemies:

> So, even if he identifies strongly as a Christian, and even if he despised the behavior of his father (as Obama said on *Oprah*); is a man who Muslims think is a Muslim, who feels some sort of psychological need to prove himself to his absent Muslim father, and who is now moving in the direction of his father's heritage, a man we want as President when we are fighting the war of our lives against Islam? Where will his loyalties be?
> Is that even the man we'd want to be a heartbeat away from the Presidency, if Hillary Clinton offers him the Vice Presidential candidacy on her ticket (which he certainly wouldn't turn down)?
> NO WAY, JOSE ... Or, is that, HUSSEIN? (Schlussel 2006)

Within the browned framework of the war on terror, Obama was not just affiliated with Islam, but was a maniacal Muslim with a psychological need to prove himself to an absent father. According to Schlussel, Obama's political mission parallels that of the 9/11 hijackers, who had a warped aspiration to prove themselves worthy of their own religious patriarch, Allah.

As with many of the tropes of Obama's othering, the Muslim slur was given some of its oxygen in the Democratic primary campaign by way of Hillary Clinton's organization. December 2007 marked the tightening up of the Clinton versus Obama polling numbers in a number of key states, including Iowa and New Hampshire, where campaigning reached a fever pitch. It was in the latter state that one of Hilary Clinton's "250 Iowa Women" took matters into her own hands and initiated an online assault on Obama's religion and background. The chain email, which went through dozens of equally pernicious and ill-advised iterations, is worth quoting in full for its encapsulation of a wide range of the Obama Islamification efforts during this period, replete with emphatic capitalization and exclamation points:

Subject: **Who is Barack Obama?**
    *_Most_* of this appears to be true! *I shutter [sic] to think!! *Scary guy!
    We checked this out on "snopes.com." It is factual. Check for yourself. *
If you do not ever forward anything else, please forward this to all your contacts ... this is very scary to think of what lies ahead of us here in our own United States ... better heed this and pray about it and share it.
THIS DEFINITELY WARRANTS LOOKING INTO. THIS COUNTRY WAS FOUNDED, "ONE NATION UNDER GOD." ALMIGHTY GOD, NOT THE GOD OF THE KORAN.
Who is Barack Obama?
Probable U.S. presidential candidate, Barack Hussein Obama was born in Honolulu , Hawaii, to Barack Hussein Obama, Sr., a black MUSLIM from Nyangoma-Kogel, Kenya, and Ann Dunham, a white ATHEIST from Wichita, Kansas.
Obama's parents met at the University of Hawaii. When Obama was two years old, his parents divorced. His father returned to Kenya. His mother then married Lolo Soetoro, a RADICAL Muslim from Indonesia. When Obama was 6 years old, the family relocated to Indonesia. Obama attended a MUSLIM school in Jakarta. He also spent two years in a Catholic school. Obama takes great care to conceal the fact that he is a Muslim. He is quick to point out that, "He was once a Muslim, but that he also attended Catholic school."
Obama's political handlers are attempting to make it appear that Obama's introduction to Islam came via his father, and that this influence was temporary at best. In reality, the senior Obama returned to Kenya soon after the divorce, and never again had any direct influence over his son's education.
Lolo Soetoro, the second husband of Obama's mother, Ann Dunham, introduced his stepson to Islam. Obama was enrolled in a Wahabi school in Jakarta.
Wahabism is the RADICAL teaching that is followed by the Muslim terrorists who are now waging Jihad against the western world. Since it is politically expedient to be a CHRISTIAN when seeking major public office in the United

States, Barack Hussein Obama has joined the United Church of Christ in an attempt to downplay his Muslim background.

ALSO, keep in mind that when he was sworn into office he DID NOT use the Holy Bible, but instead the Koran (their equivalency to our Bible, but very different beliefs).

Let us all remain alert concerning Obama's expected presidential candidacy.

The Muslims have said they plan on destroying the U.S. from the inside out, what better way to start than at the highest level—through the President of the United States, one of their own!!!!

Please forward to everyone you know. Would you want this man leading our country? . . . NOT ME!!! (Smith 2007)

The sender of the email received by a *Daily Kos* journalist was Judy Rose, a county coordinator for the Hillary Clinton campaign, and secretary of Jones County Democrats. Although there was never any evidence of consortium, many critics simply did not believe that the micromanaged campaign, or Clinton herself, was ignorant of the email's circulation. The campaign fired Rose and denied any potential endorsement of the outrageous memo:

There is no place in our campaign, or any campaign, for this kind of politics. A volunteer county coordinator made the mistake of forwarding an outrageous and offensive chain e-mail. This was wholly unauthorized and we were totally unaware of it. Let me be clear: No one should be engaging in this. We are asking this volunteer county coordinator to step down and are making it clear to every person involved in our campaign that this will not be tolerated. (Bacon 2007)

Obama responded to the incident, without descending to address the elements of the religious demonization itself. "I just think that the Iowa caucus goer is looking for an honest and real debate about their issues," he said. "If other folks want to engage in those kinds of small-time tactics, then that's their prerogative, but that's not what we're going to focus on" (Bacon 2007). There is no doubt that his reference to those "other folks" implied the involvement of the central Hillary Clinton machine.

In its own way, the email is instructive to the student of Obama's religious othering via negative and deceptive identity politics. Obama is presented as the Islamic Manchurian candidate, apparently groomed by external terrorist forces to undo the very republic from within its highest office. For completion of this ridiculous syllogism, proponents rely upon reinterpreted biographical details and skewed significations. First, according to this email, Obama received a curriculum of extremist

Wahhabi philosophy, delivered in Madrassa classrooms, alongside terrorist children. Second, Obama demonstrated his true Islamic faith by
choosing to swear his oath of office upon the Quran. Third, so devoted
is he to the anti-American Islamic cause that Obama refuses to recite the
Pledge of Allegiance or acknowledge the national flag. Ergo, Obama is
an American Osama bin Laden. The problem is that not only are the conclusions of Obama's religiosity contrary to fact, but each of the premises
upon which they are built is wildly, and often knowingly, inaccurate. To
evoke post-9/11 religious fear, Obama's opponents numb natural incredulity through sheer quantity and repetition. By way of illustration, let us
briefly examine these three premises.

Obama never attended a school that would fit the Western conception of
a madrassa—that is, an education center for the preaching of anti-American
radical Islam. Nor was Obama exposed to the fundamentalist readings of
the Quran as part of a Wahhabi syllabus. Between the years of 1967 and
1971 in Indonesia, Obama attended a Catholic school and later a public
school with a majority cohort of Muslim students, yet there is no extant
source material or corroborative testimony to even suggest that Obama
was exposed to fundamentalist theology at either location. In 2007, however, *Insight Magazine* (a sister organization to *The Washington Times*)
claimed that researchers linked to Clinton's campaign had uncovered information that Obama had attended a madrassa that taught the most radicalizing form of Islam. *Insight*'s editor, Jeff Kuhner, claimed that the Clinton
campaign was preparing to deploy the information as a weapon of character assassination. Lowell Ponte, writing for *Newsmax*, contended that
Obama might "become the first American president whose thinking was
shaped by childhood in a Muslim madrassa in Islamic Indonesia" (Press
2012, 59). Moreover, in June 2007, Michael Savage urged Obama to "say
that you proudly went to a Muslim school as a youth that indoctrinated
you in certain manners—and tell us what your indoctrination was ... and
tell us whether you believe in that doctrination or you gave up those beliefs,
Mr. Barack Hussein Obama" (Walzer 2007).

PolitiFact gave the rumor a "Pants on Fire wrong" rating on its truth-o-
meter spectrum. In doing so, it referenced conclusive investigations made by
CNN, AP, the *Los Angeles Times*, and the *Chicago Tribune*, each of which

investigated the e-mail claims by visiting the school and interviewing former
teachers and students who were there at the same time as Obama. These investigations found a public school where students wore Western clothing and prayer
was a small part of the curriculum. The *Chicago Tribune* reported the school
was "so progressive that teachers wore miniskirts and all students were encouraged to celebrate Christmas." (PolitiFact 2007)

John Vause, who debunked the claim for CNN, found that, instead of rigorous Wahhabi brainwashing, students received approximately two hours of religious instruction every week, tailored to his or her private beliefs. Akmad Solichin, the school's vice principal, told the Associated Press that the school community represents a variety of faiths including Christianity and Buddhism: "Everyone is welcome here ... it's a public school." Obama's own remembrance of his time at the school certainly does not suggest that he was magnetized to Islamic belief. "The teacher wrote to tell my mother I made faces during Koranic studies," Obama wrote. "My mother wasn't overly concerned."

Then there is the accusation that in January 2005 Obama took his senatorial oath of office while placing his hand upon the Quranic text, rather than a Christian Bible. This is yet another "Pants on Fire wrong," easily debunked narrative of right-wing irrationality channeled to form part of Obama's religious foreignization. The oath was administered by then-Vice President Dick Cheney (one of the chief architects of America's war on terror) and the ceremony was reported on by journalists, who referenced that Obama chose to use his own *Bible,* with the details confirmed by the campaign. One theory is that this story was a reapplication of a real-life event from 2007. Minnesota Congressman Keith Ellison, a Muslim American, used a copy of the Quran for his swearing-in ceremony from the collection of Thomas Jefferson, loaned to him by the Library of Congress. While both men are African American and Democratic politicians, Ellison is Muslim and Obama is Protestant. It was as though someone swapped the nametags and hoped that no one would notice.

Finally, the idea that Obama does not partake in the Pledge of Allegiance is easily disproved by the most cursory of search engine research. This accusation stems from a photograph taken during an Iowa steak-fry attended by Democratic presidential candidates, in which Obama is standing without his hand on his chest, while Hillary Clinton and Bill Richardson are. Although the context and sequence of events surrounding this image are uncertain, Obama has been pictured numerously elsewhere in traditional cross-heart posture. Obama wrote that his grandfather taught him "when I was 2" that "during the Pledge of Allegiance, you put your hand over your heart. During the national anthem you sing." Obama has also led the Pledge of Allegiance when presiding in the U.S. Senate.

The notion that Obama does not respect the star-spangled banner is similar to other claims that Obama has attempted to supplant the current flag with a red, green, and gold banner "meant to symbolize Islam and socialism." Although this rumor was initially posted by the satirical news platform *The Daily Currant* in 2012, it was still in circulation in January 2014, claiming that "the red portion sports a Soviet hammer and sickle ... the green section features the phrase 'People's Republic of America' written in Arabic."

Responding to all three claims in a Democratic primary debate in January 2008, Obama spoke with a rare directness on religious targeting by his political adversaries: "In the Internet age there are going to be lies spread all over the place. I have been victimized by these lies ... these emails were going out in Iowa, they were going out in New Hampshire and we did just fine" (Davis 2008).

Throughout 2008, insinuation turned to all-out scaremongering. Congressman Steve King, for example, predicted that Obama's successful election would be celebrated as an anti-American victory by fanatical religious constituencies abroad. Taking an overseas perspective of the visual rhetoric of Obama's ascendancy, King uttered the following words of explicit demonization:

I don't want to disparage anyone because of their race, their ethnicity, their name—whatever their religion their father might have been, I'll just say this: When you think about the optics of a Barack Obama potentially getting elected President of the United States—I mean, what does this look like to the rest of the world? What does it look like to the world of Islam? I will tell you that, if he is elected president, then the radical Islamists, the al-Qaida, the radical Islamists and their supporters, will be dancing in the streets in greater numbers than they did on September 11. (Ross 2013)

To be clear, King predicts that Obama's election would represent a terrorist triumph of a far greater magnitude than that witnessed on 9/11. Michael Bloomberg, mayor of New York City, urged the Jewish community in Florida not to be persuaded by the rhetoric claiming that the Democratic candidate was a secret Muslim and enemy of Israel: "I hope all of you will join me throughout this campaign in strongly speaking out against this fear mongering, no matter who you'll be voting for." Meanwhile, in February 2008, Obama's campaign accused Clinton's organization of pursuing a racialized dirty tricks campaign by circulating an image of Obama wearing African dress during his visit to Kenya to the press.

It was little wonder, then, that on election night in November 2008, as John McCain delivered a very amicable concession speech in light of Obama's considerable victory, members of the notably choleric crowd began shouting punctuating their boos with the shout of "terrorist." So widely distributed was the story that Obama represented a radical extremist constituency of Middle Eastern terrorist groups that even an occasion ordinarily overflowing with conciliation and gentility was polluted by an unfounded and visceral vocalization of presidential religious othering.

Throughout Obama's first presidential campaign and well into his presidency, the religion-based partisan attacks continued, peaking during the midterm and presidential elections, but never really going away. Following the Jeremiah Wright controversy (see Chapter 3), another chain email pursued Obama's complete de-Christianization by stating that the future president was the Antichrist and herald of end-times. Even as the Antichrist, however, Obama was still defined as a Muslim. Snopes.com described the accusation as another example of presage used for "denigrative fiction." In full, the email claimed:

The anti-Christ will be a man, in his 40s, of MUSLIM descent, who will deceive the nations with persuasive language, and have a MASSIVE Christ-like appeal. . . . the prophecy says that people will flock to him and he will promise false hope and world peace, and when he is in power, will destroy everything. Is it OBAMA??

I STRONGLY URGE each one of you to repost this as many times as you can! Each opportunity that you have to send it to a friend or media outlet . . . do it!

If you think I am crazy . . . I'm sorry but I refuse to take a chance on the "unknown" candidate. (Emery 2008)

Of course, the Book of Revelations says no such thing about American presidential politics, and Obama is not a Muslim. Instead, Revelations speaks of a Beast (never an Antichrist), but there is no definition of the Beast's theological descent or middle age. Indeed, any such statement would need to be doubly prophetic, considering that the Islamic religion was not founded until centuries later. Perhaps all the evidence one needs that the accusation is worthless of consideration is that the Westboro Baptist Church has adopted the conspiracy with some zeal, devoting an entire website, BeastObama.com, to its verification. YouTube is littered with videos "proving" Obama's satanic identity. For example, the 2009 creation "Did Jesus Give Us the Name of the Antichrist?" uses linguistic manipulation and stretching translations to say that "Barack Obama" is a by-phrase for "Lightning from the Skies," a Hebraic term for the coming of the Antichrist.

Obama's now-famous and unprecedented address to the Muslim world in Cairo, delivered June 4, 2009, translated the president's campaign promise of a refined tone in foreign policy into an oration calling for a new beginning between the Islamic community and the West. It cannot have escaped the listener that the speech was not just a plea for international harmony, but also a cathartic call to heal the domestic political and religious divisions rendered by his own election and the fictitious claims around him.

We meet at a time of great tension between the United States and Muslims around the world—tension rooted in historical forces that go beyond any current policy debate. The relationship between Islam and the West includes centuries of coexistence and cooperation, but also conflict and religious wars. More recently, tension has been fed by colonialism that denied rights and opportunities to many Muslims, and a Cold War in which Muslim-majority countries were too often treated as proxies without regard to their own aspirations. Moreover, the sweeping change brought by modernity and globalization led many Muslims to view the West as hostile to the traditions of Islam.

Violent extremists have exploited these tensions in a small but potent minority of Muslims. The attacks of September 11, 2001, and the continued efforts of these extremists to engage in violence against civilians has led some in my country to view Islam as inevitably hostile not only to America and Western countries, but also to human rights. All this has bred more fear and more mistrust. [...]

I've come here to Cairo to seek a new beginning between the United States and Muslims around the world, one based on mutual interest and mutual respect, and one based upon the truth that America and Islam are not exclusive and need not be in competition. Instead, they overlap, and share common principles—principles of justice and progress; tolerance and the dignity of all human beings. (Obama 2009)

Obama used the speech to reaffirm that "I'm a Christian," but also referenced his experiences of Islam "on three continents" in shaping his "conviction that partnership between America and Islam must be based on what Islam is, not what it isn't." He quoted from the Quran, hailed contributions to human progress by the Arabic world, reaffirmed the United States' alliance with Israel, and expressed support for a Palestinian state. Throughout the oration, the president spoke against crude stereotypes of both Islam and America, considering it part of his "responsibility as president of the United States to fight against negative stereotypes of Islam wherever they appear."

Remarkably, the domestic reaction to the wide-ranging speech by Obama's opponents merely revived old patterns of the president's own negative Islamification. Fox News, in particular, spent days claiming that Obama refused to acknowledge Islamic terrorism in his address, viewing the "omission" as a euphemism for Obama's soft-on-terror approach. Sean Hannity, Lou Dobbs, and Megyn Kelly seemed to suggest that Obama's conscious deployment of the term "violent extremism" instead of "terror" betrayed a form of anti-Americanism. Newt Gingrich, in conversation with Hannity, said:

Well, I think you captured part of what's going on here, which is you have a man who's in considerable conflict with himself. On the one hand, he's trying to reach out to the Muslim world and trying to open up a new dialogue. On the other hand, he just can't help himself in blaming America first. (Allison and Fong 2009)

That 10 members of the Muslim Brotherhood's parliamentary bloc were invited to attend the speech prompted Scott Wheeler, director of the National Republican Trust PAC, to assert that "The American people did not vote for President Barack Hussein Obama to make peace with Muslim terrorists." Ann Coulter denounced the speech for overestimating Muslims' contribution to intellectual progress, while Mitt Romney in 2011 and Ted Cruz in 2012 expounded the sound bite that Obama's Cairo speech was part of a larger anti-American, pro-Islamic apology tour initiated when Obama assumed office, which ultimately weakened the nation's global position.

During his presidential announcement speech, Romney attacked Obama's conciliatory foreign policy language while traveling "around the globe to apologize for America." This was not the first time the Republican candidate had made such claims. In fact, Romney named his 2010 book *No Apology* in direct contradistinction to Obama's supposed confessional presidency. In the work, Romney compared Obama's diplomatic parlance to the terrorist arson of Muslims abroad:

Never before in American history has its president gone before so many foreign audiences to apologize for so many American misdeeds, both real and imagined. . . . It is his way of signaling to foreign countries and foreign leaders that their dislike for America is something he understands and that is, at least in part, understandable. There are anti-American fires burning all across the globe; President Obama's words are like kindling to them. (Romney 2010, 25)

The demonization was relentless. Rush Limbaugh, in a self-consciously controversial move, began to describe the president as Imam Obama. Michele Bachmann, as part of her wider campaign to locate anti-American political representatives, suggested that Obama had pursued a terrorist plot to bring a swine flu epidemic to the United States.

On April 29, 2011, Obama gave the order to initiate the successful capture of America's greatest enemy from the world of extremist Islam. Two days later, at 11:35 p.m., Obama stood in the East Room of the White House and provided an extraordinary address informing the world that the architect of the September 11 attacks had been captured and killed as part of a SEAL force operation. The announcement was a landmark in the United States' fight against anti-American extremism, a therapeutic event in the post-9/11 psychology. Crowds holding banners, chanting " U.S.A.," and singing the national anthem spontaneously gathered at New York's Ground Zero site, the White House, and Times Square as part of an outpouring of national fervor and relief. Despite Obama's achievement of what Bush had failed to do, the right-wing press seized upon Obama's handling of Osama bin Laden's death as evidence of his pro-Islamic, and thus anti-American, sympathies. In an editorial published by *The Washington Times,* "America's Muslim president Obama bungled Osama killing with too much respect for Islam," the paper claimed:

The White House went out of its way to make certain that Osama bin Laden received full traditional Muslim burial rites. Obama officials claimed they did so to honor the Islamic religion, but they were also honoring bin Laden. Such acts are unacceptable on behalf of America's mortal enemy; no one suggested Adolf Hitler's remains receive a Viking funeral. (*The Washington Times* 2011)

Fox Nation picked up a story from *Right Wing Watch* and posted it on its website, claiming that "Obama Was Photoshopped into Bin Laden Raid Situation Room Photo." As the White House refused to release the pictures of Osama bin Laden's dead body, fearing that to do so would create recruitment propaganda for Islamic extremism, many have claimed that the Al Qaeda leader is still alive. Steve Doocy and Andrew Napolitano, for example, stated that the reports of Operation Neptune Spear were falsified so as to improve the president's domestic polling. Alex Jones devoted a number of his online videos to describing Osama bin Laden's capture and death as a "giant hoax." On the fringes of this anti-Obama extremism, some stated that Obama was, in fact, "100 percent" Osama bin Laden—that he was still alive as the 44th president of the United States. Others suggested that the announcement was delayed so as to conflict with Donald Trump's *Celebrity Apprentice* program schedule, as punishment for Trump's pursuit of the Birther conspiracy. From Obama's Birther critics, there now emerged an entirely new movement of Osama "Deathers." So entrenched were Obama's opponents in the narrative of Obama's Islamic otherness that they could not process the Osama bin Laden death in a conventional way because it did not comport with their anti-Obama confirmation bias.

The maligning of Obama's religious identity focused not only on his Islamification, but also on a process of de-Christianization, placing distance between the president and America's traditional monotheism. In early November 2011, the House of Representatives bizarrely tabled a debate to reconfirm the country's national motto as "In God We Trust." While the country looked to Washington for economic improvement in the midst of a depression, legislators were temporarily engaged in reaffirming the national motto, which was already guaranteed by an act of Congress in 1956 and a further bill passage in 2002. One of the bill's sponsors, Representative J. Randy Forbes (Republican-Virginia), cited the lack of awareness among public servants as to what the national motto was for the bill's introduction; no doubt he had in mind Obama's 2010 misstep when he incorrectly quoted *E pluribus Unum* as the national motto during a speech in Jakarta, Indonesia. The debate was arguably orchestrated to resurrect questions of Obama's own religiosity, suggesting that during Obama's presidency an affirmation of ceremonial deism was a necessary restorative for America's very soul. It was as though Congress was engaged in an exorcism of government, believing it to be currently inhabited by a maligned religious identity. Obama was incensed with the House's willingness to sacrifice legislative action in favor of partisan attack, calling out Majority Leader John Boehner directly:

"In the House of Representatives, what have you guys been doing, John? You've been debating a commemorative coin for baseball. You've had legislation reaffirming that 'In God We Trust' is our motto. That's not putting people back to work," Obama said. "I trust in God, "but God wants to see us help ourselves by putting people back to work." (Mason 2011)

Congress had debated the ceremonial motto within the framework of Obama's religious demonization, to the detriment of legislative focus on infrastructure projects, economic repair, and efforts to increase jobs.

During the 2012 election, the slur that the incumbent president was in some way conducting a program of American de-Christianization inspired Mitt Romney, upon reciting the Pledge of Allegiance in Virginia Beach, to say the following:

The promises that were made in that pledge are promises I plan on keeping if I'm president, and I've kept them so far in my life. That pledge says "under God." I will not take "God" out of the name of our platform. I will not take "God" off our coins and I will not take God out of my heart. (PolitiFact 2012)

His speech was notable for being heavily focused on religion, presenting Romney as *the* candidate intent on protecting theological expression in the public sphere. It followed a decision made by Democrats (sub-sequently overturned) to scrub the word "God" from the dais signs at the Democratic National Convention. With all the subtlety of a rhetorical sledgehammer, Romney attacked Obama as someone antithetical to the-istic belief. Only Romney could preserve the Pledge of Allegiance, the motto on U.S. coins, and the faith in Americans' hearts from the grab of Obama's reelected antifaith, big government.

Obama's campaign, having heard similar claims raised by Sarah Palin in 2009, was evidently concerned about the impact of the president's ongoing religious foreignization. Spokesperson Jen Psaki responded:

This is nothing more than a desperate attack based on a false premise by the Romney team and it's sad that the debate has been driven to this level of dis-course. The president believes as much that God should be taken off a coin as he does that aliens will attack Florida. It's an absurd question to be raised. (PolitiFact 2012)

In 2007, under the George W. Bush administration, the U.S. Mint began to produce a series of coins memorializing past presidents. The coins had been initially authorized with a design that placed the phrases "In God We Trust" and "E pluribus Unum" on the edge, and not the face, of the currency. The design was immediately contentious. Romney had objected to the mint's new design in September 2007, this time naming the American Civil Liberties Union (ACLU) as the de-Christianizing enemy:

Have you seen the new dollar coin? "In God We Trust" has been moved. It's not on the face of the coin anymore, it's on the edge—virtually invisible, just like the (American Civil Liberties Union) wants Him to be. I will go to work to get God back on the front of our coin. (PolitiFact 2012)

A bill was ultimately introduced, with more than 100 Republican co-sponsors, calling for the return of the national motto to a front-and-center position on all future presidential and specialist coins. Bush signed the readjustment into law, with the new design taking effect from 2009, yet the episode of Bush-era paranoia was revived and reapplied in the age of Obama to suggest the president's negative religious mutability.

If one is interested in seeing the measure and motives of presidential candidates, examination of the strategies deployed in those final desper-ate days of their campaigns is often the most instructive—and that is cer-tainly true in examining Obama's religious denigration. Even on the eve of the 2012 general election, Mitt Romney and Paul Ryan attempted to frighten God-fearing Americans into a Republican presidency. The vice presidential nominee, Paul Ryan, used the 11th hour of the GOTV campaign to reach out to the social conservative base of his party via the Faith and Freedom Coalition:

We understand the stakes of where this country is headed. We understand the stakes of our fundamental freedoms being on the line, like religious freedom—such as how they're being compromised in Obamacare ... [We're on a] path that grows government, restricts freedom and liberty and compromises those values—those Judeo-Christian, Western civilization values that made us a great and exceptional nation in the first place. (Terkel, November 4, 2012)

This talk, referencing Obamacare's inclusion of contraception within healthcare plans, was more intemperate and more revealing than that delivered for broader campaign audiences. It placed the 2012 Republican campaign within the framework of Judeo-Christian presidential normalcy and situated Barack Obama's presidency and reelection outside of that politico-theological space. Contrasting Obama with this religious belief system and with Western civilization values de-Christianizes the president and portrays him as its natural opposite, through an Orientalizing lens of anti-Founding Father exceptionalism.

A last-ditch robocall from the Romney-Ryan campaign could not have been more explicit in challenging Christians to recognize that a vote for Obama was incompatible with their system of belief:

Christians who are thinking about voting for Obama should remember what he said about people of faith: "They ... cling to guns or religion." And remember when Obama forced Christian organizations to provide insurance coverage that was contrary to their religious beliefs?

That's the *real* Barack Obama. That's the *real* threat to our religious freedom. Mitt Romney understands the importance of faith and family. That's why so many leaders of the Christian community are supporting Romney.

They know we can't underestimate the threat Barack Obama poses to our faith, our values, our freedom. (Terkel, November 2, 2012)

Using the national stage to suggest that the sitting president of the United States poses an inestimable threat to American liberty and religious freedom echoes the recent rhetorical past. As one listens to this desperate Hail Mary partisanship—a theocratic Hobson's choice—the American ear is purposefully bent to another place: the rhetoric of 9/11. Here, as with Romney's robocall dichotomy, Americans were placed within a binary of Christian versus anti-Christian, between those who kept us safe at home and those who willed our destruction abroad, between American liberty and its Islamic endangerment. In President Bush's address to Congress in September 2001, for example, one finds the same nihilistic trend of anti-extremist rhetoric, as falsely applied to Obama in the modern age:

The only way to defeat terrorism as a threat to our way of life is to stop it, eliminate it and destroy it where it grows.

From Andy Martin's cyberspace campaign to Romney's militant robo-call, and in all of Obama's religious othering in between and beyond, one sees a process of peculiarly personalized religious othering, a process of de-Christianizing and Islamifying racially informed browning that has often framed the 44th president under the same terms as our most mortal international enemies.

REFERENCES

Allen, Mike. "*New Yorker* Obama Cover Sparks Uproar." *CBS News* (July 14, 2008). http://www.cbsnews.com/news/new-yorker-obama-cover-sparks-uproar/.

Allison, Tom, and Jocelyn Fong. "Media Note Obama Did Not Say 'Terrorism,' But Don't Discuss Why." *Media Matters* (June 5, 2009). http://mediamatters.org/research/2009/06/05/media-note-obama-did-not-say-terrorism-but-dont/150914.

Aravoisis, John. "*New Yorker* Cover Shows Oval Office with Obama as Tribal African, Wife as Afro-70s-Woman with Machine Gun, Osama on the Wall, and Flag on Fire." *AmericaBlog.com* (July 13, 2008). http://americablog.com/2008/07/new-yorker-cover-shows-oval-office-with-obama-as-tribal-african-wife-as-afro-70s-woman-with-machine-gun-osama-on-the-wall-and-flag-on-fire.html.

Babbin, Jed. *How Obama Is Transforming America's Military from Superpower to Paper Tiger.* Vol. 14. New York: Encounter Books, 2010.

Bacon, Perry. "Clinton Campaign Volunteer out over False Obama Rumors." *The Washington Post* (December 5, 2007). http://voices.washingtonpost.com/44/2007/12/clinton-campaign-volunteer-out.html.

Bloodsworth-Lugo, Mary K., and Carmen R. Lugo-Lugo. "Post-9/11 Discourses of Threat and Constructions of Terror in the Age of Obama." *Altre Modernità* (2011): 261–278.

Bloodsworth-Lugo, Mary K., and Carmen R. Lugo-Lugo. *Containing (Un)American Bodies: Race, Sexuality, and Post-9/11 Constructions of Citizenship.* Vol. 219. New York: Rodopi, 2010.

Boller, Paul F. *Presidential Anecdotes.* Oxford, UK: Oxford University Press, 1996.

Coffman, Michael S. *Radical Islam in the House: The Plan to Take America for the Global Islamic State.* CreateSpace Independent Publishing Platform, 2013.

Davis, Susan. "Obama Dismisses Internet Rumors" *The Wall Street Journal* (January 15, 2008). http://blogs.wsj.com/washwire/2008/01/15/obama-dismisses-internet-rumors/.

Drum, Kevon. "That *New Yorker* Cover." *Washington Monthly* (July 13, 2008). http://www.washingtonmonthly.com/archives/individual/2008_07/014079.php.

Emery, David. "Is Barack Obama the Antichrist." *Netlore Archive* (2008). http://urbanlegends.about.com/od/barackobama/a/obamaantichrist.htm.

Falsani, Cathleen. "Interview with State Sen. Barack Obama; 3:30 p.m., Saturday March 27." March 27, 2004. http://cathleenfalsani.com/obama-on-faith-the-exclusive-interview/.

Feingold, Henry L. *A Time for Searching: Entering the Mainstream, 1920–1945.* Vol. 4. Baltimore, MD: JHU Press, 1995.

Gaffney, Frank. *The Muslim Brotherhood in the Obama Administration.* David Horowitz Freedom Center, 2012. http://www.amazon.com/The-Muslim -Brotherhood-Obama-Administration-ebook/dp/B009HIP79K.

Harrison, Maureen, and Steve Gilbert. *Barack Obama: Speeches, 2002–2006.* Excellent Books 2007.

Harsanyi, David. *Obama's Four Horsemen: The Disasters Unleashed.* Washington, DC: Regnery, 2013.

Irving, David. *Hitler's War.* Vol. 1. Viking Press, 1977. http://www.fpp.co.uk/books/Hitler/1977/html_chapter/17.html.

Jefferson, Thomas. "Address by Thomas Jefferson." Joint Congressional Committee on Inaugural Ceremonies, 1805. http://www.inaugural.senate.gov/swearing-in/address/address-by-thomas-jefferson-1805.

Jefferson, Thomas. *Memoirs, 4: Correspondence and Private Papers.* London, UK: Henry Colbura and Richard Bertley, 1829.

Kaplan, Lawrence S. *Thomas Jefferson: Westward the Course of Empire.* Wilmington, DE: Rowman & Littlefield, 1998.

Kirby, Stephen M. *Islam and Barack Hussein Obama: Handbook of Islam.* CreateSpace, 2010.

Ledeen, Michael A. *Obama's Betrayal of Israel.* New York: Encounter Broadsides, 2010.

Lincoln, Abraham. *Collected Works*, edited by Roy P. Basler. Vols. 1 and 2. New Brunswick, NJ: Rutgers University Press, 1953.

Martin, Andy. "Columnist Says Barack Obama 'Lied to the American People;' Asks Publisher to Withdraw Obama's Book." *The Free Library* (August 11, 2004). http://www.thefreelibrary.com/Columnist Says Barack Obama 'Lied to the American People;' Asks...-a0120417594.

Mason, Julie. "Godliness and Joblessness: Obama Brings God into It." *Politico* (November 2, 2011). http://www.politico.com/politico44/perm/1111/

godliness_and_joblessness_8f477498-57a2-483d-9416-b6aa6c9236b5. html.

McCarthy, Andrew C. *How Obama Embraces Islam's Sharia Agenda.* New York, NY: ReadHowYouWant.com, 2011.

McNamara, Pat. "Catholic Sisters and the American Civil War." May 30, 2011. http://www.patheos.com/Resources/Additional-Resources/Catholic-Sisters-and-the-American-Civil-War-Pat-McNamara-05-31-2011.html.

Mukasey, Michael B. *How Obama Has Mishandled the War on Terror.* New York, NY: Encounter Books, 2013.

Nightingale, Joseph R. "Joseph H. Barrett and John Locke Scripps, Shapers of Lincoln's Religious Image." *Journal of the Illinois State Historical Society* 92, no. 3 (1999): 238–273.

NPR.org. " 'New Yorker' Editor Defends Obama Cover." June 14, 2008. http://www.npr.org/templates/story/story.php?storyId=92529393.

Obama, Barack H. "Remarks by the President on a New Beginning." Speech in Cairo, Egypt, June 4, 2009. The White House. http://www.whitehouse.gov/the_press_office/Remarks-by-the-President-at-Cairo-University-6-04-09.

Pelley, William Dudley. *What Every Congressman Should Know.* Asheville, NC: Pelley, 1936.

Plaud, Joseph J. "Historical Perspectives on Franklin D. Roosevelt, American Foreign Policy, and the Holocaust." Franklin D. Roosevelt American Heritage Center and Museum. http://www.fdrheritage.org/fdr&holocaust.htm.

PolitiFact. "Obama Attended an Indonesian Public School." December 20, 2007. http://www.politifact.com/truth-o-meter/statements/2007/dec/20/chain-email/obama-attended-an-indonesian-public-school/.

PolitiFact. "Taking 'In God We Trust' off Coins Was Debunked Years Ago." September 2012. http://www.politifact.com/truth-o-meter/statements/2012/sep/11/chain-email/taking-god-we-trust-coins-was-debunked-years-ago/.

Press, Bill. *The Obama Hate Machine: The Lies, Distortions, and Personal Attacks on the President—and Who Is Behind Them.* New York, NY: Macmillan, 2012.

Reott, Martin P., and Patricia Reott. *The Unauthorized Diary of a Muslim President.* CreateSpace Independent Publishing Platform, 2012.

Romney, Mitt. *No Apology: The Case for American Greatness.* New York, NY: Macmillan, 2010.

Ross, Michael. "Bad TV's Most Wanted: Elected Instigators: #3." *The Examiner* (January 12, 2013). http://www.examiner.com/article/bad-tv-s-most-wanted-elected-instigators-3.

Sampley, Ted. "Barack Obama: Who Is He?" *U.S. Veteran Dispatch* (December 29, 2006). http://www.usvetdsp.com/dec06/obama_muslim.htm.

Sanford, Charles B. *The Religious Life of Thomas Jefferson.* Charlottesville, VA: University of Virginia Press, 1987 [1829].

Schlussel, Debbie. "Barack Hussein Obama: Once a Muslim, Always a Muslim." 2006. http://www.debbieschlussel.com/2750/barack-hussein-obama-once-a-muslim-always-a-muslim/.

Sklar, Rachel. "Yikes! Controversial *New Yorker* Cover Shows Muslim, Flag-Burning, Osama-Loving, Fist-Bumping Obama," *The Huffington Post* (July 21, 2008). http://www.huffingtonpost.com/2008/07/13/yikes-controversial-emnew_n_112429.html.

Smith, Ben. "Clinton Staffer on Anti-Obama Email Chain." *Politico* (December 5, 2007). http://www.politico.com/blogs/bensmith/1207/Clinton_staffer_on_antiObama_email_chain.html.

Terkel, Amanda. "Mitt Romney Robocall Warns Christians Obama a 'Threat to Our Religious Freedom.' " *The Huffington Post* (November 2, 2012). http://www.huffingtonpost.com/2012/11/02/mitt-romney-robocall-christians_n_2068596.html.

Terkel, Amanda. "Paul Ryan to Social Conservatives: 'Religious Freedom' at Risk If Obama Is Reelected." *The Huffington Post* (November 4, 2012). http://www.huffingtonpost.com/2012/11/04/paul-ryan-social-conservatives-religious-freedom_n_2074129.html.

Thiessen, Marc A. *Courting Disaster: How the CIA Kept America Safe and How Barack Obama Is Inviting the Next Attack*. Washington, DC: Regnery, 2010.

Veres Royal, Sue. "Fear, Rhetoric, and the 'Other.' " *Race/Ethnicity: Multidisciplinary Global Contexts* 4, no. 3 (2011): 405–418.

Walzer, Andrew. "Savage Repeated Debunked Falsehood That Obama Attended Madrassa." *Media Matters* (June 26, 2007). http://mediamatters.org/research/2007/06/26/savage-repeated-debunked-falsehood-that-obama-a/139188.

The Washington Times. "Editorial: America's Muslim Precedent" *The Washington Times* (May 3, 2011). http://www.washingtontimes.com/news/2011/may/3/americas-muslim-precedent/.

Chapter 5

Communist in Chief:
The Red Obama

If the demonization of Barack Obama on the basis of his skin color, birth place, parentage, ethnicity, or religion is rooted in antique American prejudice, intellectual inconsistency, partisan opportunism, and unnecessary hyperbole, then the foreignization of Obama's essential politic belongs, perhaps, in a league (and chapter) of its own.

In a transmogrification of his Democratic platform, Obama's policy agenda has been forced through the looking glass of the extremist political Tea Party, so that it is interpreted as simultaneously socialist, Marxist, communist, Bolshevik, and fascist, under an overall umbrella of alleging Obama's radical European influence. Obama's political identity—though recognized by analytical political science as one of the most moderate in the past half-century—has been variously described in parallel with Lenin, Stalin, Mussolini, Mao, and Hitler. Think genocide; think murderous revolution; think unqualified state domination. The country, although numbed by the shock value of the demagoguery, has been persuaded by the comparison. In April 2009, a *New York Times*/CBS poll found that two thirds of respondents described Obama as a different kind of politician, with 52 percent seeing his policies moving the country "toward socialism." Throughout 2010, surveys found that a majority of voters and Republicans believed that Obama was a committed socialist. Pew Research in 2013 discovered that "socialist" was the fifth most common one-word description of President Obama.

In the far Right's imagination, the prescriptive meanings of these discrete doctrines and their nomenclature are not deployed appropriately or rationally, but rather hybridized to suggest an overall statist, revolutionary political intention of "government takeover." The Democratic general preference for the state's more active role in solving the nation's challenges is, under Obama's charge, aestheticized as a desire for complete communist control and radical dictatorship. Obama's unsurprising Democratic pursuits for affordable healthcare legislation, more progressive taxes, economic stimulus, and the auto-industry bail-out, for example, have been cast in this epic conspiracy as landmarks on a red brick road leading toward anti-capitalism and Marxist fulfillment. This *reductio ad absurdum* dramatization of American partisan politics during Obama's tenure is sustained though a mythic interpretation of Obama's own identity, through a suppositional rewriting of his biography and life influences, and through the reinvigoration of American fears of Cold War communist infiltration. Far above the rational analysis of Obama's policy, it is a frenzied presentation of his identity, once again, as the conspiratorial codex for understanding his so-called anti-American presidency.

The charge of Obama's socialistic political identity emerged relatively late in the 2008 presidential election campaign. In June, the previous House majority leader, Tom DeLay (Republican-Texas), made the extraordinary claim—without evidence—that "unless Obama proves me wrong, he's a Marxist" (Corley 2008). Meanwhile, Representative Paul Broun (Republican-Georgia) described Obama's platform as a "philosophy of radical socialism or Marxism" (Evans 2008), and Representative Steve King (Republican-Louisiana) prophesized that Obama's policies would transform the United States into a "totalitarian dictatorship" (Burns 2008). Michael Savage, on his conservative radio show, told his listeners, "It's going to be very doubtful as to whether or not we can avoid the outright Marxism and Afro-Leninism running this country" (Kujala 2008), suggesting not only that Obama's imagined philosophy was dangerous, but also that it was made even less desirable by being wrapped within African American skin. Marcia Stirman, chair of the Republican Women of Otero Country in New Mexico, was asked to stand down for describing candidate Obama as a "Muslim socialist," another racialized portmanteau. The Right was whipped into a new terminological frenzy, deploying political ascriptions often beyond the nuanced understanding of those speaking them. A former *Saturday Night Live* cast member, Victoria Jackson, appeared on numerous television platforms describing Obama as like "Castro in Cuba" or "the guy in China [presumably Mao]" (Fernandez 2012). The Republican nominee, John McCain, when asked if Obama's policies could be classified as basic communism, replied with a tellingly paralyzed "I don't know" (Hamby 2008).

Throughout his first term, opponents from the Right pushed Obama's political character to the extreme left of the partisan continuum. "The Union of Soviet Socialist Republics may be dead," Mike Huckabee, past Republican presidential contender and Fox News contributor, mused, "but the Union of American Socialist Republics is being born" (Wharton 2009). Referring specifically to the implementation of the Troubled Asset Relief Program (TARP), established by George W. Bush and continued by Obama, Huckabee quipped, "Lenin and Stalin would love this stuff!" In 2009, Glenn Beck warned about Russian-styled policy "czars with gathering power," while leading a campaign that ended with the resignation of Van Jones, Obama's newly appointed special adviser on green jobs. Resurrecting the parlance of the Vietnam War, Michele Bachmann claimed that Obama proposed a program of back door "re-education camps . . . where young people have to go and get trained in a philosophy that the government puts forward" (Stein 2009). On the Fox News channel, Sean Hannity described the American Recovery and Reinvestment Act of 2009 as "the European Socialist Act of 2009 or the End of Capitalism as We Know It Act of 2009." Fox News president and founder Roger Ailes provided justification for that channel's editorial steer on the issue by claiming that Obama "had to be told by the French and the Germans that his socialism was too far left for them to deal with" (Kurtz 2010).

In 2009, Janet Porter, sometime senior adviser to Mike Huckabee, mythologized Obama's proposed communism within the context of a transnational, decades-long Soviet collusion. In a pejorative article on Obama's economic stimulus for *World Net Daily*, Porter recounted the unsubstantiated written record of a government contractor's experience at a Moscow dinner party in 1992 to give the conspiracy some roots. Tom Fife, who was working on a software development contract at the time, reports that during this tête-à-tête, Barack Obama was named by a Russian female as the subject of a presidential communist plot already in motion:

What if I told you that you will have a black president very soon and he will be a Communist? . . . Yes, it is true. This is not some idle talk. He is already born, and he is educated and being groomed to be president right now. You will be impressed to know that he has gone to the best schools of presidents. He is what you call "Ivy League." You don't believe me, but he is real and I even know his name. His name is Barack. His mother is white and American and his father is black from Africa. That's right, a chocolate baby! And he's going to be your president. (Fife 2008)

Obama's personal narrative was retrofitted into this implausible Manchurian-style vignette, with no corroboration or provenance. This was done as a means of timely partisan opposition to the proposed financial stimulus legislation, wrapped in a Trojan horse of a modern—racially inclined—McCarthyism.

Rush Limbaugh offered profuse commentary on the issue. The conservative radio host claimed that Obama's political ambition was to create mass unemployment to "take the nation's wealth and return it to the nation's 'rightful owners.' " Limbaugh, like many others, took full aim at the Affordable Care Act as nationalized health care, equivalent to "the first objective of . . . Hitler" in fascist Germany. Government control was so excessive that if Limbaugh "didn't know better, [he] would say that Hugo Chavez is actually running this country" (Limbaugh 2010). In more colorful language, Obama's policy actions were described as a "dictator's wet dream" leading to Americans having to "retreat into their bathrooms" to criticize government, as sometimes occurred in Soviet Russia (Limbaugh 2012). In 2011, Limbaugh lambasted presidential nominee Mitt Romney not for his own politics, but for failing to specifically label Obama as a socialist.

While Romney would not describe Obama as communist outright, as the 2012 campaign ramped up, he certainly implied it with a heavy dose of euphemism during his formal presidential announcement. Speaking to a crowd in New Hampshire, Romney critiqued Obama's stances on Israel, domestic economic policy, and progressive taxation as pointedly un-American. "He's treating Israel the same way so many European countries have," Romney claimed, "with suspicion, distrust and an assumption that Israel is at fault." Placing Obama outside of the geography of average American socioeconomic values, Romney proposed that "Here at home, the president seems to take his inspiration not from the small towns and villages of New Hampshire, but from the capitals of Europe" (Amira 2011). Put simply, "Obama's European answers are not the right solution to America's challenges." Romney was not implying that Obama was literally European, of course (as a few have done), but rather suggesting that his political bent was in keeping with the traditional seat of socialist, communist, and fascist revolutionary regimes. Other opponents have long belabored the European characterization as a slur du jour. For example, Charles Krauthammer, when speaking with Bill O'Reilly, said of the president, "He's a European social democrat" who would be more at home in "Sweden, France, Britain . . . nationalizing health care the way they have it in Europe" (O'Reilly 2013).

During his 2012 congressional campaign, Representative Allen West (Republican-Florida) used his significant Tea Party platform to rouse suspicions of Obama's hidden socialist construct. Assuming a McCarthyism-type posture, West gained national attention when he alleged that under Obama the government had been infiltrated by a network of card-carrying Communists, estimating in April 2012 that "about 78 to 81" of House Democrats were clandestine Reds. Presumably, these members were assembled by the unifying figure of the incumbent socialist president, whose 2012 campaign slogan, according to West, promoted a "Soviet Union, Marxist, socialist theme." It was only a year earlier that West had described Obama's political conduct as displaying a "Third World dictator-like arrogance," a phrase that rolls a number of othering tropes into a single almost-meaningless phrase of foreignization. According to West, this "community organizer is turning out to be . . . a low-level socialist agitator" as well as the protagonist in a high-level government takeover (Associated Press 2012; Kleefield 2011).

Upon Obama's 2012 reelection, many propagandized that the route to radical anticapitalism was secured. Sean Hannity urged his audience to fight the dawning age of a "socialist utopia." The *Drudge Report* seized upon a picture of Obama signing executive actions on gun regulation, surrounded by children, and compared it to the visual rhetoric of Hitler and Stalin—other "tyrants who have used children as props." The president of the Catholic League, Bill Donahue, used his position as a religious group leader to suggest that for the purposes of his inauguration oath, Obama should swear upon a copy of Marx's *Das Kapital* rather than the Bible. This suggestion de-Christianized Obama while cloaking him in Marxism, in a single demonizing quip removing him from the normalcy of presidential tradition on the basis of misapplied partisan labels.

The distortion of Obama's Democratic platform as Marxist-Leninist has been well established by the anti-Obama printing press, which has demonstrated a notable predilection for red dustcovers for such tomes. Aaron Klein co-wrote *The Manchurian President,* referencing the 1962 cinematic fiction, to deconstruct the president's life and expose a "far-leftist, anti-American nexus . . . aimed at reshaping our country" (Klein and Elliott 2010). Demonstrating the quotidian tactic of using Obama's biography—rather than his policy—for the assessment of his unproven communism, Klein surveys Obama's "mysterious college years," his ties to Islam and black liberation theology, and his radical colleagues to understand their influences upon the administration's destructive economic and health policies. Klein also contends that Obama's "hope and change" message is a naked reproduction of communist sloganeering.

America's Communist Revolution! Terrifying Change without Hope by Terry L. Cook similarly proposed that "B. Hussein Obama" was programmed for years to implement the agenda of his "atheist, Muslim, Communist, sex-pervert father, Frank Marshall Davis." Cook combines practically every Obama identity myth into a single narrative of political otherness, fronted by an illustration of Obama ripping open his Democratic clothes and revealing a Communist anti-superhero outfit beneath (Cook 2010).

Paul Kengor's *The Communist—Frank Marshall Davis: The Untold Story of Barack Obama's Mentor,* which was heavily plugged by Glenn Beck (a prime mover in the Obama-as-socialist frame), uses a parental Birther allegation as the lens for understanding Obama's corrupted communist-directed childhood and its manifestation in the Obama presidency. Kengor's book cover features a wreathed version of the communist hammer and sickle symbol alongside Obama's iconic campaign logo, as if the two were somehow interchangeable or analogous (Kengor 2012).

The former speaker of the House of Representatives, Newt Gingrich, wrote an exhortatory tome, *To Save America: Stopping Obama's Secular-Socialist Machine* (2011), explaining that "secular-socialist" was now the "only way describe the Left" under Obama's leadership. Obama's threat to the national construct is underlined in this text, as "greater than anything I dreamed possible after we won the Cold War and the Soviet Union disappeared in December 1991." Describing the 2012 election as an ideological crossroads, Gingrich warns, "Either we will save our country, or we will lose it." The author shores up his own future candidacy by making counterproposals to "the left-wing Democrats ... committed to a secular-socialist ideology that is alien to America's history and tradition." The insinuation here is that Obama is so fundamentally different, so "alien" from traditional presidential characters, that this identification alone poses a national threat to the American political construct (Gingrich 2011).

Other books, such as Michael Savage's *Trickle Down Tyranny: Crushing Obama's Dream of the Socialist States of America* (2012) and Dick Morris and Eileen McGann's *Revolt: How to Defeat Obama and Repeal His Socialist Programs* (2011), continue to personalize the accusation that Obama himself is the sole source of a grand socialist takeover. The literature has become so popular and self-referential that David W. Hedrick published a Christmas story, *The Liberal Claus(e)*, providing a children's parable for the Obama-as-socialist theme. "What would happen if liberal elves took over the North Pole," Hedrick asks, "and children were given the same number of toys, whether they were naughty or nice?" In this book written for the "children of the Tea Party movement," the author includes a thinly veiled scene of a "snow-covered socialist wonderland," where "Santa's workshop is unionized" and "the Sleigh manufacturers are seized because they are 'too big to fail,'" to alert his young readers to the subversive tactics of the president and the Democratic platform in a yuletide narrative. The front cover includes Obama as Santa, accompanied by cartoon images of Nancy Pelosi and Harry Reid as his attendant elves (Hedrick 2010).

Even ordinarily trusted publications engaged in furthering the Obama-as-communist meme. The U.S. business magazine *Forbes* ran pieces such as "Barack Obama: Fabian Socialist," "Comparing Obama's Policies with French Socialist Hollande," and "President Obama's Marxist-Leninist Economics: Fact and Fiction." In the last article, the tone used to skewer Obama's political direction as Marxist-Leninist was noteworthy: "Although it's too long and cumbersome a label for a generation addicted to sound bites and simplistic labels," Hendrickson (2012) wrote, "a fair description of Obama and his economic goals is to say that he is an 'interventionist, corporatist, statist, Big Government progressive, free-market-hating control freak who favors economic policies of a Marxists Leninist flavor.'" *Forbes* also came under fire for a 2010 cover story written by Dinesh D'Souza (author of *The Roots of Obama's Rage* [2011]), which argued that Obama's political agenda might be socialist or Marxist, but was even better defined as "anti-colonialism"—a worldview genetically inherited from his Kenyan father. In 2009, *Newsweek* ran a cover story by Jon Meacham discussing the U.S. government's European-style spending, under the headline "We Are All Socialists Now."

If evidence of Obama's communism could be found in ink, Glenn Beck saw the conspiracy writ large in New York's very architecture. During one of his more memorable Fox News programs, Glenn Beck delivered a hysterical television lecture on the socialist and fascist imagery found in the architecture of Rockefeller's real estate, explaining how such artwork is predictive of its second coming in Obama. A doorway leading off from Rockefeller Plaza, according to Beck, heralded two men wielding a hammer and a sickle; "This is from Moscow," he exclaimed. Turning to a bronze relief at 636 Fifth Avenue, Beck gave an extremely subjective art reading of the prophetic chariot scene: "This is the strong leader . . . using that industry [represented by the horses] to lead us into that bright future [represented by the sun], led by our children [represented by the boy]!" he said. Beck exclaimed with incredulity that the imagery was too close to home: "Gee, who's having indoctrination next week; oh yeah, that's right, the president. Totally unrelated" (Koppelman 2009). To Beck, Obama was hiding his progressive, fascist, communist objectives in plain sight. The thread of logic seemed strained. Despite the host's contention that "this administration is now beginning to use art as propaganda," this art was decades old and had been commissioned by the family of

John D. Rockefeller, an icon of capitalism. To claim that Obama is a communist agent is one thing; to "uncover" that he inspired a *Da Vinci Code*-esque art commissioning conspiracy to announce his socialist agenda 30 years prior to his birth is an example of the intense logic-defying animus aimed at his policy platform from the far Right.

The Obama-as-socialist theme has also been advanced by a visual propaganda campaign, leading to an aesthetic association of Obama with European political symbols. In 2009, the controversial political activist Lyndon LaRouche used his political action committee to circulate a manipulated version of Obama's presidential portrait. It added a Hitler-esque moustache and a byline, "I've Changed." This image was part of the fascist rendering of Obama's healthcare policy, waved at Tea Party rallies and Obamacare protests, to imply that the president's personal transformation toward extremism was representative of governmental transmutation. The extremism apparent in these claims of a parallel between Obama's healthcare policy and the mass extermination of human life in Europe is a troubling manifestation of the *reduction ad Hitlerum* presentation of Obama's Democratic platform and personal identity. Shepard Fairey's iconic red, blue and white "Hope" poster produced during Obama's first campaign has also been systematically hijacked by the blending of Obama's and Hitler's visages.

In 2009, the *Huffington Post* included an unattributed image of an Obama-style concentration camp. In this image, American people drive on a one-way street toward a high-surveillance compound, with signs warning "NOW ENTERING FASCISM" and "PREPARE TO SURRENDER ALL LIBERTY." Obama stands at the head of the site, eyes blissfully closed, framed by a red hammer and sickle. He is flanked on both sides by the spectral portraits of Hitler, Mussolini, Lenin, and Marx as cars move through the entrance marked by Obama's logo, pretending to be some fascist symbol.

During the 2010 midterm election season, the North Iowa Tea Party organization erected a large red billboard featuring Adolf Hitler, Barack Obama, and Vladimir Lenin, each sharing in the singular message of "Change." Where Hitler stood for national socialism (under the swastika), and Lenin led Marxist socialism (under the hammer and sickle), Obama was depicted as the leader of Democratic socialism (under his 2008 campaign logo). The intent of this gallery of enemy portraits was to malign the president's personality by equating his message with fascism and Marxism, so as to inculcate fear within the conservative identity-politics paradigm.

Perhaps the most iconic and influential visual rhetorical object, however, is the Obama-as-Joker poster produced in 2009 by Firas Alkhateeb.

Poster for Mass Distribution: I've Changed! President Obama with Hitler-like moustache, August 2009. (Larouchepac.com)

This antiheroic portrayal of Obama, which manipulates *Time* magazine's front cover in 2006, seeks to capture the contemporary imagination by casting Obama as a demonic, radical oppositional force. The caption "socialism" was added to Alkhateeb's creation soon after its circulation, by an anonymous user. The poster was witnessed at numerous Tea Party events, including the September 2009 march on Washington, D.C., in which Tea Party members sought to denounce Obama's economic and healthcare policies as unconstitutional. The striking iconoclastic image draws all attention not to Obama's agenda, policy implementation, or record, but rather to his whitened face of total villainy. The inverse minstrelsy of the poster—masking Obama's African American heritage, yet highlighting it by default—has led some to interpret the "socialism" label as a mere proxy for something more pernicious, more racial, and more identity politics than the standard partisan schism. Philip Kennicott, critic for art and architecture at the *Washington Post,* argued that in the Joker poster, "You have a subtly coded, highly effective racial and political argument." He continued:

Forget socialism, this poster is another attempt to accomplish an association between Obama and the unpredictable, seeming danger of urban life. It is another effort to establish what failed to jell in the debate about Obama's association with Chicago radical William Ayers and . . . Rev. Jeremiah Wright.

Obama, like the Joker and like the racial stereotype of the black man, carries within him an unknowable, volatile and dangerous marker of urban violence . . . The charge of socialism is secondary to the basic message that Obama can't be trusted, not because he is a politician, but because he's black. (Kennicott 2009)

Like the art critic, one must agree that in the Obama-as-communist strategy in general, as with the visual rhetoric, something more meta-phorical and euphemistic is to be derived from the characterization of Obama's political actions as deeds of Marx, Hitler, or Lenin. Such doc-trines are nexuses of American hatred that are used to triangulate the Right's foreignization and demonization of the first African American president, not because he is genuinely a communist in chief, but because he is Other. The president's racial identity undoubtedly contributes to at least some of the hyperbolic characterization of his Democratic policy as dangerous, unpredictable, and un-American. Tim Wise, in his article "Socialism as the New Black Bogeyman," argues:

[S]ocialism is little more than racist code for the longstanding white fear that black folks will steal from them, and covet everything they have. The fact that the fear may now be of a black president, and not just some random black bur-glar, hardly changes the fact that it is fear nonetheless: a deep, abiding suspicion that African American folk can't wait to take whitey's stuff, as payback, as repar-ations, as a way to balance the historic scales of injustice that have so long tilted in our favor. (Wise 2009)

The fetish to pursue Obama's true father as the African American poet and activist Frank Marshall Davis and the president's portrayal as an "Afro-Leninist," for example, would add credence to such interpretation of racial coding.

On literal terms, of course, Obama cannot be accurately character-ized as a fascist, communist, socialist, Marxist, Stalinist, or Leninist from a detached political science, or historical, perspective. The Holocaust, gulag camps, and *Communist Manifesto* are not equivalents to the Affordable Care Act, the Troubled Asset Relief Program, or the Cash-for-Clunkers scheme. Obama's authorization of an $80 billion emergency loan to auto industry giants General Motors and Chrysler was state intervention, for sure, but by no means was it equivalent to the socialist approach of complete nationalization. Conversely, Obama's actions strengthened the position of two iconic *Fortune* 500 companies for future private profitability. In health care, Obama's revolutionary new policy mandates all Americans to purchase health insurance on pain of fine. This policy, however, is by no stretch an act of fascist nationalization. Obama abandoned his early pursuit of a public healthcare option within the legislation and provided substantial subsidies to private insurance companies. The law, which was not supported by a single Republican member of the House of Representatives, essentially delivered 30 million new healthcare customers to the private medical insurance market, through a system that maximizes patient choice and industry competition. It is little different from the proposals made by Nixon or Clinton during their own presidencies, and is often described as a replication of healthcare legislation introduced in Massachusetts by Governor Mitt Romney. In the fiscal arena, Obama extended the Bush-era tax cuts, much to the ire of the more progressive wing of the Democratic Party. In the financial markets, the Dow Jones Industrial Average has *doubled* since Obama's inauguration. As social inequality grows in America to become the issue of our generation, many might question the logical step that conservatives undertake in interpreting Obama's sociopolitical reality as communist.

So far removed from the socialist agenda are Obama's policies that socialists themselves have denounced them. Billy Wharton, co-chair of the Socialist Party of the United States, distanced himself from the characterization, saying:

[S]ocialists know that Barack Obama is not one of us. Not only is he not a socialist, he may in fact not even be a liberal. Socialists understand him more as a hedge-fund Democrat—one of a generation of neoliberal politicians firmly committed to free-market policies. (Wharton 2009)

A left-leaning writer, Rick Ungar, also dismissed the socialism slur proposed by his *Forbes* magazine colleagues. "If Barack Obama is indeed a socialist," Ungar wrote, "he must be the absolute worst socialist in recorded history" (Ungar 2013). Brian Patrick Moore, past Socialist Party presidential nominee, agreed, attesting that "Obama's policies and actions during the entire four years of his presidency are based on his total embrace of capitalism and protecting America's capitalistic economic system." For some who had experienced first-hand the real-life meaning of communism, the political identification of Obama using 20th-century European labels was outright offensive. Czech American film director Milos Forman wrote:

I hear the word "socialist" being tossed around by the likes of Rick Perry, Newt Gingrich, Rick Santorum, Sean Hannity, Rush Limbaugh and others ... They falsely equate Western European-style socialism, and its government provision of social insurance and health care, with Marxist-Leninist totalitarianism. It offends me, and cheapens the experience of millions who lived, and continue to live, under brutal forms of socialism . . . Blood flowed through Russia's streets. The Soviet elite usurped all privileges; sycophants were allowed some and the plebes none. The entire Eastern bloc, including Czechoslovakia, followed miserably. I'm not sure Americans today appreciate quite how predatory socialism was. It was not—as Mr. Obama's detractors suggest—merely a government so central- ized and bloated that it hobbled private enterprise: it was a spoils system that killed off everything. (Forman 2012)

The Right's continued rhetorical strategy of proving Obama's covert ultra-Leftism by repeated assertion is contrary to cursory political assess- ment, the views of real socialists, and the lived experiences of fascist and communist societies.

President Obama himself has addressed accusations of his Marxist leadership with a mixture of incredulity and weariness. Late in 2013, Obama was bemused by the ongoing mischaracterization. "People call me a socialist sometimes," Obama laughed, at the *Wall Street Journal* CEO Summit, "but, no, you gotta meet real socialists." He continued, outlining his free market credentials: "I'm talking about lowering the cor- porate tax rate, my health care reform is based on the private market- place, the stock market's looking pretty good last time I checked" (Epstein 2013). Communicating a moderate Democratic position, he con- cluded, "[While] it is true I'm concerned about growing inequality in our system . . . nobody questions the efficacy of market economies in terms of producing wealth and innovation and keeping us competitive." Back in October 2008, when the rumor mill had just begun to churn out the whis- pered claims of the candidate's closeted Marxism, Obama responded to McCain's use of the attack at a North Carolina rally: "By the end of the week, he'll be accusing me of being a secret communist because I shared my toys in kindergarten," the candidate jested, confessing, "I shared my peanut butter and jelly sandwich" (Benen 2008). The childish admission was meant to ridicule and reduce the argument to the realm of the absurd, before it got off the ground. Instead, it predicated a years-long campaign of political demonization based on an *ad hominem* presentation of the president's childhood and biography as the roots of Obama's redness.

A RED DIAPER BABY IN THE WHITE HOUSE

Although there is no legitimate evidence to support the presentation of Obama's political track record as bearing the hallmarks of fascism or communism, his detractors have used the tools of identity politics to imply his Leftist extremism through the demonization of his biography and influences. By examining his life history as a site of radicalizing corruption, members of the Right rely upon a racialized counter-narrative of the president's Afro-communist upbringing in lieu of appropriate color-blind evidence from the realm of extant policy. This moves the locus of interpreting Obama's political being from the observable world to an interior, suppositional presidential pseudo-psychology, which is in turn open to negative and partisan theorization. Once exposed, one can understand the tactic as an extension of the Birtherist theme, delegitimizing Obama's presidency not only on the basis of his invalid birth, but also as a result of the foreign politics in which he was mythically cradled and nourished.

The predominant conspiracy proposes that Obama is a red diaper baby—a child of communist parents who has inherited his political perspective through ideological genetics. One online theorist outlined the broad narrative of this communistic *Bildungsroman*:

Barack Obama was born of Communist activists, mentored by a communist writer and activist, spent his college days hanging around radical activists, worked as a radical community organizer learning the radical tactics of [Saul] Alinsky, kept contact with radicals through the years, attends a radical church, and today lends his political skill to the international goals of radical activists, and has radicals working on his campaign. (ObamaConspiracy.org 2008)

Glenn Beck was driven to a frenzied state of outrage, devoting significant portions of his broadcasting platform to proselytize this theory to his audience, blackboards and all. On one program, Beck used photographs to populate Obama's "Communist Family Tree"; on another, he used images of the president's relatives and associates to build a communist "foundation" supporting Obama's deficient political "structure." Surveying each family member in turn with a socialist bias, Beck concluded, "This kid didn't have a chance to be rooted in the Founding Fathers. This guy doesn't have a chance to actually think anything but radical thoughts. Based on everybody in his life so far, who's defending capitalism?" The counter-narrative was the very definition of guilt by unfounded association; Beck was a new McCarthy, albeit one with a regular television audience (Pleat 2010).

Beginning with Obama's father, Barack Hussein Obama, Sr., Beck and others allege that the president receives a socialist spirit through paternal inheritance. For this assertion, conspirators rely upon a single piece of evidence, an article written by the senior Obama in July 1965 for the *East Africa Journal*. The president's opponents claim that his father's writing portrays a "Nairobi bureaucrat who advised government to 'redistribute' income though higher taxes," a demonizer of corporations, and a political extremist. Such an accusation, however, is a selective rendering of a single source. Obama Senior was not writing in a vacuum, but rather responding to a recently released Kenyan governmental proposal, *African Socialism and Its Applicability to Planning in Kenya*. Obama's discussion of increased taxation as a means of decreasing Kenyan reliance on foreign aid is part and parcel of this critique. Rather than proposing a firm and established socialist policy, however, Obama suggested that "African socialism is undefined" and independent from "foreign ideologies." The socialism under discussion, he clarified, is not what is understood as socialism in "Ghana, Tanzania, Great Britain or the U.S.A."; international political terminology does not apply. Despite the nuance of this half-century-old academic article, President Obama's detractors continue to quote selectively from its pages to suggest that the son is fulfilling his father's insinuated ideology (Obama 1965).

Not only did Obama inherit his father's ideological DNA, according to this line of thinking, but his questionable character, too. Dinesh D'Souza, author of *The Roots of Obama's Rage,* took the theory of biological anti-Americanism to a new level of supposition and pseudo-psychology. "Incredibly," D'Souza writes,

the U.S. is being ruled according to the dreams of a Luo tribesman of the 1950s. [A] philandering, inebriated African socialist, who raged against the world for denying him the realization of his anticolonial ambitions, is now setting the nation's agenda through the reincarnation of his dreams in his son. (D'Souza 2011)

The racialization is writ large in D'Souza's paternal analysis, which claims that through the eyes of his African father,

Obama learned to see America as a force for global domination and destruction. He came to view America's military as an instrument of neocolonial occupation. He adopted his father's position that capitalism and free markets are code words for economic plunder. Obama grew to perceive the rich as an oppressive class, a kind of neocolonial power within America. (D'Souza 2011)

In this mythology, Obama's political worldview is derived from a distant and dangerous continent, from which he inherited a red soul as well as dark complexion. Newt Gingrich provided support for D'Souza's hypothesis, describing it as the "most profound insight I have read in the last six years about Barack Obama" (Costa 2010).

While claiming that Obama's father's presence was corruptive, Glenn Beck simultaneously cites his father's *absence* as a contributory factor to the president's policies. The fact that he "abandoned Barack Obama Jr. when he was 2 years old to continue at Harvard" supposedly taught President Obama that ideology is more important than family. Obama's communist fate was apparently forged by being force fed *and* starved by the same paternal ideological force. Once again, Obama's personal foreignization is a tautologous proposition.

The other half of Obama's parental influence—from his mother—has been equally maligned as ideologically skewed. First, conspirators typically establish the importance of Obama's mother in shaping the president's outlook. Quoting the president's own description of Stanley Ann Dunham as the "dominant figure in my formative years," whose values "continue to be my very touchstone when it comes to how I go about the world of politics" (Gammell 2009), his opponents portray Dunham as a communist sympathizer, as once suggested by a *Chicago Tribune* article. As there is a dearth of evidence to support Dunham's militant Marxism, this claim centers on her alleged educational background. While she was a student at Mercer Island High School in Washington, it is claimed, radical progressive teachers pushed an atheist, antiauthority, and anarchist agenda, forcing their students to read *The Communist Manifesto* and other socialist writings. During her time at the "little red school," as Glenn Beck described it, Dunham was supposedly exposed to the Frankfurt School of Communism and "may have been a practitioner of critical theory . . . a mixture of atheism with radical leftist activist kind of stuff . . . I mean its Marx to the extreme." The incendiary rumor-mongering claimed that through this reading list, compounded for good measure by the works of Nietzsche and Freud, Obama's mother became an intellectual evangelist for the communist cause. Obama's opponents have even derided as "Marxist" his mother's careful 14-year-long anthropological study of peasant blacksmithing in Indonesia, published posthumously. While being a "radical atheist," she also supposedly attended a "little red church" well known for its communist sympathies and embarked upon a nomadic foreign adventure, leaving Hawaii for the Orientalizing influences of Indonesia and Pakistan. The accusation is that through the son's closeness with his mother, Obama received Dunham's implied politics by osmotic nurture.

In the bosom of his seemingly ordinary grandparents, Beck contends, there was no let-up in the process of Obama's communist grooming.

"At some point they changed," the Fox News host charged, from good Methodists to congregants of the East Shore Unitarian Church in Washington. This venue was known as the "little red church on the hill" because of its debates, for example, on the virtue of China's admission to the United Nations. If that was not shocking enough, Obama's grandfather (a military veteran from World War II) plotted to introduce the young president to poet and activist Frank Marshall Davis. Davis was chosen to mentor Obama as a communist revolutionary while providing a black male presence in the young boy's life. With Obama suffering from his supposed abandonment, the conspiracy maintains, Davis's mentorship represented perhaps the most important branch of this communist family tree.

There is no doubting that Davis was a radical and unorthodox figure as well as a sometime counselor of the young Obama as he tried to understand his biracial existence in 1970s Hawaii. In his own biography, *Livin' the Blues,* Davis stated that he had "worked with all kinds of groups," making "no distinction between those labeled Communist, Socialist or merely liberal. My sole criterion was this: Are you with me in my determination to wipe out white supremacy?" (Davis 1993). Obama mentions a man named "Frank" throughout *Dreams from My Father,* a person now widely understood to be Davis, who had retired to Hawaii in his later life after some notoriety as a poet. Obama describes observing his grandfather and Davis sharing drinks, poetry readings, and intellectual or often lurid conversations. The president sought advice from Frank during events of racial confusion. Yet, Davis was often described by Obama as a disconcerting and dilapidated figure, not a vital font of radical progressivism. "The visits to his house always left me feeling vaguely uncomfortable," Obama wrote, stating that Frank and others "fell short of such lofty standards" (Obama 1995).

For many, however, Davis's mere mentorship of Obama was not enough to generate the toxicity of political influence. Instead, an entirely new conspiracy was born to allege a Birther-type communist cover-up, just in time for the 2012 reelection campaign: Frank Marshall Davis, born in 1905, was the biological father of Barack Obama, providing a genetic code of Red volatility. The unsubstantiated claim found its fullest and most popular expression in Joel Gilbert's 95-minute DVD documentary, *Dreams from My Real Father: A Story of Reds and Deception* (July 2012). The documentary poses as a retort to Obama's own biographical work, suggesting alternative "chapters" such as "My Real Father Is Frank Marshall Davis," "Marxism in Paradise," and "Chicago's New Community Agitator." The film proposes that the incumbent president's assumed biography was fabricated to make his future political career easier, asking, "Was the goat herding, Kenyan father only a fairy tale to obscure a Marxist agenda, irreconcilable with American values?"

The DVD won unsurprising support from many in the Tea Party and on the far Right, reaching the top spot on Amazon.com's documentary sales charts. Jerome Corsi, of *World Net Daily* fame, praised the work, whereas more traditional Birthers (including Orly Taitz) reacted unfavorably to the alternative narrative of paternity. Gilbert claimed to have moved into mass distribution so as to bypass a biased mainstream media, supposedly mailing more than 4 million copies of his film to households in swing states, including Florida, Colorado, Iowa, Ohio, Nevada, and New Hampshire.

The film based its major premise, that Obama's biological (and ideological) father was Frank Marshall Davis, on a crude and highly racialized visual comparison of the president's physical features with those of his paternal candidates. Gilbert's basic outrageous claim is that if Obama's nose and lips look similar to Davis's features, then the two men must share political thoughts as well. This was identity politics, indeed out-and-out physical profiling, reaching the realm of scientific or anthropological racism.

"Scientific racism" denotes a pseudoscientific use of physical differences to support conclusions of racial inferiority and superiority. Early anthropology popularized the notion of racial degeneration and deviation from an ideal European white form. Such views legitimated the European and American slave trades, relying upon physiological difference, such as cranial size, skin color, and musculature, as markers of difference in personality, intelligence, temperament, character, and morality. Joel Gilbert's documentary brandishes a form of modern scientific racism to encourage the belief that if Obama looks like Davis (i.e., possesses some physiological similarities), he must be equal to him in ideology and temperament as well. If Davis's face is an anthropological form of political inferiority (here, communism), Obama's likeness is all that the racializing pseudoscience requires for evidentiary proof of its biological and ideological inheritance.

Throughout the documentary, Gilbert presents countless side-by-side comparisons and compound images of the president and Frank Marshall Davis. During the first chapter of the DVD, a voice actor impersonating Obama narrates the "real" story of his appearance:

I have my mom's long chin, but many features are from my real father. My eyes, brow, nose and lips, my smile, my body and stature, and my build. We're both 6'2". And my deep voice. We both smoke. Like my real father, as I get older, age spots are showing up. I look more and more like him every day.

Similarly, on his website, Gilbert featured a "breaking news" item, entitled "Did Obama Have a Nose Job to Hide Davis Resemblance?," which included expert cosmetic surgery testimony on Obama's "aesthetic refinement" to "the upper and middle nasal vault." Not only was Obama a socialist because he was sired by an accused Marxist poet, inheriting his facial features, skin color, and ideology all in one, Gilbert claimed, but the sitting president of the United States has undergone covert rhinoplasty to obscure that fact from the American electorate. In Gilbert's hands, and those who support him, serious presidential commentary cries out from the suffocatingly racialized realm of nasal comparisons.

Alex Jones, the consummate conspiracy theorist, welcomed Gilbert onto his *Inforwars* program and responded to the physiological examination with enthusiastic agreement. "The Kenyan dad," he said, had a "totally different-shaped skull, different nose," adding that "you can tell the different African tribes by the way they look." Cranial size and shape, as an indicator of mental faculties, has long been a component of scientific racism, deriving from a "crudely materialist proposition that identifies the qualities of one's mind by the features of one's brain." Through the assertion that Obama shares Davis's head shape, Gilbert implies that he shares his anticapitalist thoughts; by possessing the same mouth and lips, Obama breathes and speaks Davis's un-American Marxist message; through their shared eyes, Obama sees America through the lens of mid-century militant communism; and with equal stature, Obama stands shoulder-to-shoulder with Davis in a march for something radically different from the desires of the average, capitalist American.

Can one even imagine the examination of the faces or heads of Bush, Clinton, Reagan, or Roosevelt for signs of parental political inheritance as a means of partisan attack?

Beyond parentage, proponents of the Obama-as-socialist meme have scoured the president's college years for inklings of his mature political thought. In *Dreams from My Father,* Obama describes his circle of friends at Occidental College:

To avoid being mistaken for a sellout, I chose my friends carefully. The more politically active black students. The foreign students. The Chicanos. The Marxist professors and the structural feminists and punk-rock performance poets. We smoked cigarettes and wore leather jackets. At night, in the dorms, we discussed neocolonialism, Franz Fanon, Eurocentrism, and patriarchy. When we ground out our cigarettes in the hallway carpet or set our stereos so loud that the walls began to shake, we were resisting bourgeois society's stifling constraints. (Obama, 1995)

Obama's self-described college rebellion against societal constraints, with dynamic academic exchange, is not exactly an unusual form of university experimentation, nor is it anything like an admission of actual Marxist practice. Beck and his co-conspirators did not agree. If that criticism did not stick, though, Obama's detractors cited his undergraduate attendance at a socialist-leaning conference, despite the president's description of such gatherings as "like a bad dream." Ted Cruz joined the fray, implying that Obama's tenure at Harvard Law School coincided with the faculty's infiltration by card-carrying Marxists:

There were fewer declared Republicans in the faculty when we were there than Communists! There was one Republican. But there were twelve who would say they were Marxists who believed in the Communists overthrowing the United States government. (Mayer 2013)

According to Cruz, Obama "would have made a perfect president of Harvard Law School," with such willing communist disciples at his disposal. Republican Harvard Law professor Charles Fried, who served as Reagan's Solicitor General from 1985 to 1989, was perplexed by his ex-student's politically motivated arithmetic, saying, "I have not taken a poll, but I would be surprised if there were any members of the faculty who 'believed in the Communists overthrowing the U.S. government.'"

Obama's friends, associates, and distant relations have all been marshaled as radical actors in the formation of Obama's anti-American political identity. Bill Ayers and the Reverend Jeremiah Wright were formative radical players. Jim Wallis, Obama's spiritual adviser, is "yet another Marxist" in Obama's religious life, according to Beck, and one who advocates the "forced redistribution of wealth." The previous White House communications director, Anita Dunn, was viciously attacked by conspiracy theorists in 2009 for her use of a quotation from Mao Tse-tung during a high school graduation speech. Energy czar Carol Browner, manufacturing czar Ron Bloom, green jobs advocate Van Jones, SEIU president Andy Stern, and science czar John Holdren have all supposedly been handpicked by Obama's radical administration as compliant sergeants to advance the ultra-Left's redistributionist agenda. In this alternative partisan universe, Obama's long-time friend and confidant Valerie Jarrett is the Marxist architect of this West Wing coterie, on the basis that her father-in-law wrote for the African American publication *The Chicago Defender*. Americans for Limited Government have characterized Jarrett as "the Obama advisor most responsible both for originating and orchestrating the most egregious attempts to impose a socialist regime upon the American people." Some have even claimed that

Obama's Kenyan stepbrother, Abongo "Roy" Obama, and his cousin, Odinga, practice the activist Marxism in Africa that Obama endorses back at home.

Beck ran out of space on his investigative blackboard, as he concluded, "The president has aligned himself with these radical socialists . . . Fact, they're radical Marxists, they're militant communists . . ."

The guilt by (desperate) association tactics in asserting the president's communist connections are undoubtedly singular in their intensity and racialization. However, the strategy also resurrects impulses of foreignization observed during periods of U.S. political history when suspicions of alien infiltration by political extremist forces have been explored as partisan attack.

PRESIDENTS AND THE FEAR OF THE FOREIGN: TOWARD A NEW MCCARTHYISM

Since the dawning of the American Republic, the fear of foreign political doctrines and their capacity to corrupt have been at the core of constitutional and partisan debate. The American Revolutionary War had established an existential national dialectic between political freedom at home and monarchical tyranny abroad. With the emergence of the presidency in the same year as the instigation of the French Revolution, early American partisanship was heavily influenced by the positions one took in 18th-century foreign affairs. On this basis, the early presidency was energized by a divisive political "othering" based on one's opponent's perceived sympathies—with Britain or France, for example. Consequently, domestic fear-mongering and political attacks centered on associations with European forces, royalism, republicanism, and violent revolution.

Despite the stabilizing legacy of George Washington's two presidential terms and his expressed neutrality on the French Revolution, the Founding Father was the subject of substantial political demonization. For example, Benjamin Franklin Bache, a newspaper editor and Jefferson supporter, used his publication *Aurora* to disparage Washington as a "despotic, anemic counterfeit of the English Georges" with "treacherous mazes of passion." Republican journalists contended that the government was veering toward an aristocratic system, with Federalists extending their sympathy toward the British monarchy. In turn, the Federalists accused their opponents of supporting the brutal means of the French Revolution. Both sides used European political terms of reference for the nomenclature of malicious presidential campaigns: Federalists were aristocratic Anglophiles, whereas Republicans became revolutionary Francophiles.

During the notoriously contentious presidential campaign of 1800, Thomas Jefferson's opponents cast him as a revolutionist with a "cant of jacobinical illiberality." His demonization through the lens of European political experience is demonstrated most strikingly, perhaps, by a cartoon circulated to undermine Jefferson's allegiance. The image, titled "The Providential Detection," shows Thomas Jefferson kneeling upon the altar to Gallic despotism. The scene captures Jefferson on the verge of casting a parchment labeled "Constitution & Independence U.S.A." into the raging flames, that are already sustained by the kindling of radical pamphlets. A divine Seeing Eye illuminates the scene, supporting the American eagle's attempt to intercept Jefferson's unpatriotic act. During the wrangling, Jefferson's infamous letter to Philip Mazzei (in which he describes the American government as being led by an "Anglo-Monarchico-Aristocratic party") falls out of his pocket. Jefferson's altar of French radical worship is supported by Satan himself, populated by a devil-tailed snake, French philosophies, a treacherous dagger, and a fiery font etched with skull and crossbones. Such visual rhetoric from the Federalists pitted "real American values" against Jefferson's volatile French-leaning politic. In turn, Jefferson accused John Adams of being so close to Great Britain that he planned to marry his son to one of George III's daughters, undoing the work of American Independence by creating a British-American dynasty.

For those who claim that history does not repeat itself, Jefferson's cartoon image finds its 21st-century manifestation in Jon McNaughton's 2012 painting, *One Nation under Socialism*. Here, in a much less nuanced rendering, Obama stands burning the Constitution of the United States, pointing proudly toward the engulfing flames and scowling boldly outward from the canvas. Unlike Jefferson's satirical sketch, complete with a panoply of representative imagery and supplemental Francophile "props," here Obama's un-American, radical, and subversive politics is represented only by the visage of the president himself. Obama's implied identity—as the angry black president, with redistributive, revolutionary, and foreign intentions—is painted in bold brushstrokes.

President Lincoln's preservation of the Union and wartime actions opened him up to unfavorable European comparison, with Southern opponents in particular casting him as a despotic totalitarian. In 1862, the *Richmond Dispatch* railed against Lincoln's efforts in emancipation and the imposition of martial law:

**Artist Unknown, "The Providential Detection,"
1797–1800. (Courtesy of the American Anti-
quarian Society)**

The people of Yankeedom are . . . as absolutely the slaves of a military despotism as the Russians or Austrians . . . They are learning, in its full force, the
meaning of Julius Caesar's terrible saying, *"inter arma silent leges"* ("in time
of war the laws are silent"). The law indeed has no more voice in Yankeedom
at this moment than it had in Rome when the whole republic was writhing
under the iron grasp of the great Dictator . . . Those who were once his fellow
citizens, are now his timid and abject slaves . . . History does not record a
usurpation so bold, so open, so thoroughly successful. Caesar, Cromwell, or
Bonaparte never attempted a revolution so astounding. Yet Caesar, Cromwell
and Bonaparte were among the greatest men that ever lived, and Lincoln is
one of the smallest. (Tagg 2009)

So foreign was Lincoln's mode of politics that it was more suited to
Russia, Austria, ancient Rome, Britain, and France than to America,
according to the opprobrium. Just as Obama was accused of turning to
the old ideologies of 20th-century communism, so Lincoln was characterized as "a believer in the savageries of old Europe." In 1864, one newspaper asked, "By whom and when was Abraham Lincoln made dictator

in this country?" During his 1864 reelection campaign, the *Illinois State Register* warned that "the most powerful monarchy in Europe would not dare commit the outrages which have been put upon us by the Lincoln administration" (Oates 1979).

In the early 20th century, the foreignization of presidential policy and personality as somehow European and tyrannical turned into a specific accusation of actively complicit communism. The United States underwent two discrete periods known as Red Scares. The first, between 1919 and 1921, was a product of a nationalist fervor in the wake of the U.S. involvement in World War I. Having witnessed the Russian Bolshevik Revolution in 1917, American leaders feared its violent manifestation in the United States. Authorities alleged that communism had contaminated America's labor movement, a claim that, combined with anarchist bomb plots in 1919, spread fear throughout the nation. Woodrow Wilson's Sedition Act of 1918 clamped down on antigovernment speech, with the strictures created by this legislation being compounded by heated rhetoric; illegal arrests, searches, and seizures; and the deportation of political undesirables and ideological "others." Between this period and the second Red Scare, epitomized by McCarthyism, Franklin Delano Roosevelt and his progressive economic reforms were the subject of a prolonged campaign of socialist accusations and Marxist conspiracies levied by his political detractors.

Roosevelt's inheritance of the Great Depression, and his subsequent enactment of the New Deal agenda, unemployment insurance, and social security as means to remedy the pain of the ongoing economic downtown, led to swift changes in governmental organization and assistance. In 2009, while appearing on the comedy chat show *Late Night with David Letterman,* Obama spoke seriously about the comparison of his own vilification to that suffered by FDR during the 1930s. "What's happened is that whenever a president tries to bring about significant changes, particularly during times of economic unease, then there is a certain segment of the population that gets very riled up," Obama said, before adding that "FDR was called a socialist and a communist." Obama was aware of the historicity of his foreignization.

As reported by the *Chicago Daily Tribune* in 1934, Senator Simeon D. Fess (Democrat-Ohio) described the New Deal agenda as a "policy of state socialism, which necessitates increased activities of the government in either ownership or operation of industry, or both." On the House floor in July 1935, Robert Rich, Republican from Pennsylvania, denounced President Roosevelt as "a socialist, not a Democrat," insisting that Roosevelt's actions went beyond ordinary partisan terminology. During his 1936 reelection campaign, the vilification increased. The

American Liberty League, a conservative organization sharply opposed to
the New Deal (and often described as a predecessor to the Tea Party),
described the election as a simple choice: "The people could either
breathe the clear fresh air of America, or the foul breath of Soviet
Russia." Senator Thomas Schall (Republican-Minnesota) tried to align
Roosevelt even more strongly with the Soviet cause, claiming that "the
Russian newspapers during the last election published the photograph
of Franklin D. Roosevelt over the caption, 'The first communistic
President of the United States.' " Schall interpreted this as Russia's
"knowledge concerning the ultimate intent of the President, which had
been carefully withheld from the voters in this country."

Although an initial supporter of FDR until 1935, newspaper publisher
William Randolph Hearst became a propagator of the Roosevelt-as-
communist theme throughout the 1936 presidential campaign; Hearst
alleged in his publications that the Democrat enjoyed support from senior
and influential Reds. After the White House denounced such claims,
Hearst issued a rebuttal to the "conglomerate party of socialists, communists and renegade democrats" arguing that Roosevelt "received the
support of the Karl Marx socialists, the Frankfurter radicals, communists and anarchists, the Tugwell Bolsheviks and the Richberg
revolutionists." Winning the election by a veritable landslide, Roosevelt
well understood the partisan nature of the socialistic demonization.
In a 1934 fireside conversation, Roosevelt—whose words Obama would
echo nearly 80 years later—dismantled the tactic of ultra-Leftist name-
calling:

Sometimes they will call it "Fascism," sometimes "Communism," sometimes
"Regimentation," sometimes "Socialism." But in so doing, they are trying to
make very complex and theoretical something that is really very simple and very
practical . . . Plausible self-seekers and theoretical die-hards will tell you of the loss
of individual liberty. Answer this question out of the facts of your own life. Have
you lost any of your rights or liberty or constitutional freedom of action and
choice? (Roosevelt 1992, 51)

The landmark phenomenon of a national, years-long, predominantly
unfounded communist witch-hunt—known as McCarthyism, so named
after the efforts of Senator Joseph McCarthy (Republican-Wisconsin)—
emerged in a post-World War II era of palpable national anxiety. In the
midst of the emerging Cold War, the threat of communism and all associated persons and organizations led to the overnight *prima facie* enemization of thousands of suspect Americans. Throughout more than 100
hearings and many more closed-door investigations, McCarthy whipped

the national psyche into a frenzy, making continuous, inflammatory, and vague allegations that government and industry had been infiltrated by communist sympathizers and activists. The tactics of political intimidation, guilt by association, and character assassination became poisonous for anyone who was investigated by the various committees and panels established for that purpose. Incarceration, job losses, and social ostracism were common outcomes for those subjected to McCarthyite examination. On various occasions, McCarthy claimed to have lists of Communist Party members working within government. He claimed that he knew of 205 subversives in the State Department, and also suggested that approximately 130 communist activists had gained access to U.S. nuclear facilities. Turning from people to their literature, McCarthy claimed that his aide, Roy Cohn, had discovered that the Overseas Library Program (administered by the State Department) had also been infiltrated, such that it now contained 30,000 books written by pro-communist authors. President Dwight Eisenhower acquiesced to McCarthy's book banning, leading to the confiscation—and in some cases burning—of McCarthy's subversive bibliography.

For McCarthy, the anticommunist cause was a matter of partisan principle as well as national duty. "The Democratic label," he argued, "is now the property of men who have been unwilling to recognize evil or who bent to whispered pleas from the lips of traitors." But McCarthy's extreme methods, and his continuation of the investigations despite GOP control of the executive office of government, also irked many leading Republicans, including Eisenhower. As with many transgressions in human history, the breadth and depth of McCarthy's agenda were made possible only by a lack of vociferous objection and resistance from moderate voices in an era of manipulated fear. Former President Harry Truman, whom McCarthy had labeled as a "dangerous liberal," lamented the ramifications of this period of history for the American soul: "Character assassination is their stock and trade. Guilt by association is their motto. They have created such a wave of fear and uncertainty that their attacks upon our liberties go almost unchallenged. Many people are growing frightened—and frightened people panic."

The public cross-examination of Obama's biographical, political, and moral character, in front of a jury made up of the American public, with false witnesses, incendiary and unsubstantiated evidence, character assassination, vague and unprovable charges, and guilt by tenuous association, aimed at whipping up fear and politically motivated slurs, with a less than thinly veiled prosecution of communistic infiltration, is undoubtedly a resurrection of McCarthyism. Whether it was Allen West's list of approximately 80 communist Congressional representatives; Spencer

Bachus's accusation that 17 of his House of Representatives colleagues were socialists; or Michele Bachmann's wish that "the American media would take a great look at the views of the people in Congress and find out if they are pro-America or anti-America"—a conservative ethos to question the patriotism of liberals in the age of Obama has reemerged as a partisan mode of being.

The difference between then and now is that McCarthy did not pursue President Truman or President Eisenhower as the source of communism itself; he had Russia for that. Instead, he cast a wide net of investigation from Hollywood to industry, from the federal government to the armed forces. Today, in contrast, the new McCarthyism is laser focused on a single individual as the source of national political corruption. President Obama is the direct subject of communist infiltration, it is claimed. The threat is no longer a foreign power, but rather an African American president who channels an intrinsic biographical foreignness to enact an anti-American agenda.

In conclusion, Obama's foreignization not only reinvigorated patterns of presidential attack on the basis of perceived European or otherwise un-American politics, but also exposed a modern ethos of racialized Cold War accusation. The anxieties surrounding Obama's politics of change, and his identity of difference, became the focus of a right-wing campaign of unsubstantiated allegations of national disloyalty, communist sympathy, and government infiltration, re-imagining an America replete with re-education camps and government mandated death panels.

REFERENCES

Amira, Dan. "Mitt Romney: President Obama Is European" *New York Magazine* (June 2, 2011). http://nymag.com/daily/intelligencer/2011/06/mitt_romney_to_save_america_ju.html.

Associated Press. "Rep. Allen West Says 'about 78 to 81' House Democrats in Communist Party," *NYDailyNews.com* (April 11, 2012). http://www.nydailynews.com/news/politics/rep-allen-west-78-81-house-democrats-communist-party-article-1.1060137.

Benen, Steve. "By the End of the week, He'll Be Accusing Me of Being a Secret Communist Because I Shared My Toys in Kindergarten." *Alternet.org* (October 29, 2008). http://www.alternet.org/story/105228/obama_mocks_socialist_attacks%3A_%22i_shared_my_toys_in_kindergarten%22.

Burns, Douglas. "King: Electing Obama Could Lead to 'Totalitarian Dictatorship.' " *The Iowa Independent* (October 25, 2008). http://iowaindependent.com/7522/king-electing-obama-could-lead-to-totalitarian-dictatorship.

Cook, Terry L. *America's Communist Revolution! Terrifying Change without Hope.* CreateSpace Independent Publishing Platform, 2010.

Corley, Matt. "DeLay On Obama: 'Unless He Proves Me Wrong, He Is a Marxist.' " *ThinkProgress.org* (June 5, 2008). http://thinkprogress.org/politics/2008/06/05/24302/delay-obama-marxist/.

Costa, Robert. "Gingrich: Obama's 'Kenyan, Anti-colonial' Worldview." *The National Review* (September 11, 2010). http://www.nationalreview.com/corner/246302/gingrich-obama-s-kenyan-anti-colonial-worldview-robert-costa.

Davis, Frank Marshall. *Livin' the Blues: Memoirs of a Black Journalist and Poet.* Madison, WI: University of Wisconsin Press, 1993.

D'Souza, Dinesh. *The Roots of Obama's Rage.* Washington, DC: Regnery, 2011.

Epstein, Jennifer. "Obama Scoffs at People Who Call Him a 'Socialist': 'You Gotta Meet Real Socialists.' " *Politico.com* (November 19, 2013). http://www.politico.com/politico44/2013/11/obama-scoffs-at-people-who-call-him-a-socialist-you-177886.html.

Evans, Ben. "Georgia Congressman Warns of Obama Dictatorship." *Fox News* (November 10, 2008). http://www.foxnews.com/printer_friendly_wires/2008Nov10/0,4675,CongressmanObamaMarxist,00.html.

Fernandez, Maria. "The Road to Victoria Jackson's Election Meltdown on Twitter." *The Daily Beast* (November 7, 2012). http://www.thedailybeast.com/articles/2012/11/07/the-road-to-victoria-jackson-s-election-meltdown-on-twitter.html.

Fife, Tom. "The First Time I Heard of Barack." *Rense.com* (2008). http://www.rense.com/general84/brck.htm.

Forman, Milos. "Obama the Socialist? Not Even Close." *The New York Times* (July 10, 2012). http://www.nytimes.com/2012/07/11/opinion/obama-the-socialist-not-even-close.html?_r=0.

Gammell, Caroline. "Academic Prowess of Barack Obama's Mother Disclosed." *The Telegraph* (September 16, 2009). http://www.telegraph.co.uk/news/worldnews/barackobama/6196237/Academic-prowess-of-Barack-Obamas-mother-disclosed.html.

Gingrich, Newt. *To Save America: Stopping Obama's Secular-Socialist Machine.* Washington, DC: Regnery, 2011.

Hamby, Peter. "McCain: 'I Don't Know' If Obama Is Socialist." *CNN Political Ticker Blog* (July 18, 2008). http://politicalticker.blogs.cnn.com/2008/07/18/mccain-%E2%80%9Ci-don%E2%80%99t-know%E2%80%9D-if-obama-is-socialist/.

Hedrick, David W. *The Liberal Claus(e).* Freedoms Answer, 2010.

Hendrickson, Mark. "President Obama's Marxist-Leninist Economics: Fact and Fiction." *Forbes* (July 26, 2012). http://www.forbes.com/sites/markhendrickson/2012/07/26/president-obamas-marxist-leninist-economics-fact-and-fiction/2/.

Kengor, Paul. *The Communist—Frank Marshall Davis: The Untold Story of Barack Obama's Mentor.* New York, NY: Simon and Schuster, 2012.

Kennicott, Philip. "Philip Kennicott on Images: Obama as the Joker Betrays Racial Ugliness, Fears." *The Washington Post* (August 6, 2009).

http://www.washingtonpost.com/wp-dyn/content/article/2009/08/05/AR2009080503876.html.

Kleefeld, Eric. "Allen West: 'Barack Hussein Obama' Is a 'Low-Level Socialist Agitator' (Video)." *TalkingPointsMemo.com* (April 22, 2011). http://talkingpointsmemo.com/dc/allen-west-barack-hussein-obama-is-a-low-level-socialist-agitator-video.

Klein, Aaron, and Brenda J. Elliott. *The Manchurian President: Barack Obama's Ties to Communists, Socialists and Other Anti-American Extremists.* Washington, DC: WND Books, 2010.

Koppelman, Alex. "Glenn Beck Exposes Obama's Communist Art Scheme." *Salon.com* (September 3, 2009). http://www.salon.com/2009/09/03/beck_art/.

Kujala, Jordan R. "Savage Repeatedly Called Obama an 'Afro-Leninist.'" *MediaMatters.org* (June 10, 2008). http://mediamatters.org/video/2008/06/10/savage-repeatedly-called-obama-an-afro-leninist/143714.

Kurtz, Howard. "Roger Ailes Lets Rip." *The Daily Beast* (November 16, 2010). http://www.thedailybeast.com/articles/2010/11/16/fox-news-chairman-roger-ailes-slams-white-house-in-exclusive-interview.html.

Limbaugh, Rush. "This Regime Doesn't Like America; Vilifies, Targets Americans Citizens." *The Rush Limbaugh Show* (April 15, 2010). http://www.rushlimbaugh.com/daily/2010/04/15/this_regime_doesn_t_like_america_vilifies_targets_american_citizens.

Limbaugh, Rush. "Pearls of Wisdom." *The Rush Limbaugh Show* (June 25, 2012). http://www.rushlimbaugh.com/daily/2012/06/25/pearls_of_wisdom.

Mayer, Jane. "Senator Ted Cruz Our New McCarthy?" *The New Yorker* (February 22, 2013). http://www.newyorker.com/online/blogs/comment/2013/02/ted-cruz-sees-red-not-crimson-at-harvard.html.

Morris, Dick, and Eileen McGann. *Revolt! How to Defeat Obama and Repeal His Socialist Programs.* New York, NY: Harper Collins, 2011.

Oates, Stephen B. *Our Fiery Trial: Abraham Lincoln, John Brown, and the Civil War Era.* Amherst, MA: University of Massachusetts Press, 1979.

Obama, Bara(c)k H. Sr. "Another Critique of Sessional Paper No. 10: Problems Facing Our Socialism" *The East Africa Journal* (July 1965). http://www.politico.com/static/PPM41_eastafrica.html.

ObamaConspiracy.org. "Barack Obama Is a Communist." December 31, 2008. http://www.obamaconspiracy.org/2008/12/barack-obama-is-a-communist/.

O'Reilly, Bill. "Krauthammer: Obama Using SOTU Speech to Crush the Republicans." *The O'Reilly Factor, Fox News* (February 13, 2013). http://www.foxnews.com/on-air/oreilly/2013/02/13/krauthammer-obama-using-sotu-speech-crush-republicans.

Pleat, Zachary. "Beck Lies about His History of 'Dragging' Obama's Family 'into the Debate.'" *MediaMatters.org* (June 1, 2010). http://mediamatters.org/research/2010/06/01/beck-lies-about-his-history-of-dragging-obamas/165604.

Roosevelt, Franklin Delano. *FDR's Fireside Chats*. Norman, OK: University of Oklahoma Press, 1992.

Savage, Michael. *Trickle Down Tyranny: Crushing Obama's Dream of the Socialist States of America*. New York, NY: Harper Collins, 2012.

Stein, Sam. "Bachmann: Obama Wants 'Re-education Camps for Young People.' " *The Huffington Post* (May 7, 2009). http://www.huffingtonpost .com/2009/04/06/bachmann-obama-wants-re-e_n_183552.html.

Tagg, Larry. *Unpopular Mr. Lincoln: The Story of America's Most Reviled President*. New York: Savas Beatie, 2009.

Ungar, Rick. "Still Believe That Barack Obama Seeks a Permanent American Socialist State?" *Forbes.com* (January 6, 2013). http://www.forbes.com/ sites/rickungar/2013/01/06/still-believe-that-barack-obama-seeks-a-permanent -american-socialist-state/.

Wharton, Billy. "Obama's No Socialist. I Should Know." *The Washington Post* (March 15, 2009). http://www.washingtonpost.com/wp-dyn/content/ article/2009/03/13/AR2009031301899.html.

Wise, Tim. "Socialism as the New Black Bogeyman: Red Baiting and Racism." *CounterPunch.org* (August 11, 2009). http://www.counterpunch.org/2009/ 08/11/red-baiting-and-racism/.

Chapter 6

The Outside(r) Advantage: Social Media, Participatory Culture, and a Rhetoric of Difference[1]

And so we arrive at our startling—and motivating—paradox.

Barack Obama is undoubtedly the most demonized, foreignized, and "othered" political personality in recent memory, exposed to a metamorphic campaign of identity denigration by virtue of his birth, race, politics, and religion. He has been cast as an illegitimate baby; a foreign interloper; a communist revolutionary; an ignorant, apathetic, and aggressive black man; a secret Muslim; a covert terrorist; a Kenyan anticolonialist; a tyrannical monarch—and worse. Such characterizations revived antique modes of racial prejudice and patriotic belonging in an attempt to force Obama's very existence to the outskirts of American normalcy. His unique personal biography has been transmogrified into the bildungsroman of some malevolent antihero to support the vignettes of his demonization. His elections have inspired protests, secession petitions, and the creation of the Tea Party movement and SuperPACs with the mission of removing him from office. Political representatives and media personalities have initiated, and legitimated the various identity-based conspiracy theories conjured against the 44th president, which, at their heart, "other" Obama as a national aberration of the political construct.

Yet despite all of this, and in the very same America, that supposedly Afro-Marxist, red-diaper, extremist, anti-Christian, Black Panther

---

[1]Parts of this chapter are reproduced from Martin A. Parlett, "Barack Obama, the American Uprising and Politics 2.0," in *Social Media Go to War*, 2013. (Copyright retained by Martin A. Parlett.)

president has inspired a grassroots coalition of electoral support of Nobel Prize–winning consequence, and has been twice elected and twice legitimized as the executive representative of the people, having gained majority approbation at the ballot box.

This chapter aims to provide a rumination on this oxymoron—that is, how President Obama has been able to recognize the problematic markers of his potential marginalization and transform them, through rhetorical manipulation, strategic intent, and participatory social media, into positive electoral attributes. More specifically, this chapter underlines how Obama uses elements of his own "otherness" to appeal to distinct, and often alienated, constituents in building one of the most formidable coalitions of support in the last century.

Put another way, for Obama, "othering" has been both disease and cure. His right-wing (and some left-wing) opponents have seized on Obama's identity as evidence of an interior political malignancy, calling upon the tropes of discrimination to equate the president's uniqueness with a foreign and anti-American danger. Conversely, Obama has embraced his own heterogeneity as political capital, using it as a metaphor for American diversity and as a symbol for his grassroots movement of total inclusion. With the potential to realign the axis of a nation haunted by slavery, he became—and often presented himself as—the symbolic representation of racial and general transformational projects. In doing so, Obama became the icon of diversity and the visual proclamation of change.

As a mixed-race man, born off the American mainland to an unconventional mother and a largely absent African father, schooled for a time in Indonesia while living with a Muslim stepfather, with an unusual and foreign-sounding name, Barack Hussein Obama's successful nomination and elections signaled a *prima facie* triumph of the outsider against a tradition of racial (and other) exclusions. Obama's varietal iconicity—teamed with a lexicon of "Change," "Hope," and "Belief"—became the organizational principle of the campaign proper. Obama's individual atypicality was the figurehead of a wide-scale movement founded upon the tenet of unlimited outreach. His melting-pot mantra of "young and old, rich and poor, Democrat and Republican, black, white, Hispanic, Asian, Native American, gay straight, disabled and not disabled" worked to democratize the then-Senator Obama's potential base of support. The strategy, of course, was by no means new: politics is a game of extending appeal. Nevertheless, its efficacy was undoubtedly assisted by the presence of an icon who from and within himself validated the concept of inclusion. It was a marketing tool of exceptional skill through which the specific difference of the leader was cascaded to appeal to the disenfranchised groups excluded from the white male status quo of a presidential "elite."

Obama was aware of his all-encompassing strategy years prior to his candidacy for president. As well as describing himself as a "blank screen" to receive the projections of others in *The Audacity of Hope,* he responded to the question posed by television host Oprah Winfrey, "What do you want to do with your politics?," by saying, in perhaps one of his most self-revelatory statements:

I'm well situated to help the country understand how we can both celebrate our diversity in all its complexity and still affirm our common bonds. That will be the biggest challenge, not just for this country but for the entire planet. How do we say we're different, yet the same? Of course, there will be times when we'll argue about our differences, but we have to build a society on the belief that you are more like me than different from me. That you know your fears, your hopes, your love for your child are the same as what I feel. Maybe I can help with that because I've got so many different pieces in me. (Obama 2004)

Those "different pieces" within Obama became the micro-equivalent to the macro-organizational principle of Obama's campaign, rhetoric, and social media utilization. Obama's election success was to celebrate, then amalgamate, complex diversities under the unifying power of his own narrative.

A largely unreported phenomenon of the 2008 campaign—and testament to Obama's ability to bring together supporters of widely disparate backgrounds, identities, and beliefs—was the demographic make-up of his volunteer and activist community. In Virginia, for example, I heard the British, Australian, Irish, and German accents that collided with the more domestic dialects from Boston, Maine, Maryland, Pennsylvania, Iowa, and Hawaii. True to Obama's mantra, staff and volunteers spanned the entire gamut of social, racial, physical, religious, sexual, and political spectra. In essence, the icon of Obama had proliferated into a series of demi-icons of diversity. The strategy was more than just words, though words were important, as we shall later explore; rather, it was a thorough and meaningful project of acceptance. A hand was a hand, and a voice was a voice. If you could speak, you could make calls; if you could walk, you could knock on doors; if you could fold paper, you could prepare mailings; if you were shy, you could deal with administration; and if you were hopeless at all of the above, you could provide lunch. The campaign was based on a simple, but powerful three-column principle: "Respect. Empower. Include."

It was the campaign workers' responsibility not only to recruit and retain volunteers, but also to actively recognize and harness the particular symbolic qualities of each individual who walked through the door. While being inclusive, the campaign made no apologies for subdividing its volunteers into miniature taskforces covering specific political, racial, and gender issues. "Women for Obama Wednesdays," for example, saw female volunteers deployed to personally contact female voters on issues with the most demographic pull for the female vote. Veteran affairs canvassing drew upon the unique resources surrounding the nearby military bases through which military families were contacted to set out Obama's policies for Afghanistan and Iraq. "Republicans for Obama" revealed their own stories of political conversion to those potential voters who had expressed only leaning support for John McCain. County and state organizers were involved with the temporary iconization of volunteers to inspire wider participation and electoral interests.

The campaign framework was built upon a highly complex information database, called *Votebuilder*, in partnership with the national Democratic Party. Each "contact" with an individual voter was recorded on his or her personal log, and the technology allowed the campaigner to append to that long seemingly extraneous details of that conversation: "likes Hillary," "owns a dog," "anti-war," "pro-life," and "gun ownership" were common enough epithets. Mailing strategies were developed that converted the concerns from the doorstep into targeted and personalized responses from the campaign. Within 24 hours of a telephone or threshold conversation with Obama volunteers, a personal letter, factsheet, and specific item of literature, reflecting the issue of concern, were distributed in the mail. This mailing was then followed up in the next 48 hours to confirm delivery and to open up dialogue about the nature of the potential voter's indecision and the details of Obama's plans. While being a campaign of blanket inclusion inspired by a political "CEO" who authenticated diversity, the quotidian strategy on the ground identified, celebrated, and deployed difference. This paradoxical, but winning formula sought mass incorporation as an organizational ideal, but achieved this ideal through a sensitivity to uniqueness. The campaign was inclusive in membership, but effectively discriminatory in its method. Six million separate volunteering psychologies could have descended into organizational chaos, yet Obama's communication strategy purposefully attempted to sustain ideological unity.

The peculiar extent of diversification in the campaigns in 2008 and 2012 was matched by a linguistic strategy of maximizing relevance—a political *lingua franca*, if you will, that found resonance with the greatest number of voters in the largest number of contexts. Obama's primary slogan "Yes We Can," for example, embraced the campaign's ethic of embracing difference as advantageous in building an alliance of supporters. This simple trisyllabic phrase,

> Yes (Affirmative interjection)
> We (First person plural pronoun)
> Can (Modal auxiliary verb of potential)

as I have discussed in an earlier paper, is a masterfully ambiguous phrase of positive perception and collective action:

The purposeful incompleteness functions to increase the flexibility of the slogan's application to a variety of campaign literatures and ephemera, whilst permitting innumerable political participants to act as interlocutors, supplying the denouement of their choice … Accordingly the central pronoun "we" equalizes the politician and his supporters, whilst also providing a particularly useful generality of identification. The innate elasticity of the first person plural pronoun—appropriate for two or two million—allows the umbrella of inclusion to be as broad or narrow as the speaker chooses to define it. As such it enables Obama to relate to a national or general audience, as well as social groups with specific mandates or policy positions. It allows Obama to perform an acute conceit by expressing an image of unity, and simultaneously encouraging diverse identifications with his campaign. Thus, Yes We Can is a slogan which manages a set of collective attitudes without explicitly discriminating between constituencies (although this was often the way in which the phrase was used). When ingratiated into particular contexts (religious, racial, political) the "we" is provided with boundaries of definition—*Yes African Americans Can*, for example—but these are able to coexist with a number of other identifications (Yes Latinos Can, Yes American Christians Can, Yes American Jews Can) without ever explicitly marginalizing any electoral "target." In short, the ambiguity of this pronominal pivot encourages voters to construct their own associative meanings surrounding the candidate …
The use of the affirmative adverb "Yes" is also rhetorically significant in presenting the slogan as some kind of well-rehearsed responsorial to any criticisms or doubts which might be proffered against the candidate. This technique draws upon the traditional rhetorical argumentative device known as *prolepsis*—also understood as a form of prebuttal—predictively anticipating and complicating potential future criticisms … Yes We Can, therefore, severely problematizes any possible accusation of inability (No You Can't) by posing that claim as an antiquated ventriloquization of age-old prejudices. That is, Yes We Can energetically promises to dismantle the walls of exclusion (in terms of race, class, sex, gender, etc.) which surround the traditional presidential arena. Thus Obama has framed his own campaign as a movement to some sort of post-racial utopia, rendering any straightforward refutation as a kind of discriminatory institutional spasm. (Parlett 2011)

Thus, Obama's slogan functioned to extend the candidate's "Yes I Can" challenge to institutional whiteness and other forms of identity opposition to the individuals' own "Yes I Can" agendas, under a collective and powerful voice. There is no literal "I" in Obama's slogan, but beneath the surface it sustained a host of innumerable and potentially irreconcilable, political aims. The use of Obama's own symbolism and a lack of specificity in the slogan itself sustained a collective imagination for the satisfaction of primarily individual aims.

To explicate this concept further, I devote the remainder of this chapter to an analysis of Obama's utilization of campaign technologies (primarily during the 2008 election) to proactively optimize his greatest weakness: his difference.

SOCIAL MEDIA, SYMBOLIC CONVERGENCE, AND HARNESSING DIFFERENCE

In 2008, Barack Obama's election to the U.S. presidency was heralded as an identifiable locus of the emerging yet potent force of social media and the collective energy of its users. For the first time in American history, an African American had been elected to the stratosphere of political power, an underdog achievement, laying to rest the myth of absolute white political supremacy. In parallel, the dominant role of social media in this election cycle indicated a seismic shift in the dynamics of journalism, through which, to a significant extent, broadcast gave way to interactivity and multicast with greater opportunity for viewer response. If the destabilization of the Ben Ali, Mubarak, Saleh, and Gadhafi regimes represents how social media, infused with civic engagement and lit by the flame of democracy, can promote disunion between a political leader and his publics, Obama's relationship with Web 2.0 technology demonstrates its converse power to galvanize mass political support for a political leader who purportedly represents and speaks to the shared ideals of his participants.

This chapter uses Obama's utilization of social media technologies as an exemplar of the president's ability to positively engineer and reorient the denigration of his identity, taking into account the following factors in giving rise to Obama's outside(r) advantage:

1. The recognition of, and attendance to, the expectations of an established participatory culture

2. The recognition of, and attendance to, the expectations of a youth movement of the Millennial generation

3. A milieu in which opposition politicians failed to completely recognize and attend to points 1 and 2

4. A campaign that was able to translate Obama's personal identity of "difference" so as to sustain a multitude of interests by pursuing a molecularized strategy of appealing to specific constituencies, while maintaining an overarching appeal to the mass electorate

5. The creation of a stable rhetorical vision, in accordance with symbolic convergence theory

6. An embrace of the terrifying and glorious uncontrollability of Web 2.0 technologies

Recent studies (Baumgartner and Morris, 2010; Gulati and Williams March 11, 2008, August 28–31, 2008; Kim and Geidner, 2008; Vitak et al., 2011) have attempted to quantify and correlate the relationship between measures of social network support (i.e., friends on Facebook) and electoral success, suggesting the existence of direct correspondence between online friendship and offline votes. Indeed, by Election Day, Obama had 2 million Facebook friends, whereas McCain had only 600,000; on Twitter, McCain had a following of only 4,500 in comparison to Obama's 112,000 followers; and on YouTube, Obama's subscribers outnumbered his opponent's by four to one.

While these findings are intriguing, such research of simple causality neglects the very significant multifaceted interactions of rhetoric, culture, and medium at play in the 2008 (or indeed any) political election. Moreover, such social science quantifications do not reveal the qualitative explanations for such a correlation: Obama might have had more Facebook friends, for example, because his general outreach to voters was more sophisticated, which in turn led to his electoral success. We will therefore examine the Obama election campaign primarily through the lens of participatory culture and symbolic convergence theory to explain why the Illinois senator alone seemed to intuitively seize the contemporary social zeitgeist and fully utilize its related technologies.

PARTICIPATORY CULTURE AND THE MILLENNIAL GENERATION

Barack Obama's online and offline political movement was both a response to and a form of participatory culture. A participatory culture is an antonymic response to consumerism, in which individuals are no longer simply passive consumers, but also significant producers of cultural content—a new generation of *prosumers,* if you will. A participatory culture is defined as one with relatively low barriers to artistic expression and civic engagement, strong support for generating and sharing creations, and some type of informal mentorship whereby experienced participants pass along knowledge to novices. In a participatory culture, members also believe their contributions matter and feel some degree of social connection with one another (Jenkins 2009, 3).

While participatory culture predates the Internet, new research has emerged over the last decade as society increasingly finds in new media technologies and social media platforms the possibility to enact, more freely than ever before, the impulses of prosumerism. The culture of participation is developing in potency as that culture imbibes, and reacts to, the breakneck emergence of Web 2.0 technologies.

Audiencehood has been reconceptualized by participatory culture research as an interactive and complicated mode of being. Media and communications specialist Henry Jenkins has written extensively on the nature of participatory culture and the movement toward a " 'convergence culture,' where old and new media intersect, where grassroots and corporate media collide" (Jenkins 2006, 259). In an important and readable report commissioned by the MacArthur Foundation for Digital Media and Learning, Jenkins, as part of his recommendations for improving youth competencies in this new media landscape, reiterates the four central avenues for involvement in a participatory culture: *affiliation* (e.g., membership in online communities), *expression* (e.g., the production of new or appropriated content), *collaborative problem solving* (e.g., working in teams to complete tasks or develop knowledge and skills), and *circulation* (e.g., influencing the flow of media through vlogging) (Jenkins 2009, 8).

Throughout 2007–2008, Obama's embrace of online tools opened all four of these avenues for his grassroots dimension, while energizing a youth base most literate in the technology and its expectations. Through his own social network, MyBO, and his presence on others such as Facebook, MySpace, and LinkedIn, Obama enabled his supporters to build profiles connected to the campaign and express *affiliation* with certain policy groups or pages. Members could *express* themselves through the creation of new content—on widely read MyBO blogs or YouTube channels, for example. Indeed, the campaign hierarchy often released "how to" and response content to encourage this expression and assure users of its value. *Collaborative problem solving* is at the core of a political campaign, and Obama's online and offline advances in collective activity (hosting house parties, attending policy roundtable discussions, canvassing potential voters, and using the *Neighbor-to-Neighbor* function on MyBO) viewed gathering the perspectives of the ordinary citizen as valuable and constructive. Similarly, *circulation* was facilitated by Obama's own website and his links to immediate news-making social networks such as Facebook, Twitter, and YouTube.

Participatory culture and the "culture of Obama" became almost interchangeable philosophies. As the former represented a "new generation of media-makers and viewers . . . which could lead to a sea change in how media is made and consumed" (Blau 2005, 3), the Obama culture represented a new generation of politically and technologically engaged activists who could lead a sea change in how the very theory of democracy is enacted in U.S. presidential elections. Prior to the dawn of participatory cultural practice and its associated Web 2.0 media, young people were, on the whole, disempowered from the political process and the traditional media that communicated it. Referencing the work of David Buckingham, professor of education at the University of London, Jenkins maintains:

[P]olitics, as constructed by the news, becomes spectator sport, something we watch but do not do. Yet the new participatory culture offers many opportunities for youths to engage in civic debates, participate in community life, and even become political leaders, even if sometimes only through the "second lives" offered by online communities. (Jenkins 2009, 10)

Yet, just as Obama did not create participatory culture, so he did not magically call into being a new generation of democratic youth activism with a penchant for social media. Indeed, as youth vote researcher Kathleen Barr has traced, a high liberal youth turnout in 2008 was on schedule: partly because of the characteristics of the new generation and partly because of the outreach of political campaigns (Barr 2009). It was, however, the Obama campaign's ability to empower this generation as valuable civic actors, particularly through a social media strategy that placed interaction above broadcast, that positioned Obama as the candidate of youth identification and cultural participation.

The Millennial generation (an unsatisfactory and variably interpreted label), understood here as those persons born between 1981 and 2000, has emerged as the most liberal, ethnically and racially heterogeneous, and technologically minded generation in history. The Millennials are statistically more likely to volunteer and to engage in politics and community organization. According to a 2010 Pew Research Center report, *Millennials: A Portrait of Generation Next*, this generation is more likely to connect to wireless Internet, use social networking multiple times a day, post a Tweet, use cell phones only, send text messages, and access their news online. They are "confident, self-expressive, liberal, upbeat and open to change" (Taylor and Keeter 2010, 1). Yet the Millennials are also perceived as the most politically mobile cohort, more likely than any other age group to boycott a product or service when dissatisfied. As a consequence, mere token gestures toward Millennials' aspirations would not guarantee long-standing allegiance, nor would a superficial engagement of the media tools with which they are so highly familiar. Authentic empowerment in the political process is the means to appeal to this young participatory culture, which had all the markings of a king-maker in the 2008 election.

It came as little surprise that a youthful campaign, meaningfully employing new media tactics from the Left, attracted the support of the 18- to 29-year-old cohort. Indeed, throughout the primary stage of the voting process, young Republicans' share of voters rose from 9.7 percent in the 2000 Republican primary to 10.7 percent in 2008. Even more significantly, Democratic youth voting surged from 9.4 percent of all voters in 2000 to 14.3 percent in 2008. In the general election, 23 million, or 53 percent, of under-30s voted—more than in any other election in presidential history, surpassing even the turnout in 1972, when 18-year-olds were first permitted to vote in federal contests. Youth-geared organizations such as Rock the Vote, founded in 1991, worked with an unprecedented intensity to register first-time voters (mainly liberal-leaning Millennials) on college campuses across key battleground states. Electoral strategists and pundits have invariably agreed that without the youth vote, Obama would not have beaten McCain to the White House. Obama, however, conscientiously attended to this newly participatory generation at their locale of revolution: the Internet—defined by Tapscott as the Millennials' "tract, megaphone, teach-in, bookstore, fundraising event, demonstration, makeshift stage, and war room all in one" (Tapscott 1998, 300).

Similarly, unlike McCain, Obama established an entire staff concentrated on youth outreach efforts and grassroots organizations intended to register, train, mobilize, educate, and persuade the Millennial community and beyond. Kathleen Barr succinctly describes the disparity between the campaigns' reactions to the inevitable "perfect storm" of youth turnout:

By fall 2008, the Obama youth effort had full-time paid organizers in 18 states, plus a National Youth Vote Director ([Leigh] Arsenault) and a National Voter Registration Director, Jason Green. Other youth outreach arms, most notably Students for Barack Obama, had grown from independent efforts to crucial parts of the campaign infrastructure … By contrast McCain still had just one youth-focused staff person. (Barr 2009, 120)

Despite this evident investment in youth engagement, the Obama campaign did not distinguish between this and his overall strategy of civic transformation. MyBO, social network presence, and volunteer training were not tools developed for Obama youth per se, but rather for the entire participatory culture. Obama merely translated the expectations of the Millennials into the 21st-century political experience. Millennial knowledge, perspective, and practice were just some components of Obama's overall appeal to what Pierre Levy defines as a networked "collective intelligence"—a system in which no one knows everything, but everyone knows something (Levy 2009). Obama's organization promoted the importance of this demographic's contribution toward a collective intelligence, which could be facilitated through a "communalized media." Quite simply, youth were at the core, and not the fringe, of the Obama movement, and this centrality paid dividends. According to a Pew Research Center report, *Young Voters in the 2008 Election,* McCain managed to make contact with only one in eight young voters prior to Election Day, whereas the Obama campaign interacted with at least one fourth of the same group (Keeter, Horrowitz, and Tyson 2008). That this is the only age group to report such a differential points to the success of a meaningful Web 2.0 strategy and the appeal to a Millennial generation prepared for a revolution in politico-cultural practice.

BEFORE OBAMA: SOCIAL MEDIA AND PRESIDENTIAL POLITICS

Prior to analyzing the 2008 race, it is important to recognize the prehistory of presidential campaign technology. In 1996, personality-oriented candidate websites emerged; in 1998, email was used as an outreach tool primarily by Jesse Ventura's short-lived presidential bid; in 2000, John McCain (in an ironic twist) heralded the new frontier of campaign fundraising, raising $2.2 million in a week of online contributions; in 2003, blogs—both official and not—flourished in a golden age of online political commentary. As far back as 1992, presidential candidate Ross Perot proposed a radical system of electronic town halls, through which democracy was enacted via a theoretical live electronic voting system, allowing immediate referenda on current legislative issues. But perhaps the most important precursor to the Obama new media strategy, Howard Dean's campaign of 2003–2004, provided a narrow glimpse of the future.

Without doubt, the advancement of social media usage in political organization finds its origins in Dean's failed bid for the Democratic presidential nomination. The Dean campaign was the first to seriously enable its supporters to utilize nascent social media tools in any significant way, primarily through a community organization website, MeetUp.com. MeetUp was founded in 2001 as a platform for online users to create, join, and attend offline meetings or "affinity spaces"—ranging from Harry Potter enthusiasts, to fine wine aficionados, to political activists. Two years after its founding, Dean incorporated the MeetUp function on the homepage of his own website, encouraging sympathetic activists to self-organize within their local communities, under the name of the Howard Dean campaign. Dean supporters sought out this online outlet for their participatory cultural impulses, meeting across the country to knock on doors, plan local meetings or rallies, and write personal letters to voters. The candidate's website enabled electronic distribution of policy points, forum chats, and monetary donations. Furthermore, Dean's creation of *Blog for America* enabled supporters to circumvent the broadcast nature of traditional media and create what Steven Jones describes as a "complex, palpable, but elusive entity . . . a computer mediated or cyber community" in which members could exchange self-affirming expressions of support (Kerbel and Bloom 2005, 4).

Despite exiting the race is early 2004, Dean set an example that was quickly appropriated by the opposition, perhaps most strikingly by George W. Bush's get-out-the-vote stage strategy of presidential house parties—offline community festivities for political proselytization, organized primarily through an online platform based on Dean's effort. From this point onward, no serious campaigner for residency of 1600 Pennsylvania Avenue could avoid the emergent Web 2.0, and that offline battle had an important counterpart in a virtual media. Dean also exemplified one of the unique dangers of online electioneering; through its very elusiveness, it is difficult to quantify actual support from a social media community. As researcher danah boyd remarked:

[O]ffline you know if a door has been slammed in your face; online it is impossible to determine the response that the invisible audience is having to your message. (boyd 2008a, 115)

The marriage of Campaigning 1.0 and Web 2.0 was vital, and necessitated greater understanding by the candidates themselves. It is no surprise, therefore, that the forays of politicians into this online warfare during the 2008 election cycle were marked by tentativeness and traditionalism, which often did not capture the interconnectivity of old and new media, and old and new campaigning alike. Hillary Clinton, Barack Obama, Joe Biden, John Edwards, and Sam Brownback were among those who turned away from traditional media and toward new media to announce their candidacy for executive office. The majority of these announcements were made through the online video hosting and sharing website YouTube, which had been founded in 2005. YouTube is in many ways a formalization of participatory cultural media proliferation and interactivity, allowing various levels of public engagement. In *YouTube: Online Video and Participatory Culture*, Jean Burgess and Joshua Green define the online facility as "one of a number of competing services aiming to remove the technical barriers to the widespread sharing of video online," and Jenkins further suggests it might represent "the epicenter of today's participatory culture" (Burgess and Green 2009, 1, 109). As such, presidential candidates keen to *appear* to attend to this new cultural phenomenon gravitated toward YouTube, which in turn created a politically structured subsite, known as You-Choose08, to accommodate them.

To build the momentum for his own grassroots political movement, Senator John Edwards was the first mainstream presidential candidate in the 2008 election cycle to utilize a social medium for campaign organization. Edwards pursued an expansive presence on 23 different social networks. The North Carolina senator released a saccharine battle cry on YouTube.com, entitled *Tomorrow Begins Today*, on December 27, 2006. In it, Edwards stands among a group of black youths engaged in a reconstruction effort in post-Hurricane Katrina New Orleans with desolated houses as the backdrop. The senator attempts to use the visual grassroots efforts of his surroundings as a call to arms for political support and low-level participation in "rebuilding a broken America." The address makes all of the right noises ("ground up" effort, "I wanted you to hear it first," and "forward this video to all of your friends") and features the patois of participatory culture (inclusion, empowerment, and respect for the ordinary citizen). After just 48 hours, the message had received more than 50,000 views.

The rhetoric, however, was undermined by a certain primitiveness that misses the full opportunities of the medium. Despite the tagline "Exclusive to YouTube," there is very little in the video's content to signal the announcement as online specific. The 2.5-minute video is a static, single-view direct-to-camera setup, in the style of a traditional satellite broadcast link-up for television news segments. That it ends with an on-screen signpost to "www.johnedwards.com" and a text message registration service ("text 'hope' 30644") does little to rectify the internal problems of the preceding "broadcast." The result is an altogether strange and ill-advised initiation of the online presidential battle that eventually gathered only 170,000 views before Election Day.

New York Senator Hillary Clinton—Barack Obama's prime opponent for the Democratic nomination—also settled upon YouTube users as the premier audience for her candidacy announcement. Almost a month after Edwards's attempt, Clinton released *I'm In,* a declaration of political intent and an invitation to a national online conversation. Sitting on a sofa, the senator remarked, "I'm beginning a conversation ... So let's talk. Let's chat. Let's start a dialogue." In doing so, she attempted to lower the barriers of access for political participation. This was not a top-down imposition from the establishment, she claimed (a prescient concern for the spouse of a former president), but rather a leveling of presidential and public registers.

However, the video actually communicated a different message. Rather than learning from the lessons of the Edwards strategy, the Clinton video found its point of reference in an old-media-style broadcast. The entire video is wrapped in a televisual cliché: through a pastel hue glaze, we see the former First Lady perched upon a velvet chaise, flanked by a lamp and family pictures. The lines are faultless, but delivered with smiling consistency and a lack of authenticity. The result is a corporate, fake domestic setting where participation is more a prop than the central concern. Clinton is still dutifully in charge; she is visiting our living rooms, but we are certainly not visiting hers. The incongruity of medium, delivery, and message is further intensified by Clinton's scripted line, "with a little help from modern technology," which seems an age-defined and almost nontechnological expression, out of touch with the social tools the candidate professes to engage. Team this with Clinton's preselection of user questions and well-rehearsed responses during her subsequent online webchats, and it was felt by many that the candidate was offering a form of participatory culture-lite.

The contrived nature of the *I'm In* video and its underestimation of the interactive desires of a participatory culture were seized upon by a YouTube user, ParkRidge47 (also known as Phil De Vellis), and transmogrified into an anti-Clinton video entitled *Vote Different*. Mashed up with a 1984 commercial for Apple's *Think Different* campaign, De Vellis exemplified the potential for new-media impact. Clinton was recast as a Big Brother suppressor, utilizing technology as a unidirectional brainwashing instrument under the veil of participation. In this video, the pseudo-coziness of the original version becomes the metallic grayish nightmare of George Orwell's universe, as she is projected upon the inescapably large hypnotizing screen. The hammer thrower bears a passing resemblance to Clinton, giving a possible interpretation of self-destruction. The subtle glitches of the Clinton version are magnified by a scrutinizing online eye, a random opponent extracting their ultimate and damaging ironies. The senator had submitted herself not just to a conversation, but to a territory populated by intelligent, skilled, and potentially dangerous political actors. At the time of writing this chapter, Clinton's original video had accumulated close to 72,000 views online, whereas its spoliation, *Vote Different,* had received 6.2 million.

Later revealing his identity via *The Huffington Post,* De Vellis revealed much about the nature of new media dynamics:

I wanted to show that an individual citizen can affect the process ... This shows that the future of American politics rests in the hands of ordinary citizens ... the underlying point was that the old political machine no longer holds all the power ... The game has changed. (De Vellis 2007)

Edwards and Clinton had assumed the new media represented only a change of channel rather than a vehicle for, and a marker of, a change of cultural practice. In these efforts, both politicians released official broadcast messages under the guise of "bilateral communication" (Henke 2008), making a mockery, for some, of the true potential of websites such as YouTube for meaningful civic involvement. Communication expert danah boyd's supplication for candidates to "interact, not broadcast" went unheeded, as both Democrats "buil[t] structured, formalized content for citizens to passively consume" (boyd 2008b).

The online venue necessitated an embrace of a new political reality: that presidential candidates must submit themselves to very nontraditional media over which they have relatively little control. Only a true understanding of, and strategic response to, the essential powerlessness of Web 2.0 can provide the foundation for a genuine political movement based on participation and diversity.

OBAMA'S EMBRACE OF LACK OF CONTROL

The Barack Obama campaign, though with some misjudgments of its own, submitted itself to the creativity of user-generated content rather than presenting a unified, centrally dominating online messaging process. It was able to achieve this through an overarching campaign strategy that celebrated and symbolized difference—a mode of umbrella leadership, which was fueled by the participation and energy of diverse constituencies and authenticated by a leader who encapsulated multiplicity. The Obama campaign was political participatory culture defined, sustained by a grassroots civic engagement (from below) and energized by an icon of diversity (from above). With an unusual name, mixed-race parentage, an age close to 40, and a history of both low-level community organization *and* meteoric legal and academic achievement, Obama became a sort of metamorphic candidate with the potential—through symbolism alone—to uproot the presidency's inherited racial and social hegemony. The Illinois senator's genuine atypicality, in contrast to the presidential standard, was buoyed by, and reflected in, a grassroots campaign arguably more diverse than any other in U.S. presidential history. Both leader and followers radiated a sort of welcoming heterogeneity that authenticated a strategy of unrestrained membership and provided a universalism of appeal.

The symbolism was matched by the rhetoric. Obama's stump speeches were littered with this common *paradeigma*—young and old, rich and poor, Democrat and Republican, black, white, Hispanic, Asian, Native American, gay, straight, disabled and not disabled—that sought to universally lower the sociopolitical barriers to involvement in his organization, and perhaps even the American Dream itself, which Obama professed to represent. Obama's precampaign writing also offered glimpses into his early understanding of participatory culture and his almost unique ability to sustain an American smorgasbord. In *The Audacity of Hope,* Obama self-analyzes his role:

I serve as a blank screen on which people of vastly different political stripes project their own views. (Obama 2006, 16)

The future president realized that the age of traditional electioneering—with its emphasis on broadcast, unified messaging, and personal image—had given way to a modern civic sensibility of multimodal engagement. The candidate must become, in part, a passive component in this democratized political landscape in which members of the voting public are led to interpret and project their own context-informed "Obamas."

Obama's iconicity of diversity and access, as well as his social media strategy, might be better understood through the communication theory of *symbolic convergence* (Bormann 1972, 1985; Bormann, Cragan, and Shields, 1994, 1996, 2001, 2003). Symbolic convergence theory (SCT) explores how communities of agreement are constructed based on shared meanings or values, through the formation of fantasy themes. That is, reality is a social and symbolic construction, formed through our interaction with, and positive selection of, meanings shared with others. All perceptions are composites of our "adoption of, and addition to, the meanings of these interactions using symbols" (Larson 2009, 300). The theory "is one approach to account for human communication in terms of *Homo narrans.* It assumes that human beings are social storytellers who share fantasies and thus build group consciousness and create social realities" (Bormann 1985, 136). For *Homo narrans,* social media allow the rapid and horizontal dissemination or, and attraction to, shared narrative experiences. Obama's campaign in particular emphasized the importance of personal narration in the process of political persuasion, as Horace Campbell accounts in *Barack Obama and Twenty First Century Politics: A Revolutionary Moment:*

[T]he Obama team encouraged volunteers to tell their story in order to motivate other volunteers and activists. Just as Obama told his story in *Dreams from My Father,* each volunteer was encouraged to tell their story so that the power of their narrative could inspire others ... thus the very act of telling stories acted as one way to attract social forces who wanted change. (Campbell 2010, 99)

Introduced by Bormann and following the work of sociologist Robert Bales in the mid-20th century, SCT research demonstrated that groups of individuals would construct shared meanings (or fantasies) through the co-creation of particular rhetorics. When people come into contact with particular narratives or fantasies, they can choose to ignore them, accept them, or participate in them. Through our participation in particular, "we create social reality and come together in social convergence" (Larson 2009, 299). When a number of fantasy themes are constructed within a society, they may form a grand *rhetorical vision*—a super-fantasy on a potentially national or international scale, shared among a number of Burkean associates of substance. Bormann describes a rhetorical vision as a unified putting-together of the various scripts that gives the participants a broader view of things. Rhetorical visions are often integrated by the sharing of a dramatizing message that contains a master analogy, which pulls the various elements together into a more or less elegant and meaningful whole. A rhetorical vision is usually indexed by a key word, slogan, or label (Bormann 1985, 133). In Obama's case, the master analogy is that of his own "outsiderness" extended to appeal to all narratives of difference, sustained under the indexing and all-encompassing slogan, "Yes We Can."

The important underlying assumption throughout all of this research is that the world around us is a cooperative communicative creation, horizontal rather than vertical in nature. As a result, meanings formed through such communities of agreement are typically *more* stable than those delivered by sources of authority from, say, a governmental body.

All rhetorical visions begin with a genesis story, and if this narrative is "widely believed, we have a national rhetorical vision that can motivate nations to take drastic action" (Larson 2009, 300). Obama's presidential campaign was successful in allowing its supporters to organically form a rhetorical vision (that Obama was the symbol for a brighter American future), which was constructed by an accumulation of more specific fantasy themes. Through Obama's encouragement of a political participatory culture, the campaign allowed a maximal number of versions of these fantasies to be compiled without conflicting with one another, because of the sheer openness of Obama's rhetoric and his self-casting as the icon of multiple elements of difference (Parlett 2011, 29).

More importantly, the Obama campaign, while appearing universal, discretely encouraged the compartmentalization of communities of agreement. The paradoxical nature of the Obama campaign was that it represented a form of antidiscrimination and yet pursued a strategy that was, at its core, discriminatory. In segmenting the campaign into stratified portions—Students for Obama, Virginian Students for Obama, and University of Mary Washington Students for Obama, for example—the Obama grassroots movement was defined through the creation of robust fantasies that were chained together and sustained by an overarching rhetorical vision that Obama was the right choice at the ballot box in the general election. This strategy of micro-targeting, described by some as the "long tail" and likened to fractal geometry by others, "involved repeating self-similar patterns of community organizing by the grassroots" (Campbell 2010, 121) and was assisted by the opportunities afforded by social network messaging, through which contact lists could be created on the basis of location or interest. This unusual structure was relentlessly implemented across 50 states. It securely locked Obama supporters in a double community of agreement—one specific, one general—but both with socially constructed shared values that implored support for the Democratic candidate. In this sense, Obama's supporters literally created their own rhetorical visions of Obama due in part to the reflexivity with which he presented himself, but also due to the anti-paternalistic attitude of the politician. With little influence from Obama as to how his fantasy should be specifically constructed, activists and voters alike were able to indulge in particularly accommodating realms of fantasy themes (Parlett 2011, 29).

Aside from *genesis* stories, which are the points of origin for rhetorical visions, symbolic convergence is achieved through two further stages known as *consciousness-raising* and *consciousness-sustaining*. Consciousness-raising represents a preliminary stage of fantasy chain creation and, in the political context, might include a commitment to support the candidate, such as by attending a meeting or volunteering for a campaign. Consciousness-sustaining gives solidity to a fully formed rhetorical vision. During this stage, member retention and member recruitment are essential, as is the rhetorical vision's ability to survive among alternative and competing rhetorical vision creations (i.e., oppositional political campaigns or philosophies). Apart from Obama's open rhetoric, it was through his use of social media that his campaign was most obviously able to appeal to a participatory culture and to foster the consciousness-raising and consciousness-sustaining elements of symbolic convergence.

In February 2007, Barack Obama launched his online headquarters, my.barackobama.com, soon abbreviated—as is ubiquitous in the medium—to MyBO. In the words of digital strategist Rahaf Harfoush:

[I]t was the hub that captured all activists in the Obamaverse and shared them with the world. The blog was the campaign's repository, a place where stories, videos, news, and pictures were captured and pushed out to Obama's many social network profiles. (Harfoush 2009)

The sweep and intelligence of MyBO were unprecedented, partly because throughout the campaign it maintained a tone and functionality unparalleled by opposition versions, but mainly because it responded to—and was shaped by—a respected preexisting online community of supporters. The grassroots participation forced the top campaign advisers to expand their social networking capacity, not the other way around. The abbreviated name for the website, MyBO, borrowed from the success of MySpace and communicated the locus of control in the individual, a vital ingredient for peer-to-peer empowerment. The initialization of the candidate's name (BO) neutralized the ego of the candidate, as Obama stepped back from the center stage, a departure from the majority of heavily branded campaign websites and online tools.

While his political rivals introduced sound platforms for social media during the 2008 campaign, Obama's virtual hub was technically superior and more explicitly geared toward user participation. As far as possible, MyBO was designed to simulate offline campaign relationships, providing equal value to online and offline interactions. In the words of leading digital strategist Julie Barko Germany, the system attempted to harness all of the excitement and energy—the echo chamber effect that benefited candidates like Ron Paul and John Edwards early in the primaries—of a charismatic online candidate and channel that energy into real activities that met the goals of the campaign (Barko 2009, 156).

Sharing aspects of established social media while still maintaining traditional expectations of a campaign website, MyBO appealed to the expectations and sensibilities of a wide online community. At the point of entry, members were able to set up their own profiles—in a similar way to Facebook—which were accessible to all fellow members. New users were encouraged to complete their profiles with details including location, age, reasons for supporting Obama, and policy concerns. This promoted data collection *and* initiated members into ready-made communities based on shared preferences. Profiles were created automatically, not subject to any process of top-down authentication. Immediately, new members were led to their personalized homepages or dashboards furnished with a range of functions geared toward assisting Obama's organizational and electoral success. From here, users could join online groups (or communities of agreement) in one click, which in turn would advertise offline campaign events to their members. Diverse "constituency" groups such as tango dancers, single mothers, and cat owners could congregate and, if no suitable community was available, new groups could be formed to provide refuge for almost any interest, philosophy, or quirk. At all times, the user was in control of the level and energy of membership in both online and offline groups, creating more stable foundations for symbolic convergence and a tightly knit participatory culture. As members progressed, they were awarded points based on their level of activity (e.g., blogging, hosting events, creating groups), providing a clear incentive to perform as a "good" and "rewardable" participant in full view of their peers.

MyBO also allowed users to take ownership of the fundraising process by enabling members to create and name their own monetary campaign, set a fundraising goal, view a real-time success "thermometer," and send invitations to potential donors. The imperative to "donate" of the traditional campaign was democratized into a cooperative and voluntary pursuit. This innovation goes some way in explaining Obama's ability to raise an incomparable $650 million by Election Day, much of it from small donations, compared with McCain's $360 million.

Perhaps the most impressive function of the MyBO platform was its development of users' ability to act as campaign activists from the comfort of their own homes. Using a contact voter service, later renamed *Neighbor-to-Neighbor* (N2N), MyBO users could direct their own micro-campaigns either on the doorstep (by printing walk sheets, maps, and flyers for local neighborhoods) or by telephone canvassing of a number of locally situated voters. During the GOTV stage of the campaign, an app was launched for the iPhone, which had the facility to generate personalized call lists based on saved contacts. Each member was entrusted with accurately inputting the response data back into the MyBO system, which would enhance the accuracy and effectiveness of future voter contact. MyBO community members were becoming "their own generals," training for the momentous political battle ahead (Feld and Wilcox 2008, 135). Uniquely, N2N was tailored to a user's local environs and useful only insofar as the campaign fully trusted the data reports of their armies of casual activists.

MyBO was a transparent example of the performative participatory culture upon which the Obama campaign pivoted, eliding the impulses of new media and old campaigning. The figures speak for themselves: by Election Day, MyBO had facilitated the creation of more than 2 million profiles, 30,000 volunteer groups, 200,000 offline host events, and nearly 500,000 blog posts.

In contrast to the MyBO machine, John McCain's online platform, McCainSpace, was launched in the latter stages of the campaign, almost a year later than Obama's version. This delay halved the time during which the McCain campaign was able to mobilize its army of online-to-offline volunteers; it also severely reduced the effectiveness of McCain's consciousness-raising and consciousness-sustaining efforts for securing his own rhetorical vision. Obama's early introduction of MyBO had communicated a symbiosis between Obama and Web 2.0, whereas McCainSpace seemed to arrive as an overt strategic tool in response to opposition technology rather than any groundswell of grassroots dynamism.

McCainSpace—also borrowing from the MySpace portmanteau—maintained a candidate-centric online campaign. Profiles could be created, but membership was subject to approval from a campaign authority, often taking more than 48 hours to become fully active. As such, the conversation between McCainSpace members and the campaign hierarchy was burdened by a stuttering process, replete with the markers of top-down old media. The website was generally overbranded, and the functionality of the homepage appeared nebulous.

In isolation, McCainSpace was an innovation—more interactive than any previous Republican presidential campaign hub—yet MyBO had already elevated the standard. Though subsequently there was little difference in what the social networks could achieve, Republican supporters were putting on their chainmail as Democratic activists had already begun a momentous advance toward them. Neither electoral successes nor rhetorical visions are built in a day, despite the speed of new media.

NEW MEDIA AND THE THREAT OF RHETORICAL "VISION IMPLOSION"

Obama's progress, of course, was due to his submission to his essential lack of control over social media, and the senator's campaign clearly benefited from the collective intelligence and ingenuity of user-generated content. This meant that while rhetorical visions of Obama supporters were distributed for positive effect, those who shared alternative fantasy chains or rhetorical visions were able to use the very same media to disseminate their messages.

Two rhetorical communities living side by side in the same culture may have mirror-image rhetorical visions. That is, the same historical personages may be heroes in one community and villains in another, or one group may celebrate certain courses of action as laudable while the other denigrates the same scenarios (Bormann 1985, 135).

Thus, new media technologies had a particular propensity not only for forming communities of agreement, but also for initiating misinformation and rumor for communities of collective disagreement. While the beneficiary of social media advantage, Obama was also the recipient of the majority of social media disadvantage. Rumors reverberated throughout the conservative media echo chamber: Obama was communist, Muslim, satanic, a terrorist, and an illegal alien; he would ban your guns; he was endorsed by the Black Panthers; he was not the author of his own books; and he had gained entry to Harvard in spite of his own achievement, not because of it. It is important to note that the rumors that did persist might be characterized as fantasies of Obama's alienation. Accusations that Obama does not belong (religion, citizenship, political extremism) permit more subtle and veiled expressions of racism—a rhetorical vision prevalent in a number of American homes, transmitted through generations of prejudice, and reinvigorated by a potentially opposite rhetorical vision of black-man-as-president. A cursory search on YouTube reveals that user-generated content on such topics received vast viewing figures: "Obama Admits He Is a Muslim" (4.9 million views); "Obama Kenyan Birth Certificate" (800,000); "OBAMA TELLS AMERICA—'Serve Satan!'—This will floor you!" (2.4 million). Despite clear arguments to the contrary from official sources (e.g., the White House's eventual release of the birth certificate in April 2011) and as predicted by the stability theory of symbolic convergence, the horizontally formed rhetorical visions of Obama-as-outsider remain prevalent, perpetuated by online communities. Participatory culture has a Janus face, and Obama has looked into both pairs of eyes.

Perhaps Obama's most strained relationship with Web 2.0 arrived in March 2008—a *mensis horribilis* for the campaign during which the Reverend Jeremiah Wright controversy threatened to derail the senator's entire candidacy. Following ABC News research, damaging excerpts from the sermons of Obama's Chicago pastor were thrown like grenades into the online minefield. The clipped videos of Wright's distinctively aggressive preaching style showed the Reverend straying into areas of social and political commentary. The edited segments presented Wright as an antipatriot, preaching against the country's historical treatment of the black community in violently Biblical terms: "They wants [sic] us to sing *God Bless America*? No! No! No! Not *God Bless America*, God

DAMN America!" Even more damaging was the climax of a sermon delivered only days after the terrorist attacks of September 11, 2001. In it, Wright claimed:

We bombed Hiroshima. We bombed Nagasaki. And we nuked far more than the thousands in New York and the Pentagon, and we never batted an eye ... and now we are indignant? ... America's chickens are coming home to roost.

Soon YouTube users were appropriating the broadcast material, editing it to enhance its potency, and mashing it up with damaging imagery, music, and commentary. Online video sharing seemed to take over from the broadcast media in advancing the story, with the online world's participation applying pressure on the candidate to respond. The coverage was continuous, rebounding from old and new media alike. The Illinois senator was seeking nomination to the U.S. presidency, while spiritually aligned in the public's eye with a preacher who sought to "damn" the country and its misuse of executive power. Obama's symbolic quality was under threat and his rhetorical vision in a state of decline.

As Albert May has maintained, the Wright story became the first feeding frenzy of the digital age, illustrating

a new ecosystem of communication [which] has erased the boundaries of media and dramatically elevated the importance of images conveyed by video to millions of Americans on their televisions and computers. (May 2009, 79)

Through the perspective of symbolic convergence, those users disseminating the Wright YouTubery did so to disturb the consciousness-sustaining stage of convergence. The controversy and the general Obama-as-outsider rumor mill attempted to advance the rhetorical vision of Obama as a viable candidate to the final and destructive stage of symbolic convergence, known as *vision implosion*. This stage represents the irrecoverable end of a previously stable super-fantasy. The speed of social media publication and the very potent visual and aural qualities of the Wright videos catapulted the Obama campaign to the precipice of vision implosion, yet (as we know) he was able to eventually maintain a necessary symbolic convergence until Election Day. While Obama did not own participatory culture, as was evidenced by the extension of the scandal, he was protected by the stability of his long-term relationships with his prosumers. Returning to Web 2.0 to launch his strategic response, Obama's official YouTube channel, BarackObamadotcom, released two videos of Obama's *More Perfect Union* speech—a famous example of crisis rhetoric wrapped in an historic call for racial reparation—which gained more than 8 million collective views. It was an impressive feat for a 37-minute political speech, unedited for multicast.

During this crisis, Obama exemplified the perils and fortunes of presidential campaigning 2.0. Without his early understanding of participatory culture and his facilitation of stable rhetorical visions, Obama might not have survived the feeding frenzy of modern Internet electoral politics. Sarah Palin, who arrived relatively late in the campaign cycle, was unable to defend herself against the rumor mill with comparable power. In turn, the mainstream rhetorical vision of Palin was soon imploded by online communities that attempted to discredit the intelligence and suitability of the vice presidential hopeful.

Conversely, Obama demonstrated a striking ability to harness his online community to protect his rhetorical vision from Republican jibes. During her vice presidential nomination acceptance speech, Palin attempted to undermine the work of Obama as a community organizer, juxtaposing that experience with her own political background. "I guess a small-town mayor is sort of like a community organizer, except that you have actual responsibilities," she quipped, and was rewarded with cheers and laughter from the audience. The Obama machine moved to shield its candidate by using his social network platform, MyBO, and his text messaging and email databases to launch a national fundraising fight-back campaign under the guise of defending the work of grassroots activists across America. In a matter of hours, messages reached nearly every voter whom the Obama campaign had on record, supplicating them: "Let's clarify something for them right now. Community organizing is how ordinary people respond to out-of-touch politicians and their failed policies." In the month after Palin's threat to Obama's communities of agreement, the Obama campaign raised $151 million—a significant financial and philosophical affirmation of the security of Obama's symbolic convergence and its translation into real participatory action.

Obama's relaxed attitude toward the online activities of his supporters resulted in masterpieces of unofficial positive content. At the professional level, will.i.am's production of "Yes We Can" in February 2008—a music video in which the lyrics were formed entirely by digitally enhanced lines from Obama's New Hampshire primary concession speech—was released on Dipdive.com and on YouTube under the username WeCan08. The Obama campaign had no involvement in the musical innovation in which celebrities ventriloquized Obama's call for hopeful participation. Yet, its evident affinity with the campaign ethic of collective possibility, teamed with a faultless delivery, led the Obama machine to immediately adopt it. It was plastered across the campaign website and MyBO, and became a viral tool for youth outreach.

The most famous appropriation of, and response to, will.i.am's effort was the comically charged YouTube video "john.he.is," released only 10 days after the original. In it, user Election08 (actually a group of Los Angeles-based comics) used excerpts from McCain's speeches that detail a depressing and potentially infinite continued presence in foreign wars, set to the same rhythm and backdrop of Obama's expression of national hope. Throughout the anti-McCain video, each contributor begins to question his or her agreement with the repeated words, reenacting a collective disbelief in the alternative to Barack Obama. Again, john.he.is was adopted as a legitimate campaign video because it was essentially an attack ad, with a gentility and intelligence that complicated the opposition, in that it was a parody of a Republican campaign response. The video received more than 2.2 million views.

Face-swapping technology was utilized to create YouTube videos such as *The Empire Strikes Barack* and *SUPERBARACK* (titles that exemplify the often-heroic nature of co-created Obama fantasies). Such videos work in two ways: first because they are evidently parodied versions of a shared reality, revealing the stability of the rhetorical vision to which they relate and gently tease, and second because they are not delivered univocally. They are valuable precisely because of their unofficial, rather than authoritative, origins.

Importantly, when the Obama campaign did release videos on its official website and through its official accounts on social media networks, it was intent on sustaining the grassroots aesthetic of the participatory culture at large. A significant number of the channel's campaign videos turned attention away from the candidate and toward the image of the public or the crowd. Capturing the essence of what an official video for a participatory movement should look like, the campaign released *Barack in the Virginia Rain: "There's Nothing We Can't Do,"* only days before Election Day on YouTube. The video was a reworking of a speech made by Obama during a storm in Fredericksburg, Virginia, at the end of September 2008. The three-minute clip begins with an appeal to his participatory culture's fear of failure by suggesting a future reality in which the rhetorical vision does not come to pass: "November 5, 2008. The day after the election / Will you have done all that you could have?" As a section from Obama's speech begins to emerge, the video focuses on amateur recordings of the listening crowd rather than the candidate's face. The crowd is gargantuan and diverse. Soon, an instrumental piece of music begins to complement the speech. Video footage of various counties throughout the state (e.g., Richmond, Chester, Newport News) passes across the screen, showing groups through Virginia diligently engaged in communal activism: making phone calls, interacting on the doorstep, making posters—essentially performing a political participatory culture. The "listing" of this amateur grassroots footage builds force as the crowd from Obama's speech begins to chant "Yes We Can." Image, music, and speech come together in a polyphonous crescendo toward the climax of Obama's dramatic oration, targeting specifically the energy of the Millennials:

And this young generation that's out here . . . if you're willing to work for us, if you're willing to roll up your sleeves, if you're willing to lock arms and march and talk to your friends, and talk to your neighbors, make a phone call, do some organizing, yes do some community organizing, then I promise you, Fredericksburg, we will win Virginia, we will win this general election, and you and I together we will change the country and change the world.

As the staccato music trails off at the end of the video, the images return to concentrate on the moonlit applause of the excited crowd, as their anonymous hands are raised, representing the cooperative call for change. Although Obama is speaking throughout, he is subjugated by the presence of a participatory culture that is imagined as performing the important bread-and-butter work of political revolution. The video, with its focus on the individual, small community groups, entire counties, the state of Virginia, and the nation as a whole, visually extrapolates the process of multilayered communities of agreement coming together in a synchronized rhetorical vision that "there's nothing we can't do." It was not only a call to arms for the GOTV stage of the election cycle, but also an overt celebration of the Obama campaign's structure of symbolic convergence.

By the visual rhetoric alone, it was clear that Obama had an *a priori* advantage in being the figurehead of a technologically informed movement. Characterized as the BlackBerry candidate and dogged by an accusation of teleprompter over-reliance, the senator was, even as the subject of criticism, elided with the techno-landscape of his fellow revolutionaries. The in-touch politician contrasted with a septuagenarian John McCain and running mate Sarah Palin, who, during a now-infamous piece of YouTubery of Katie Couric's CBS interview-gone-wrong, refused to even acknowledge her print media consumption. Indeed, John McCain's admission during the campaign that he did not know how to use a computer was perhaps more damning than his previous self-effacement, "I don't really understand economics."

But Obama's 2008 victory was about more than simple imagery. It was a confluence of accidental and purposeful strategies. By 2007–2008, demographic patterns and technological enhancements had created a burgeoning participatory culture eager to enact the principles of American citizenship both online and offline. Barack Obama's investment in MyBO and other social network platforms, combined with a campaign that valued the Web 2.0 innovations of its supporters, were most successful in garnering a positive cooperative community of volunteers and activists. Obama's success came through his ability to share with his followers his quality as an almost universal symbol for national optimism and societal inclusion. Through the lens of symbolic convergence theory, we understand how new media allowed Obama to align his stories of struggle, alienation and otherness with the narratives of millions of Americans, and how these social platforms permitted the creation of a vast number of communities of agreement that shared fantasies of Obama's political potential. These shared fantasies were sustained by submission to the essential lack of control that can be exerted over social media, and united under the central rhetorical vision of Obama as the hero of the American future. Through this symbolic convergence, anti-rhetorical visions, political controversy, and rumor were more easily avoided because of the stability of that convergence. Obama clearly understood the possibilities for online communities to freely self-perpetuate the campaign's elemental message and to stabilize political belief through horizontal (peer-to-peer) affirmation. Obama was a revolutionary identity, navigating a technologically revolutionary moment.

Difference has been, and continues to be, both lock and key to Obama's political and personal acceptance.

REFERENCES

Barr, K. "A Perfect Storm." In *Campaigning for President 2008: Strategy and Tactics, New Voices and New Techniques,* edited by D. Johnson, 105–125. New York, NY: Routledge, 2009.

Baumgartner, J. C., and J. S. Morris. "MyFaceTube: Politics Social Networking Web Sites and Political Engagement of Young Adults." *Social Science Computer Review* 28, no. 1 (2010): 24–44.

Blau, A. "The Future of Independent Media." *Deeper News* 10, no. 1 (2005). http://www.namac.org/deep-focus-report.

Bormann, E. "Fantasy and Rhetorical Vision: The Rhetorical Criticism of Social Reality." *Quarterly Journal of Speech* 58 (1972): 396–407.

Bormann, E. "Symbolic Convergence Theory: A Communication Formulation Based on *Homo narrans." Journal of Communication* 35 (1985): 128–138.

Bormann, E., J. Cragan, and D. Shields. "In Defense of Symbolic Convergence Theory: A Look at the Theory and Its Criticisms after Two Decades." *Communication Theory* 4 (1994): 259–294.

Bormann, E., J. Cragan, and D. Shields. "An Expansion of the Rhetorical Vision Concept of Symbolic Convergence Theory: The Cold War Paradigm Case." *Communication Monographs* 63 (1996): 1–28.

Bormann, E., J. Cragan, and D. Shields. "Three Decades of Developing, Grounding, and Using Symbolic Convergence Theory." In *Communication Yearbook, Vol. 25*, edited by W. B. Gudykunst, 271–313. 2001.

Bormann, E., J. Cragan, and D. Shields. "Defending Symbolic Convergence Theory from an Imaginary Gunn." *Quarterly Journal of Speech* 89 (2003): 366–372.

Bowie, N. "Voting, Campaigns, and Elections in the Future: Looking Back from 2008." In *Democracy and New Media,* edited by H. Jenkins and D. Thorburn. Cambridge, MA: MIT Press, 143–170, 2004.

boyd, d. "Can Social Network Sites Enable Political Action?" In *Rebooting America: Creative Commons,* edited by A. Fine, M. Silfry, A. Raslej, and J. Levy, San Francisco, Ca: Creative Commons. 112–116. 2008a.

boyd, d. "Digital Handshakes in Networked Publics: Why Politicians Must Interact, Not Broadcast." In *Mobilizing Generation 2.0,* edited by B. Rigby. San Francisco, CA: Jossey-Bass, 91–94. 2008b.

Burgess, J., and J. Green. *YouTube: Online Video and Participatory Culture.* Cambridge, UK: Polity Press, 2009.

De Vellis, Phil. "I Made the 'Vote Different' Ad." *The Huffington Post* (March 21, 2007). http://www.huffingtonpost.com/phil-de-vellis-aka-parkridge/i-made-the-vote-different_b_43989.html

Campbell, H. *Barack Obama and Twenty-First Century Politics: A Revolutionary Moment in the USA.* London, UK: Pluto Press, 2010.

Feld, L., and N. Wilcox. *Netroots Rising: How a Citizen Army of Bloggers and Online Activists Is Changing American Politics.* Westport, CT: Praeger, 2008.

Gulati, G. J., and C. B. Williams. "The Political Impact of Facebook: Evidence from the 2006 Midterm Elections and 2008 Nomination Contest." *Politics & Technology Review* 1(1): 272–291 (March 11, 2008).

Gulati, G. J., and C. B. Williams. "What Is a Social Network Worth? Facebook and Vote Share in the 2008 Presidential Primaries." Unpublished paper presented at the Annual Meeting of the American Political Science Association, Boston, MA, August 28–31, 2008.

Harfoush, R. *Yes, We Did: An Inside Look at How Social Media Built the Obama Brand.* Berkley, CA: New Riders, Pearson Education, 2009.

Henke, J. "Campaigns Need to Listen to the Internet Media." *The Next Right.Com* (October 24, 2008). http://thenextright.com/jonhenke/campaigns-need-to-listen-to-the-inter-net-media.

Jenkins, H. *Convergence Culture: Where Old and New Media Collide.* New York, NY: NYU Press, 2006.

Jenkins, H. *Confronting the Challenge of Participatory Culture: Media Education for the 21st Century.* Cambridge, MA: MIT Press, 2009.

Keeter, S., J. Horowitz, and A. Tyson. "Young Voters in the 2008 Election." Pew Research Center, 2008. http://pew-research.org/pubs/1031/young-voters-in-the-2008-election.

Kerbel, M., and J. Bloom. "Blog for America and Civic Involvement." *Press/ Politics* 10, no. 4 (Fall 2005): 3–27.

Kim, Y., and N. W. Geidner. "Politics as Friendship: The Impact of Online Social Networks on Young Voters' Political Behavior." Paper presented at the Annual Meeting of the International Communication Association, Montreal, Quebec, 2008.*Canada Online.* http://www.allacademic.com/meta/ p233811_ index.html.

Larson, C. *Persuasion: Reception and Responsibility,* Boston, MA: Cengage Learning, 2009.

Levy, P. *Collective Intelligence: Mankind's Emerging World in Cyberspace.* New York, NY: Perseus Books, 2009.

May, A. "The Preacher and the Press: How the Jeremiah Wright Story Became the First Feeding Frenzy in the Digital Age." In *Campaigning for President 2008: Strategy and Tactics, New Voices and New Techniques,* edited by D. Johnson. New York, NY: Routledge, 78–101, 2009.

Obama, B. "Interview with Oprah Winfrey." *O Magazine* (November 2004). http://www.oprah.com/world/Oprah-Winfrey-Interviews-Barack-Obama/6.

Obama, B. *The Audacity of Hope.* New York, NY: Crown, Random House, 2006.

Parlett, M. "Yes We Can and the Making of a (Post) Racial Super Slogan?" *Journal of American, British and Canadian Studies* 16 (2011): 13–41.

Tapscott, D. *Growing up Digital: The Rise of the Net Generation.* New York, NY: McGraw-Hill, 1998.

Taylor, P., and S. Keeter. "Millennials: A Portrait of Generation Next." Pew Research Center, 2010. http://pewsocialtrends.org/files/2010/10/ millennials-confident-connected-open-to-change.pdf.

Vitak, J., P. Zube, A. Smock, C. T. Carr, N. Ellison, and C. Lampe. "It's Complicated: Facebook Users' Political Participation in the 2008 Election." *Cyberpsychology, Behavior, & Social Networking* 14, no. 3 (2011): 107–114.

Bibliography

8 U.S. CODE § 1403:- Persons Born in the Canal Zone or Republic of Panama on or after February 26, 1904.

Allen, Mike. "*New Yorker* Obama Cover Sparks Uproar." *CBS News* (July 14, 2008). http://www.cbsnews.com/news/new-yorker-obama-cover-sparks -uproar/.

Allison, Tom, and Jocelyn Fong. "Media Note Obama Did Not Say 'Terrorism,' But Don't Discuss Why." *Media Matters* (June 5, 2009). http://media matters.org/research/2009/06/05/media-note-obama-did-not-say-terrorism -but-dont/150914.

Amira, Dan. "Mitt Romney: President Obama Is European." *New York Magazine* (June 2, 2011). http://nymag.com/daily/intelligencer/2011/06/mitt _romney_to_save_america_ju.html.

Aravoisis, John. "*New Yorker* Cover Shows Oval Office with Obama as Tribal African, Wife as Afro-70s-Woman with Machine Gun, Osama on the Wall, and Flag on Fire." *AmericaBlog.com* (July 13, 2008). http://americablog .com/2008/07/new-yorker-cover-shows-oval-office-with-obama-as-tribal -african-wife-as-afro-70s-woman-with-machine-gun-osama-on-the-wall -and-flag-on-fire.html.

Ashton, J. Hubley, ed. *Official Opinions of the Attorneys General of the United States.* Washington, DC: W. H. & O. H. Morrison, 1868.

Associated Press. "Rep. Allen West Says 'about 78 to 81' House Democrats in Communist Party." *NYDailyNews.com* (April 11, 2012). http://www .nydailynews.com/news/politics/rep-allen-west-78-81-house-democrats -communist-party-article-1.1060137.

Babbin, Jed. *How Obama Is Transforming America's Military from Superpower to Paper Tiger.* Vol. 14. Encounter Books, 2010.

Bacon, Perry. "Clinton Campaign Volunteer out over False Obama Rumors."
    The Washington Post (December 5, 2007). http://voices.washingtonpost
    .com/44/2007/12/clinton-campaign-volunteer-out.html.

Baldwin, James. In "James Baldwin, Nathan Glazer, Sidney Hook, and Gunnar
    Myrdal: 'Liberalism and the Negro: A Round-Table Discussion.' " *Commen-*
    tary 37 (1964): 25–42.

Baldwin, James. "The White Problem." In *100 Years of Emancipation*, edited by
    Robert A. Goldwin. Chicago, IL: Rand McNally, 1964.

"Barack Obama 1995 Interview on *Dreams from My Father*: Part 1." YouTube
    video from a televised video with Connie Martinson on *Talks Books,* posted
    by "Andrew Kaczynski," November 20, 2011. http://www.youtube.com/
    watch?v=Rx_XS4s6aA4.

Barr, K. "The Online Revolution." In *Campaigning for President 2008: Strategy*
    and Tactics, New Voices and New Techniques, edited by D. Johnson. New
    York: Routledge, 2009.

Baum, Bruce. "Barack Obama and the White Problem." Paper presented at the
    Annual Meeting of the Western Political Science Association, San Antonio,
    TX, April 21–23, 2011.

Baumgartner, J. C., and J. S. Morris. "MyFaceTube: Politics Social Networking
    Web Sites and Political Engagement of Young Adults." *Social Science Com-*
    puter Review 28, no. 1 (2010).

Benen, Steve. "By the End of the Week, He'll Be Accusing Me of Being
    a Secret Communist Because I Shared My Toys in Kindergarten."
    Alternet.org (October 29, 2008). http://www.alternet.org/story/
    105228/obama_mocks_socialist_attacks%3A_%22i_shared_my_toys_in
    _kindergarten%22.

Bergo, Bettina. "Emmanuel Levinas." In *The Stanford Encyclopedia of Philoso-*
    phy, edited by Edward N. Zalta. Summer 2013. http://plato.stanford.edu/
    archives/sum2013/entries/levinas.

Berman, Dan. "Mitt Romney: President Obama Won Because of 'Gifts.' "
    Politico (November 14, 2012). http://www.politico.com/news/stories/1112/
    83878.html.

Bernasconi, Robert. "Othering." In *Critical Communities and Aesthetic Prac-*
    tices: Contributions to Phenomenology 64, edited by Francis Halsall et al.,
    151–157. New York, NY: Springer, 2012.

Blackstone, William, St. George Tucker, and Edward Christian.
    Blackstone's Commentaries, William Young Birch and Abraham Small,
    1803.

Blake, John. "Why Obama Doesn't Dare Become the 'Angry Black Man.' " *CNN*
    (June 10, 2010). http://edition.cnn.com/2010/POLITICS/06/08/rage.obama/.

Blau, A. "The Future of Independent Media." *Deeper News* 10, no. 1 (2005).
    http://www.namac.org/deep-focus-report.

Bloodsworth-Lugo, Mary K., and Carmen R. Lugo-Lugo. *Containing (Un)*
    American Bodies: Race, Sexuality, and Post-9/11 Constructions of Citizen-
    ship. Vol. 219. Rodopi, 2010.

Bloodsworth-Lugo, Mary K., and Carmen R. Lugo-Lugo. "Post-9/11 Discourses of Threat and Constructions of Terror in the Age of Obama." *Altre Modernità* (2011): 261–278.

Boller, Paul F. *Presidential Anecdotes*. Oxford, UK: Oxford University Press, 1996.

Bormann, E. "Fantasy and Rhetorical Vision: The Rhetorical Criticism of Social Reality." *Quarterly Journal of Speech* 58 (1972): 396–407.

Bormann, E. "Symbolic Convergence Theory: A Communication Formulation Based on *Homo narrans*." *Journal of Communication* 35 (1985): 128–138.

Bormann, E., J. Cragan, and D. Shields. "In Defense of Symbolic Convergence Theory: A Look at the Theory and Its Criticisms after Two Decades." *Communication Theory* 4 (1994): 259–294.

Bormann, E., J. Cragan, and D. Shields. "An Expansion of the Rhetorical Vision Concept of Symbolic Convergence Theory: The Cold War Paradigm Case." *Communication Monographs* 63 (1996): 1–28.

Bormann, E., J. Cragan, and D. Shields. "Three Decades of Developing, Grounding, and Using Symbolic Convergence Theory." In W. B. Gudykunst (Ed.), *Communication Yearbook 25*, edited by W. B. Gudykunst, 271–313. 2001.

Bormann, E., J. Cragan, and D. Shields. "Defending Symbolic Convergence Theory from an Imaginary Gunn." *Quarterly Journal of Speech* 89 (2003): 366–372.

Bowie, N. "Voting, Campaigns, and Elections in the Future: Looking back from 2008." In *Democracy and New Media*, edited by H. Jenkins and D. Thorburn. Cambridge, MA: MIT Press, 2004.

boyd, d. "Can Social Network Sites Enable Political Action?" In *Rebooting America: Creative Commons*, edited by A. Fine, M. Silfry, A. Raslej, and J. Levy, 112–116. 2008.

boyd, d. "Digital Handshakes in Networked Publics: Why Politicians Must Interact, Not Broadcast." In *Mobilizing Generation 2.0*, edited by B. Rigby. San Francisco, CA: Jossey-Bass, 2008.

Brewer, Justin. "White Elitism: The 'Othering' Theory Applied to Colonial America." 2007.

Brooks, David. "The Oil Plume." *The New York Times* (May 31, 2010). http://www.nytimes.com/2010/06/01/opinion/01brooks.html?gwh=C5C9CAEA2BF3952237EE3CBBF91E9E90&gwt=pay.

Brooks, David. "Trim the 'Experts,' Trust the Locals." *The New York Times* (June 17, 2010). http://www.nytimes.com/2010/06/18/opinion/18brooks.html.

Burgess, J., and J. Green. *YouTube: Online Video and Participatory Culture*. Cambridge, UK: Polity Press, 2009.

Burns, Douglas. "King: Electing Obama Could Lead to 'Totalitarian Dictatorship.'" *The Iowa Independent* (October 25, 2008). http://iowaindependent.com/7522/king-electing-obama-could-lead-to-totalitarian-dictatorship.

Bush, George W. "Address to the Republican National Convention." Speech in Saint Paul, MN, September 2, 2008. http://elections.nytimes.com/2008/president/conventions/videos/transcripts/20080902_BUSH_SPEECH.html.

Campbell, H. *Barack Obama and Twenty-First Century Politics: A Revolutionary Moment in the USA*. London, UK: Pluto Press, 2010.

Campbell, John F. "How Free Is Free? The Limits of Manumission for Enslaved Africans in Eighteenth-Century British West Indian Sugar Society." In *Paths to Freedom*, edited by Rosemary Brana-Shute and Randy J. Sparks. Columbia, SC: University of South Carolina Press, 2009.

Cartwright, Samuel A. "'Report on the Diseases and Physical Peculiarities of the Negro Race." *Health, Disease, and Illness: Concepts in Medicine* (2004): 28–39.

Cassidy, John. "Obama and the 'Angry Black Man' Factor." *The New Yorker* (October 17, 2012). http://www.newyorker.com/online/blogs/johncassidy/2012/10/obama-and-the-angry-black-man-factor.html.

Chen, Adrian. "Maher Wants Obama to Act Like a Real Black President with Guns and Stuff." *Gawker* (May 30, 2010). http://gawker.com/5551249/bill-maher-wants-obama-to-act-like-a-real-black-president-with-guns-and-stuff.

Cirilli, Kevin. "Newt Gingrich: Like NFL Refs, President Obama 'Not Real.'" *Politico* (September 26, 2012). http://www.politico.com/news/stories/0912/81688.html.

Coates, Ta-Nehisi. "Fear of a Black President." *The Atlantic* (August 22, 2012). http://www.theatlantic.com/magazine/archive/2012/09/fear-of-a-black-president/309064/?single_page=true.

Coffman, Michael S. *Radical Islam in the House: The Plan to Take America for the Global Islamic State*. CreateSpace Independent Publishing Platform, 2013.

Condon, Stephanie. "Poll: One in Four Americans Think Obama Was Not Born in U.S." *CBS News* (April 21, 2011). http://www.cbsnews.com/news/poll-one-in-four-americans-think-obama-was-not-born-in-us/.

Cook, Terry L. *America's Communist Revolution! Terrifying Change without Hope*. CreateSpace Independent Publishing Platform, 2010.

Cooper, Frank Rudy. "Our First Unisex President: Black Masculinity and Obama's Feminine Side." *Denver University Law Review* 86 (2008): 633.

Corley, Matt. "DeLay On Obama: 'Unless He Proves Me Wrong, He Is a Marxist.'" *ThinkProgress.org* (June 5, 2008). http://thinkprogress.org/politics/2008/06/05/24302/delay-obama-marxist/.

Corn, David. "SECRET VIDEO: Romney Tells Millionaire Donors What He REALLY Thinks of Obama Voters." *Mother Jones* (September 17, 2012). http://www.motherjones.com/politics/2012/09/secret-video-romney-private-fundraiser.

Corsi, Jerome. *The Obama Nation*. New York, NY: Simon and Schuster, 2008.

Corsi, Jerome R. *Where's the Birth Certificate? The Case That Barack Obama Is Not Eligible to Be President*. Washington, DC: WND Books, 2011.

Costa, Robert. "Gingrich: Obama's 'Kenyan, Anti-colonial' Worldview." *The National Review Online* (September 11, 2010). http://www.nationalreview.com/corner/246302/gingrich-obama-s-kenyan-anti-colonial-worldview-robert-costa.

Criddle, Laura. "Oxford Don Embroiled in Obama Smear." *The Cherwell* (November 6, 2008). http://www.cherwell.org/news/2008/11/06/oxford-don-embroiled-in-obama-smear.

Curry, Tom. "How Obama Won the White House." MSNBC.com (November 5, 2008).

Davis, Frank Marshall. *Livin' the Blues: Memoirs of a Black Journalist and Poet.* Madison, WI: University of Wisconsin Press, 1993.

Davis, Susan. "Obama Dismisses Internet Rumors." *The Wall Street Journal* (January 15, 2008). http://blogs.wsj.com/washwire/2008/01/15/obama-dismisses-internet-rumors/.

Deggans, Eric. "Rev. Jeremiah Wright's Media Blitz Forces Barack Obama to Face the Angry Black Man Test—Again." *The Huffington Post* (April 28, 2008). http://www.huffingtonpost.com/eric-deggans/rev-jeremiah-wrights-medi_b_98957.html.

Denton, Robert E. Jr., ed. *Studies of Identity in the 2008 Presidential Campaign.* Lanham, MD: Lexington Books, 2009.

Devos, Thierry, and Mahzarin R. Banaji. "American = White?" *Journal of Personality and Social Psychology* 88, no. 3 (March 2005): 447–466.

Devos, Thierry, Debbie S. Ma, and Travis Gaffud. "Is Barack Obama American Enough to Be the Next President? The Role of Ethnicity and National Identity in American Politics." Poster presented at the IXth Annual Meeting of the Society for Personality and Social Psychology, Albuquerque, NM, 2008. http://www-rohan.sdsu.edu/~tdevos/thd/Devos_spsp2008.pdf.

Dixon, Thomas. *The Clansman: An Historical Romance of the Ku Klux Klan.* Pelican, 2002.

Douglass, Frederick, and Harriet Jacobs. *Narrative of the Life of Frederick Douglass, an American Slave & Incidents in the Life of a Slave Girl.* Random House Digital, 2007.

Dowd, Maureen. "Obama, Legally Blonde?" *The New York Times* (February 14, 2007).

Dowd, Maureen. "Boy, oh, Boy." *The New York Times* (September 12, 2009). http://www.nytimes.com/2009/09/13/opinion/13dowd.html.

Dowd, Maureen. "Once More, with Feeling." *The New York Times* (May 29, 2010). "http://www.nytimes.com/2010/05/30/opinion/30dowd.html.

Drum, Kevin. "Barack Obama Is Dumb and Lazy." *Mother Jones* (March 29, 2013). http://www.motherjones.com/kevin-drum/2013/03/barack-obama-dumb-and-lazy.

Drum, Kevin. "That *New Yorker* Cover." *Washington Monthly* (July 13, 2008). http://www.washingtonmonthly.com/archives/individual/2008_07/014079.php.

D'Souza, Dinesh. *The Roots of Obama's Rage.* Regnery Publishing, 2011.

Du Bois, W. E. B. *The Souls of Black Folk*. New York, NY: New American Library, 1903.

Edwards, David, and Muriel Kane. "MSNBC Analyst: Rove Obama Attack Close to 'Outright Racist.' " *The Raw Story* (January 11, 2008). http://rawstory.com/news/2007/MSNBC_Analyst_Rove_Obama_attack_almost_0111.html.

Emery, David. "Is Barack Obama the Antichrist." *Netlore Archive* (2008). http://urbanlegends.about.com/od/barackobama/a/obamaantichrist.htm.

Enck-Wanzer, Darrel. "Barack Obama, the Tea Party, and the Threat of Race: On Racial Neoliberalism and Born Again Racism." *Communication, Culture & Critique* 4, no. 1 (2011): 23–30.

Epstein, Jennifer. "Obama Scoffs at People Who Call Him a 'Socialist': 'You Gotta Meet Real Socialists.' " *Politico.com* (November 19, 2013). http://www.politico.com/politico44/2013/11/obama-scoffs-at-people-who-call-him-a-socialist-you-177886.html.

Evans, Ben. "Georgia Congressman Warns of Obama Dictatorship." *Fox News* (November 10, 2008). http://www.foxnews.com/printer_friendly_wires/2008Nov10/0,4675,CongressmanObamaMarxist,00.html.

Falsani, Cathleen. "Interview with State Sen. Barack Obama; 3:30 p.m., Saturday March 27." March 27, 2004. http://cathleenfalsani.com/obama-on-faith-the-exclusive-interview/.

Feingold, Henry L. *A Time for Searching: Entering the Mainstream, 1920–1945*. Vol. 4. JHU Press, 1995.

Feld, L., and N. Wilcox. *Netroots Rising: How a Citizen Army of Bloggers and Online Activists Is Changing American Politics*. Westport, CT: Praeger, 2008.

Feldman, Josh. "Palin Bashes Obama over Snowden Manhunt: 'The Community Organizer in Our President' Leading from Behind." *Mediaite* (June 29, 2013). http://www.mediaite.com/tv/palin-bashes-obama-over-snowden-manhunt-the-community-organizer-in-our-president-leading-from-behind/.

Fernandez, Maria. "The Road to Victoria Jackson's Election Meltdown on Twitter." *The Daily Beast* (November 7, 2012). http://www.thedailybeast.com/articles/2012/11/07/the-road-to-victoria-jackson-s-election-meltdown-on-twitter.html.

Fife, Tom. "The First Time I Heard of Barack." *Rense.com* (2008). http://www.rense.com/general84/brck.htm.

Foner, Eric. *Reconstruction: America's Unfinished Revolution, 1863–1877*. New York, NY: Harper and Row, 1988.

Forman, Milos. "Obama the Socialist? Not Even Close." *The New York Times* (July 10, 2012). http://www.nytimes.com/2012/07/11/opinion/obama-the-socialist-not-even-close.html?_r=0.

Gaffney, Frank. *The Muslim Brotherhood in the Obama Administration*. David Horowitz Freedom Center, 2012.

Gammell, Caroline. "Academic Prowess of Barack Obama's Mother Disclosed." *The Telegraph* (September 16, 2009). http://www.telegraph.co.uk/news/

worldnews/barackobama/6196237/Academic-prowess-of-Barack-Obamas
-mother-disclosed.html.

Gibbs, Robert. "Press Briefing by Press Secretary Robert Gibbs." The White
House, June 1, 2010. http://www.whitehouse.gov/the-press-office/press
-briefing-press-secretary-robert-gibbs-6110.

Gingrich, Newt. *To Save America: Stopping Obama's Secular-Socialist Machine.*
Regnery Publishing, 2011.

Goldberg, Michelle. "Donald Trump's New Obama Conspiracy Theory." *The
Daily Beast* (April 26, 2011). http://www.thedailybeast.com/articles/2011/
04/26/donald-trump-takes-up-birthers-obama-college-conspiracy-theory.
html.

Green, Joshua. "Penn Strategy Memo, March 19, 2008." *The Atlantic*
(August 11, 2008). http://www.theatlantic.com/politics/archive/2008/08/
penn-strategy-memo-march-19-2008/37952/.

Gregory, Derek, Ron Johnston, Geraldine Pratt, Michael Watts, and Sarah
Whatmore, eds. *The Dictionary of Human Geography*, 5th ed. Oxford,
UK: Wiley-Blackwell, 2009.

Griffith, D. W. *Birth of a Nation.* Epoch Producing Co., 1915.

Gulati, G. J., and C. B. Williams. "The Political Impact of Facebook: Evidence
from the 2006 Midterm Elections and 2008 Nomination Contest." *Politics
& Technology Review* (March 11, 2008).

Gulati, G. J., and C. B. Williams. "What Is a Social Network Worth? Facebook
and Vote Share in the 2008 Presidential Primaries." Unpublished paper presented at the Annual Meeting of the American Political Science Association,
Boston, MA, August 28–31, 2008.

Hall, G. Stanley. "The Negro in Africa and America." *The Pedagogical Seminary*
12, no. 3 (1905): 350–368.

Hamby, Peter. "McCain: 'I Don't Know' If Obama Is Socialist." *CNN Political
Ticker Blog* (July 18, 2008). http://politicalticker.blogs.cnn.com/2008/07/
18/mccain-%E2%80%9Ci-don%E2%80%99t-know%E2%80%9D-if
-obama-is-socialist/.

Haney-Lopez, Ian. *White by Law: The Legal Construction of Race.* New York,
NY: NYU Press, 2006.

Harfoush, R. *Yes, We Did: An Inside Look at How Social Media Built the
Obama Brand.* Berkeley, CA: New Riders, Pearson Education, 2009.

Harris Interactive. " 'Wingnuts' and President Obama." *Harris Interactive*
(March 24, 2010). http://www.harrisinteractive.com/NewsRoom/
HarrisPolls/tabid/447/ctl/ReadCustom%20Default/mid/1508/ArticleId/223/
Default.aspx.

Harrison, Maureen, and Steve Gilbert. "Barack Obama: Speeches, 2002–2006.
Carlsbad." 2007.

Harris, Frank III. "Calling Obama Lazy Crosses Racial Line." *The Courant*
(October 10, 2012). http://articles.courant.com/2012-10-10/news/hc-op
-harris-obama-weak-in-debated-not-lazy-1011-20121010_1_lazy-person
-republican-challenger-mitt-romney-president-barack-obama.

Harsanyi, David. *Obama's Four Horsemen: The Disasters Unleashed.* Regnery Publishing, 2013.

Hedrick, David W. *The Liberal Clause.* Freedoms Answer, 2010.

Hegel, Georg. W. F. *Phenomenology of Spirit.* Digireads.com Publishing, 2009.

Hendrickson, Mark. "President Obama's Marxist-Leninist Economics: Fact and Fiction." *Forbes* (July 26, 2012). http://www.forbes.com/sites/markhendrickson/2012/07/26/president-obamas-marxist-leninist-economics-fact-and-fiction/2/.

Henke, J. "Campaigns Need to Listen to the Internet Media." *The Next Right.Com* (October 24, 2008). http:// thenextright.com/jonhenke/campaigns-need-to-listen-to-the-inter-net-media.

Hinman, Arthur P. *How a British Subject Became President of the United States.* New York, NY: 1884.

Hitchens, Christopher. "White Fright." *Slate* (August 30, 2010). http://www.slate.com/articles/news_and_politics/fighting_words/2010/08/white_fright.html.

Hitchens, Christopher. "From the N-Word to Code Words." *Slate* (September 20, 2010). http://www.slate.com/articles/news_and_politics/fighting_words/2010/09/from_the_nword_to_code_words.html.

Holpuch, Amanda. "White House Petition for Texas Independence Qualifies for Response." *The Guardian* (November 13, 2012). http://www.theguardian.com/world/2012/nov/13/white-house-petition-texas-independence.

Hughey, Matthew W. " 'Show Me Your Papers': Obama's Birth and the Whiteness of Belonging." *Qualitative Sociology* 35, no. 2 (2012): 163–181.

Husle, Carl. "McCain's Canal Zone Birth Prompts Queries about Whether That Rules Him Out." *The New York Times* (February 28, 2008). http://www.nytimes.com/2008/02/28/us/politics/28mccain.html?pagewanted=print.

Irving, David. *Hitler's War.* Vol. 1. Viking Press, 1977.

"Jack Cashill: Deconstructing Obama." *YouTube* (March 21, 2011). http://www.Youtube.com, http://www.youtube.com/watch?v=xxPhnhQ7Tr0.

Jackman, Simon, and Lynn Vavreck. "Obama's Advantage? Race, Partisanship and Racial Attitudes in Context." Annual Meeting of the Midwest Political Science Association, 2010.

Jackson, David. "Obama: No Moratorium on Golf." *USA Today* (June 21, 2010). http://content.usatoday.com/communities/theoval/post/2010/06/obama-no-moratorium-on-golf/1#.UvQQHfl_vX8.

James, Frank. "Can a President Be an Angry Black Man?" *NPR* (June 8, 2010). http://www.npr.org/blogs/thetwo-way/2010/06/could_america_handle_an_angry.html.

Jay, John, to George Washington, July 25, 1787. In *History of the Formation of the Constitution of the United States of America,* edited by George Bancroft. New Jersey: Lawbook Exchange Limited, 2000.

Jefferson, Thomas. *Notes on the State of Virginia.* 1787.

Jefferson, Thomas. "Address by Thomas Jefferson." Joint Congressional Committee on Inaugural Ceremonies, 1806. http://www.inaugural.senate.gov/
swearing-in/address/address-by-thomas-jefferson-1805.

Jefferson, Thomas. *Memoirs, 4: Correspondence and Private Papers*. Henry
Colbura and Richard Bertley, 1829.

Jenkins, H. *Convergence Culture: Where Old and New Media Collide*. New
York, NY: NYU Press, 2006.

Jenkins, H. *Confronting the Challenge of Participatory Culture: Media Education for the 21st Century*. Cambridge, MA: MIT Press, 2009.

Jenkins, Lynnette R. "Politics as Usual: Black Stereotypes and President Obama's
Racialization." 2012.

Johnson, James W. *The Autobiography of an Ex-Colored Man*. Boston:
Sherman, French & Company, 1912. http://www.ibiblio.org/eldritch/jwj/
auto.htm.

Journal Editorial Report. "Is Romney's Lead the Real Deal?" *Journal Editorial
Report* video, 7:23, October 27, 2012. http://www.foxnews.com/on-air/
journal-editorial-report/2012/10/29/romneys-lead-real-deal.

Kaplan, E. A. "Who's Afraid of Michelle Obama?" *Salon* (April 20, 2008). http://
www.salon.com/mwt/feature/2008/06/24/michelle_obama/index.html.

Kaplan, Lawrence S. *Thomas Jefferson: Westward the Course of Empire*.
Rowman & Littlefield, 1998.

Keeter, S., J. Horowitz, and A. Tyson. "Young Voters in the 2008 Election." Pew
Research Center, 2008. http://pew-research.org/pubs/1031/young-voters-in
-the-2008-election.

Kengor, Paul. *The Communist*. Simon and Schuster, 2012.

Kennicott, Philip. "Philip Kennicott on Images: Obama as the Joker Betrays
Racial Ugliness, Fears." *The Washington Post* (August 6, 2009). http://
www.washingtonpost.com/wp-dyn/content/article/2009/08/05/AR2009080
503876.html.

Kent, James. *Commentaries on American Law*. O. Halsted: 1826–1830.

Kerbel, M., and J. Bloom. "Blog for America and Civic Involvement." *Press/
Politics* 10, no. 4 (Fall 2005): 3–27.

Kessler, Glenn. "Barack Obama: The 'Food-Stamp President'?" *The Washington
Post: The Fact Checker* (December 8, 2011). http://www.washingtonpost.
com/blogs/fact-checker/post/barack-obama-the-food-stamp-president/2011/
12/07/gIQAzTdQdO_blog.html.

Kim, Y., and N. W. Geidner. "Politics as Friendship: The Impact of Online Social
Networks on Young Voters' Political Behavior." Paper presented at the
annual meeting of the International Communication Association, Montreal,
Quebec, 2008. *Canada Online*. http://www.allacademic.com/meta/
p233811_index.html.

Kirby, Stephen M. *Islam and Barack Hussein Obama: Handbook of Islam*.
CreateSpace, 2010.

Kleefeld, Eric. "Allen West: 'Barack Hussein Obama' Is a 'Low-Level
Socialist Agitator' (Video)." *TalkingPointsMemo.com* (April 22, 2011).

http://talkingpointsmemo.com/dc/allen-west-barack-hussein-obama-is-a
-low-level-socialist-agitator-video.

Klein, Aaron, and Brenda J. Elliott. *The Manchurian President: Barack Obama's Ties to Communists, Socialists and Other Anti-American Extremists.* WND Books, 2010.

Klein, Ezra. "People Don't Fully Appreciate How Committed the Tea Party Is to Not Compromising." *The Washington Post* (October 4, 2013). http://www.washingtonpost.com/blogs/wonkblog/wp/2013/10/04/people -dont-fully-appreciate-how-committed-the-tea-party-is-to-not-compromising/.

Koppelman, Alex. "Glenn Beck Exposes Obama's Communist Art Scheme." *Salon.com* (September 3, 2009). http://www.salon.com/2009/09/03/beck _art/.

Kujala, Jordan R. "Savage Repeatedly Called Obama an 'Afro-Leninist.' " *MediaMatters.org* (June 10, 2008). http://mediamatters.org/video/2008/06/ 10/savage-repeatedly-called-obama-an-afro-leninist/143714.

Kurtz, Howard. "Roger Ailes Lets Rip." *The Daily Beast* (November 16, 2010). http://www.thedailybeast.com/articles/2010/11/16/fox-news-chairman -roger-ailes-slams-white-house-in-exclusive-interview.html.

Lacan, Jacques. "Some Reflections on the Ego." In *Influential Papers from the 1950s*, edited by Andrew C. Furman and Steven T. Levy, 293–306. London, UK: Karnac, 2003 [1953].

Larson, C. *Persuasion: Reception and responsibility.* Boston, MA: Cengage Learning, 2009.

Lavender, Paige. "Morgan Griffith, GOP Rep, Compares Default to American Revolution." *The Huffington Post* (October 12, 2013). http://www .huffingtonpost.com/2013/10/12/default-american-revolution-morgan -griffith_n_4089911.html.

Ledeen, Michael A., and Michael Ledeen Ledeen. *Obama's Betrayal of Israel.* Encounter Books, 2010.

Levi-Strauss, Claude. *Triste Tropiques,* translated by John Russell. London: Criterion, 1961.

Levy, P. *Collective Intelligence: Mankind's Emerging World in Cyberspace.* New York, NY: Perseus Books, 2009.

Limbaugh, Rush. "ACORN's Aim: Chaos at the Polls." *The Rush Limbaugh Show* (October 14, 2008). http://www.rushlimbaugh.com/daily/2008/10/ 14/acorn_s_aim_chaos_at_the_polls.

Limbaugh, Rush. "This Regime Doesn't Like America; Vilifies, Targets Americans Citizens." *The Rush Limbaugh Show* (April 15, 2010). http:// www.rushlimbaugh.com/daily/2010/04/15/this_regime_doesn_t_like_america _vilifies_targets_american_citizens.

Limbaugh, Rush. "Pearls of Wisdom." *The Rush Limbaugh Show* (June 25, 2012). http://www.rushlimbaugh.com/daily/2012/06/25/pearls_of_wisdom.

Limbaugh, Rush. "Obama Got Worst Grades in Harvard History—and It's Up to Him to Prove He Didn't." *The Rush Limbaugh Show* (August 2, 2012).

http://www.rushlimbaugh.com/daily/2012/08/02/obama_got_worst_grades
_in_harvard_history_and_it_s_up_to_him_to_prove_he_didn_t.

Lincoln, Abraham. *Collected Works,* edited by Roy P. Basler. Vols. 1 and 2. New Brunswick, NJ: Rutgers University Press, 1953.

Long, Breckenridge. "Is Mr. Charles Evans Hughes a 'Natural Born Citizen' within the Meaning of the Constitution?" *Chicago Legal News,* 146–148 (1916): 220–222. http://libertylegalfoundation.org/wp-content/uploads/2012/01/Breckinridge-Long.pdf.

Madison, James. 1789, statement. In *The Founders' Constitution,* edited by Philip B. Kurland and Ralph Lerner. Chicago, IL: University of Chicago Press, 1987.

Martin, Andy. "Columnist Says Barack Obama 'Lied to the American People'; Asks Publisher to Withdraw Obama's Book." *The Free Library* (August 11, 2004). http://www.thefreelibrary.com/Columnist Says Barack Obama 'Lied to the American People;' Asks...-a0120417594.

Mason, Julie. "Godliness and Joblessness: Obama Brings God into It." *Politico* (November 2, 2011). http://www.politico.com/politico44/perm/1111/godliness_and_joblessness_8f477498-57a2-483d-9416-b6aa6c9236b5.html.

May, A. "The Preacher and the Press: How the Jeremiah Wright Story Became the First Feeding Frenzy in the Digital Age." In *Campaigning for President 2008: Strategy and Tactics, New Voices and New Techniques,* edited by D. Johnson. New York, NY: Routledge, 2009.

Mayer, Jane. "Senator Ted Cruz Our New McCarthy?" *The New Yorker* (February 22, 2013). http://www.newyorker.com/online/blogs/comment/2013/02/ted-cruz-sees-red-not-crimson-at-harvard.html.

McCain, John, and Mark Salter. *Worth the Fighting for: A Memoir.* Random House, 2002.

McCarthy, Andrew C. *How Obama Embraces Islam's Sharia Agenda.* ReadHowYouWant.com, 2011.

McNamara, Pat. "Catholic Sisters and the American Civil War." *Patheos.com* (May 30, 2011). http://www.patheos.com/Resources/Additional-Resources/Catholic-Sisters-and-the-American-Civil-War-Pat-McNamara-05-31-2011.html.

McPherson, Edward. *The Political History of the United States of America, during the Great Rebellion, from November 6, 1860, to July 4, 1864.* Philip and Solomons, 1865.

Mendible, Myra. "The Politics of Race and Class in the Age of Obama." *Revue de recherche en civilisation américaine* 3 (March 2012). http://rrca.revues.org/489.

Moon, Robert. "Obama Classmate: There Is a Reason Obama Refuses to Release His College Records." *The Examiner* (August 7, 2012). http://www.examiner.com/article/obama-classmate-there-is-a-reason-obama-refuses-to-release-his-college-records.

Morris, Dick, and Eileen McGann. *Revolt! How to Defeat Obama and Repeal His Socialist Programs*. Harper Collins, 2011.

Mukasey, Michael B. *How Obama Has Mishandled the War on Terror*. ReadHowYouWant.com, 2011.

Newby, Joe. "Al Sharpton, Touré: Ailes Used Racist 'Dog Whistle' in Calling Obama 'Lazy.' " *The Examiner* (March 8, 2013). http://www.examiner .com/article/al-sharpton-tour-ailes-used-racist-dog-whistle-calling-obama -lazy.

New York Times Archive, "Material for a Democratic Lie; St. Albans, Vt." *The New York Times* (December 22, 1880). http://query.nytimes.com/ mem/archive-free/pdf?res=FA0C15F8395B1B7A93C0AB1789D95F448 884F9.

Nightingale, Joseph R. "Joseph H. Barrett and John Locke Scripps, Shapers of Lincoln's Religious Image." *Journal of the Illinois State Historical Society* 92, no. 3 (1999): 238–273.

NPR.org. " 'New Yorker' Editor Defends Obama Cover." June 14, 2008. http:// www.npr.org/templates/story/story.php?storyId=92529393.

Oates, Stephen B. *Our Fiery Trial: Abraham Lincoln, John Brown, and the Civil War Era*. Amherst, MA: University of Massachusetts Press, 1979.

Obama, Barack H. *Dreams from My Father*. New York, NY: Times Books, 1995.

Obama, B. "Interview with Oprah Winfrey." *O Magazine* (November 2004). http://www.oprah.com/world/Oprah-Winfrey-Interviews-Barack-Obama/6.

Obama, B. *The Audacity of Hope*. New York, NY: Crown, Random House, 2006.

Obama, Barack H. "A More Perfect Union." Speech in Philadelphia, PA, March 18, 2008. http://blogs.wsj.com/washwire/2008/03/18/text-of -obamas-speech-a-more-perfect-union/.

Obama, Barack H. "Victory Speech." Speech in Chicago, IL, November 4, 2008. *BBC News*. http://news.bbc.co.uk/1/hi/world/americas/us_elections_2008/ 7710038.stm.

Obama, Barack H. "Remarks by the President on a New Beginning." Speech in Cairo, Egypt, June 4, 2009. The White House. http://www.whitehouse .gov/the_press_office/Remarks-by-the-President-at-Cairo-University-6-04 -09.

Obama, Barack H. "Remarks by the President." Speech in Washington, DC, April 27, 2011. The White House. http://www.whitehouse.gov/the-press -office/2011/04/27/remarks-president.

Obama, Barack H. "Remarks by the President on Trayvon Martin." Speech in Washington, DC, July 19, 2013. The White House. http://www .whitehouse.gov/the-press-office/2013/07/19/remarks-president-trayvon -martin.

Obama, Bara(c)k H. Sr. "Another Critique of Sessional Paper No. 10: Problems Facing Our Socialism." *The East Africa Journal* (July 1965). http://www .politico.com/static/PPM41_eastafrica.html.

ObamaConspiracy.org. "Barack Obama Is a Communist" *ObamaConspiracy. org* (December 31, 2008). http://www.obamaconspiracy.org/2008/12/ barack-obama-is-a-communist/.

"Obama's Lost Years." *The Wall Street Journal* (September 11, 2008). http:// online.wsj.com/news/articles/SB122108881386721289.

O'Reilly, Bill. "Is Obama Not Emotional Enough?" *The O'Reilly Factor* (June 2, 2010). http://www.billoreilly.com/show?action=viewTVShow&showID =2615.

O'Reilly, Bill. "Krauthammer: Obama Using SOTU Speech to Crush the Republicans." *The O'Reilly Factor, Fox News* (February 13, 2013). http://www .foxnews.com/on-air/oreilly/2013/02/13/krauthammer-obama-using-sotu -speech-crush-republicans

Owen, David. "Othering Obama: How Whiteness Is Used to Undermine Authority." *Altre Modernità* 3 (March 2010): 112–119. doi: 10.13130/2035-7680/ 517.

Owen, Samuel. *The New-York Legal Observer: Containing Reports of Cases Decided in the Courts of Equity and Common Law, and Important Decisions in the English Courts.* S. Owen, 1845.

Pareene, Alex. "How Can Michele Bachman Be President If She Won't Release Her Birth Certificate?" *Salon* (March 17, 2011). http://www.salon.com/ 2011/03/17/bachmann_birth_certificate/.

Parlett, M. "Yes We Can and the Making of a (Post) Racial Super Slogan?" *Journal of American, British and Canadian Studies* 16 (2011): 13–41.

Parlett, Martin. "Like a Lion Bound, Hear Him Roar: Richard Harvey Cain and a Rhetoric of Reconstruction." In *Before Obama: A Reappraisal of Black Reconstruction Era Politicians*, edited by Matthew Lynch. ABC-CLIO, 2012.

Parlett, M., and L. Graves. *Respect. Empower. Include.: Barack Obama and the Limitations of Umbrella Leadership.* Oxford, UK: Oxford Leadership Prize, 2010.

Pelley, William Dudley. *What Every Congressman Should Know.* Asheville, NC: Pelley Publishers, 1936.

Pierce, Charles P. "What Is Not about Race." *Esquire* (August 8, 2013). http:// www.esquire.com/blogs/politics/The_President_In_Arizona.

Pilgrim, David. "The Coon Caricature." Jim Crow Museum of Racist Memorabilia, 2012. http://www.ferris.edu/jimcrow/coon//

Pilgrim, David. "The Sapphire Caricature." Jim Crow Museum of Racist Memorabilia, 2012. http://www.ferris.edu/jimcrow/sapphire/.

Pilgrim, David. "What Was Jim Crow?" Jim Crow Museum of Racist Memorabilia, 2012. http://www.ferris.edu/jimcrow/what.

Piston, Spencer. "How Explicit Racial Prejudice Hurt Obama in the 2008 Election." *Political Behavior* 32 (2010): 431–451.

Plaud, Joseph J. "Historical Perspectives on Franklin D. Roosevelt, American Foreign Policy, and the Holocaust." Franklin D. Roosevelt American Heritage Center and Museum, 2007. fdrheritage.org.

Pleat, Zachary. "Beck Lies about His History of "Dragging" Obama's Family "into the Debate." *MediaMatters.org* (2010). http://mediamatters.org/research/2010/06/01/beck-lies-about-his-history-of-dragging-obamas/165604.

PolitiFact.com. "Obama Attended an Indonesian Public School." December 20, 2007. http://www.politifact.com/truth-o-meter/statements/2007/dec/20/chain-email/obama-attended-an-indonesian-public-school/.

PolitiFact.com. "Mitt Romney Says Barack Obama's Plan for Welfare Reform: 'They Just Send You Your Check.'" August 7, 2012. http://www.politifact.com/truth-o-meter/statements/2012/aug/07/mitt-romney/mitt-romney-says-barack-obamas-plan-abandons-tenet/.

PolitiFact.com. "Taking 'In God We Trust' off Coins Was Debunked Years Ago." September 2012. http://www.politifact.com/truth-o-meter/statements/2012/sep/11/chain-email/taking-god-we-trust-coins-was-debunked-years-ago/.

Potok, Mark. "Rage on the Right: This Year in Hate and Extremism." *Southern Poverty Law Centre Intelligence Report*, 137 (Spring 2010). http://www.splcenter.org/get-informed/intelligence-report/browse-all-issues/2010/spring/rage-on-the-right.

Powell, Michael, and Jodi Kantor. "After Attacks, Michelle Obama Looks for a New Introduction." *The New York Times* (2008).

Press, Bill. *The Obama Hate Machine: The Lies, Distortions, and Personal Attacks on the President—and Who Is Behind Them*. Macmillan, 2012.

Ramsay, David. *Observations on the Decision of the House of Representatives of the United States, on the 22d Day of May, 1789: Respecting the Eligibility of the Hon. William Smith, of South-Carolina, to a Seat in that House*. Hodge, Allen and Campbell, 1789.

Rawle, William. *A View of the Constitution of the United States of America*. P. H. Nicklin, 1829.

Real Clear Politics. "Andrea Mitchell Asks Sununu to Apologize for Calling Obama 'Lazy.'" October 4, 2012. http://www.realclearpolitics.com/video/2012/10/04/andrea_mitchell_asks_sununu_to_apologize_for_calling_obama_lazy.html.

Reott, Martin P., and Patricia Reott. *The Unauthorized Diary of a Muslim President*. CreateSpace Independent Publishing Platform, 2012.

Rice, Kym S., and Martha B. Katz-Hyman. *World of a Slave: Encyclopedia of the Material Life of Slaves in the United States*. Westport, CT: 2010.

Riggins, Stephen Harold. "The Rhetoric of Othering." *The Language and Politics of Exclusion: Others in Discourse* (1997): 1–30.

Robinson, Eugene. "Black Boys Denied the Right to Be Young." *Washington Post* (July 15, 2013). http://www.washingtonpost.com/opinions/eugene-robinson-black-boys-denied-the-right-to-be-young/2013/07/15/d3f603d8-ed69-11e2-9008-61e94a7ea20d_story.html.

Rodriguez, Junius P., ed. *The Historical Encyclopedia of World Slavery: AK; Vol. II, LZ*. Vol. 1. ABC-CLIO, 1997.

Romney, Mitt. *No Apology: The Case for American Greatness*. Macmillan, 2010.

Roosevelt, Franklin Delano. *FDR's Fireside Chats*. Norman, OK: University of Oklahoma Press, 1992.

Ross, Michael. "Bad TV's Most Wanted: Elected Instigators: #3." *The Examiner* (January 12, 2013). http://www.examiner.com/article/bad-tv-s-most-wanted-elected-instigators-3.

Rossing, Jonathan P. "Comic Provocations in Racial Culture: Barack Obama and the 'Politics of Fear.'" *Communication Studies* 62, no. 4 (2011): 422–438.

Rove, Karl. "Why Hillary Won." *The Wall Street Journal* (January 10, 2008). http://online.wsj.com/news/articles/SB119992615845679531.

S.Res.511: A Resolution Recognizing That John Sidney McCain, III, Is a Natural Born Citizen. http://www.opencongress.org/bill/110-sr511/text.

Said, Edward W. *Orientalism*. London, UK: Routledge & Kegan Paul, 1978.

Sammon, Bill. *The Evangelical President: George Bush's Struggle to Spread a Moral Democracy throughout the World*. Regnery Publishing, 2007.

Sampley, Ted. "Barack Obama: Who is He?" *U.S. Veteran Dispatch* (December 29, 2006). http://www.usvetdsp.com/dec06/obama_muslim.htm.

Sanford, Charles B. *The Religious Life of Thomas Jefferson*. Charlottesville, VA: University of Virginia Press, 1987 [1829].

Sartre, Jean-Paul. *Being and Nothingness,* translated by Hazel E. Barnes. New York, NY: Washington Square Press, 1993.

Savage, Michael. *Trickle Down Tyranny: Crushing Obama's Dream of the Socialist States of America*. Harper Collins, 2012.

Schlussel, Debbie. "Barack Hussein Obama: Once a Muslim, Always a Muslim." 2006. http://www.debbieschlussel.com/2750/barack-hussein-obama-once-a-muslim-always-a-muslim/.

Schneider, William. "What Racial Divide?" *National Journal Magazine* (November 8, 2008).

Scott, J. "Transcript: 'Fox News Watch,' June 14, 2008." *FoxNews.com* (June 14, 2008). http://www.foxnews.com/story/2008/06/16/transcript-fox-news-watch-june-14-2008/.

Sklar, Rachel. "Yikes! Controversial New Yorker Cover Shows Muslim, Flag-Burning, Osama-Loving, Fist-Bumping Obama." *The Huffington Post* (July 21, 2008). http://www.huffingtonpost.com/2008/07/13/yikes-controversial-emnew_n_112429.html.

Smith, A. "22% of Online Americans Used Social Networking or Twitter for Politics in 2010 Campaign." Pew Research Center, 2011. http://www.pewInternet.org/Reports/2011/Politics-and-social-media/Report/Voters-of-all-political-stripes-were-using-SNS.aspx.

Smith, Ben. "Clinton Staffer on Anti-Obama Email Chain." *Politico* (December 5, 2007). http://www.politico.com/blogs/bensmith/1207/Clinton_staffer_on_antiObama_email_chain.html.

Smith, Ben. "Palin: Obama Birth Certificate 'a Fair Question." *Politico* (December 3, 2009). http://www.politico.com/blogs/bensmith/1209/Palin_Obama _birth_certificate_a_fair_question.html.

Southern, Ed. "Observations Gathered out of a Discourse of the Plantation of the Southern Colony in Virginia by the English, 1608. Written by That Honorable Gentleman, Master George Percy." In *The Jamestown Adventure: Accounts of the Virginia Colony, 1605–1614*, 20–36. Winston-Salem, NC: John F. Blair, 2004.

Speigel, Lee. "McCain Confronts the Anger." *ABC News* (October 10, 2008). http://abcnews.go.com/blogs/politics/2008/10/mccain-confront/.

Steele, Shelby. "Obama's Post-Racial Promise." *The Los Angeles Times* (November 5, 2008).

Stein, Sam. "Bachmann: Obama Wants 'Re-education Camps for Young People.' " *The Huffington Post* (May 7, 2009). http://www.huffingtonpost .com/2009/04/06/bachmann-obama-wants-re-e_n_183552.html.

Steyn, Mark. "Mrs Grievance. . ." *National Review* (April 21, 2008).

Swaine, Jon. "Birther Row Began with Hillary Clinton." *The Telegraph* (April 27, 2011). http://www.telegraph.co.uk/news/worldnews/barackobama/ 8478044/Birther-row-began-with-Hillary-Clinton.html.

Swift, Zephaniah. *A System of the Laws of the State of Connecticut*. John Byrne, 1795.

Tagg, Larry. *Unpopular Mr. Lincoln: The Story of America's Most Reviled President*. Casemate, 2009.

Taitz, Orly. "Demand for Emergency Hearing to NH Speaker of House Regarding Obama's Ballot Access." November 20, 2011. http://www.birtherreport .com/2011/11/demand-for-emergency-hearing-to-nh.html.

Tapscott, D. *Growing up Digital: The Rise of the Net Generation*. New York, NY: McGraw-Hill, 1998.

Taylor, P., and S. Keeter. "Millennials: A Portrait of Generation Next." Pew Research Center, 2010. http://pewsocialtrends.org/files/2010/10/ millennials-confident-connected-open-to-change.pdf.

Terkel, Amanda. "Mitt Romney Robocall Warns Christians Obama a 'Threat to Our Religious Freedom.' " *The Huffington Post* (November 2, 2012). http:// www.huffingtonpost.com/2012/11/02/mitt-romney-robocall-christians_n_20 68596.html.

Terkel, Amanda. "Paul Ryan to Social Conservatives: 'Religious Freedom' at Risk If Obama Is Reelected." *The Huffington Post* (November 4, 2012). http://www.huffingtonpost.com/2012/11/04/paul-ryan-social-conservatives -religious-freedom_n_2074129.html.

Terman, Lewis Madison. *The Measurement of Intelligence c. 2*. Boston, MA: Houghton Mifflin, 1916.

Tesler, Michael. "The Return of Old-Fashioned Racism to White Americans' Partisan Preferences in the Early Obama Era." *Journal of Politics* 75, no. 1 (2013): 110–123.

Tesler, Michael, and David Sears. "President Obama and the Growing Polarization of Partisan Attachments by Racial Attitudes and Race." Presentation
at the Annual Meeting of the American Political Science Association,
Washington, DC, 2010.

Thernstrom, Abigail. "Great Black Hope? The Reality of President-Elect
Obama." *National Review Online* (November 6, 2008).

Thiessen, Marc A. *Courting Disaster: How the CIA Kept America Safe and How
Barack Obama Is Inviting the Next Attack.* Regnery Publishing, 2010.

Tracy, Susan J. *In the Master's Eye: Representations of Women, Blacks, and
Poor Whites in Antebellum Southern Literature.* Amherst, MA: University
of Massachusetts Press, 2009.

Ungar, Rick. "Still Believe That Barack Obama Seeks a Permanent American
Socialist State?" *Forbes.com* (January 6, 2013). http://www.forbes.com/
sites/rickungar/2013/01/06/still-believe-that-barack-obama-seeks-a-permanent
-american-socialist-state/.

Valentino, Nicholas A., Vincent L. Hutchings, and Ismail K. White. "Cues That
Matter: How Political Ads Prime Racial Attitudes during Campaigns."
American Political Science Review 1 (March 2002). http://journals
.cambridge.org/action/displayAbstract?fromPage=online&aid=208457.

Vattel, Emer de. *The Law of Nations.* G. G. and J. Robinson, 1797.

Velasco, Eric. "Man Fighting Obama Candidacy Asks Black Jefferson County
Judge to Step Aside due to Racial Bias." *The Birmingham News* (January 11,
2012). http://blog.al.com/spotnews/2012/01/man_challenging_obama
_candidac.html.

Veres Royal, Sue. "Fear, Rhetoric, and the 'Other.' " *Race/Ethnicity: Multidisciplinary Global Contexts* 4, no. 3 (2011): 405–418.

Vitak, J., P. Zube, A. Smock, C. T. Carr, N. Ellison, and C. Lampe. "It's Complicated: Facebook Users' Political Participation in the 2008 Election." *Cyberpsychology, Behavior, & Social Networking* 14, no. 3 (2011): 107–114.

Walzer, Andrew. "Savage Repeated Debunked Falsehood That Obama Attended
Madrassa." *Media Matters* (June 26, 2007). http://mediamatters.org/
research/2007/06/26/savage-repeated-debunked-falsehood-that-obama-a/
139188.

Washington Times. "Editorial: America's Muslim Precedent." May 3, 2011.
http://www.washingtontimes.com/news/2011/may/3/americas-muslim
-precedent/.

Webster, Yehudi O. *The Racialization of America.* New York, NY: Palgrave
Macmillan, 1993.

Wharton, Billy. "Obama's No Socialist. I Should Know." *The Washington Post*
(March 15, 2009). http://www.washingtonpost.com/wp-dyn/content/
article/2009/03/13/AR2009031301899.html.

Wilson, John K. "Limbaugh Falsely Smears Obama's Harvard Record." *The
Daily Kos* (August 2, 2012). http://www.dailykos.com/story/2012/08/02/
1116174/-Limbaugh-Falsely-Smears-Obama-s-Harvard-Record.

Winston, George T. "The Relation of the Whites to the Negroes." *Annals of the American Academy of Political and Social Science* 18 (1901): 105–118.

Wise, Tim. "Socialism as the New Black Bogeyman: Red Baiting and Racism." *CounterPunch.org* (August 11, 2009). http://www.counterpunch.org/2009/08/11/red-baiting-and-racism/.

Wong, Curtis M. "Jerome Corsi, Tea Party Activist, Reports Obama Is Gay and Familiar with Chicago Bathhouse Scene." *The Huffington Post* (September 12, 2012). http://www.huffingtonpost.com/2012/09/12/obama-gay-rumors-chicago-jerome-corsi-_n_1877990.html.

Index

About the Author

MARTIN A. PARLETT is a communications professional and researcher in political communication, rhetoric, and strategy. He is a graduate of Oxford University and the recipient of the Canadian Rhodes Foundation Scholarship. In 2008, Martin worked with the Barack Obama campaign in Virginia, directing volunteer activities and creating a nationally adopted communication initiative, receiving recognition from the future president. His work focused particularly on developing "in the field" micro-targeting—a key feature of the 2008 and 2012 elections. His work on political communication and history has been recognized by the Oxford Leadership Prize and published in the press, the *Journal of American, British and Canadian Studies*; *Social Media Go to War: Rage Rebellion and Revolution in the Age of Twitter*; and *Before Obama: A Reappraisal of Black Reconstruction Era Politicians* (Praeger, 2012).

www.ingramcontent.com/pod-product-compliance
Lightning Source LLC
Chambersburg PA
CBHW050414280326
41932CB00013BA/1854